Electronic Design of Microprocessor-Based Instruments and Control Systems

Abund Ottokar Wist
and
Z. H. Meiksin

Prentice-Hall, Inc.
Business and Professional Division

Englewood Cliffs
New Jersey

Prentice-Hall International, Inc., *London*
Prentice-Hall of Australia, Pty. Ltd., *Sydney*
Prentice-Hall Canada Inc., *Toronto*
Prentice-Hall of India Private Ltd., *New Delhi*
Prentice-Hall of Japan, Inc., *Tokyo*
Prentice-Hall of Southeast Asia Pte. Ltd., *Singapore*
Whitehall Books, Ltd., *Wellington, New Zealand*
Editora Prentice-Hall do Brasil, Ltda., *Rio de Janeiro*
Prentice-Hall Hispanoamericana, S. A., *Mexico*

Third Printing.....April 1987

Editor: George E. Parker

Library of Congress Cataloging in Publication Data

Wist, Abund Ottokar.
  Designing microprocessor-based electronic
instruments and control systems.

  Includes index.
  1. Microprocessors. 2. Electronic instruments—
Design and construction. 3. Electronic controllers—
Design and construction. I. Meiksin, Z. H. II. Title.
TK7895.M5W57 1985   621.381   85-3586

ISBN 0-13-25031-2

Printed in the United States of America

Dedicated to the memory of my parents

Abund Ottokar Wist

To my children Tamar, Avery, Judith, and Dan

Z.H. Meiksin

A Word from the Authors on This Book's Practical Value

This unique reference guide shows how to select the right microprocessor chips and peripheral components for a range of applications, and how to interconnect these components into functional equipment for instrumentation, data processing, inventory, display, and control systems. The book goes far beyond the presentation of block diagrams, microcomputer architecture, and software programming. It shows step-by-step development of hardware and software, how to combine them most effectively, and how to interface the microprocessor with input devices such as sensors or data sources, and output devices, such as relay actuators or display devices.

Microprocessor chips for electronic and other applications are available at low cost. The rapid progress made in the manufacture and supply of microprocessors expands enormously the opportunities to design and build highly effective equipment and systems. The microprocessor has simplified the design and implementation of many projects, and opened up many new areas that previously were impractical or too costly. This book shows how to make full use of these developments. You are shown step by step how to build simple and sophisticated projects with all the necessary details. Many proven examples are included throughout the book for industrial, laboratory, health-care, and home use.

The microprocessor is a relatively new and complex electronic device. For its proper application, the designer must acquire knowledge beyond that needed for the application of conventional integrated circuits. The information needed to follow the many design examples in this book is given in a simple, direct manner with supporting tables to keep mathematics to a minimum. Once this know-how is acquired, you will be able to build systems with less effort and less time than ever before.

Chapters 1 and 2 of the book explain the basic microprocessor and building blocks of the microcomputer, computer arithmetic and logic, and computer operation. Chapter 3 covers the programming required for system design. Chapter 4 provides help in understanding microprocessor families and their respective advantages and limitations. To write information into the microprocessor and then read it, interface devices or systems are required. Chapter 5 shows how such interface devices can be built with minimum effort and at a cost that is often a small fraction of the price of commercial products. Chapter 6 gives a practical selection guide for microcomputers and peripherals.

Productive use of the material introduced in the first six chapters is demonstrated in Chapters 7 through 11 through application of the material to different broad fields such as how to build microprocessor-based equipment for use in the laboratory, industry, medicine, and the automotive industry. Not only are present uses shown, but the information given will also help you capitalize on future developments.

The microprocessor industry has reached a level where standardization has become necessary to benefit both the manufacturer and the user. Chapter 12 presents hardware and software standards most applicable in the USA and worldwide.

Each chapter contains examples with detailed diagrams where necessary.

This book will familiarize you with microprocessors so that you will be able to incorporate microprocessors into your own designs. You will find the helpful guidelines in this reference work to be of an extraordinary practical value in your efforts to fully capitalize on the opportunities offered by the microprocessor.

Acknowledgments

I thank my students for suggesting the book, my coauthor for encouraging me to get started, and Roger Kirk for giving it uniform style. I am grateful for the unending patience of the editor, and I would also like to thank all those who contributed many additional suggestions for the book.

Abund Ottokar Wist

I thank my coauthor for his enthusiasm and untiring dedication. I am grateful to my teachers from whom I learned much and to my students, from whom I learned even more.

Z. H. Meiksin

CONTENTS

CHAPTER 1

Developing a Practical View of the Microprocessor

1.1 INTRODUCTION

Ultrafast and powerful computers keep space probes on target, drastically shorten astronomy calculations, automatically run whole refineries, and make our check cashing system possible. Today's computers have come a long way since the first true electronic computer in the U.S., ENIAC (Electronic Numeric Integrator and Computer) became operational in 1946. Despite its huge size—it filled a room 20 × 40 feet—it had approximately the power of a hand-held calculator costing thirty dollars three decades later. Nonetheless, it was a worldwide sensation because it could multiply two ten-digit numbers in a few milliseconds, proving that a machine could be built that was fast enough to make midcourse corrections during the flight of missiles. Still, transmissions of midcourse correction signals from a ground computer are errorprone, but computers at that time were too large to be built into the missile itself making it necessary to reduce the size of the computer.

Early electronic computers used large components such as relays, switches, and electronic tubes. Later, small transistors became available, which were continuously further reduced in size until today one electronic device package, measuring ¾ inch × 2 inches, may contain over 250,000 transistors including the many other components necessary for its operation.

1.2 COMPUTER CATEGORIES

Continuing microminiaturization of electronic parts has reduced the size of computers approximately fifty percent every two

Developing a Practical View of the Microprocessor

years with a corresponding reduction in price. According to industry estimates, this reduction rate will continue, leading finally to button- and needle-head-size computers by the end of this century.

There is also another interesting side to this development. Every time the miniaturization leads to a new technology such as transistors or integrated circuits (ICs), a new type of computer is created, such as hand-held and wristwatch computers. This development is shown in more detail in Figure 1-1.

The vertical, logarithmic scale shows the cost of full computer systems, while the horizontal axis gives years on a linear scale, from the development of the first electronic computer, ENIAC, in 1946 to the present-day computers, and to a projection of computer developments in the future.

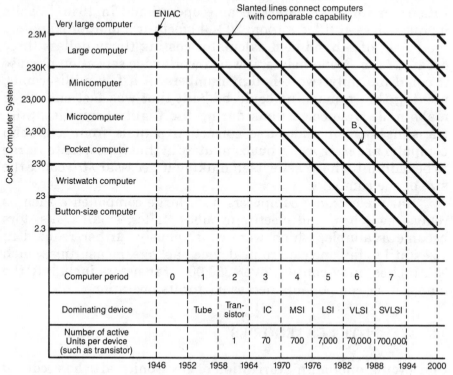

Figure 1-1

Computer Development

At the start of the 1950s, only "very large" computers were available. Then "large" computers came on the market. "Mini" computers followed, and so forth, until we may have a computer system the size of a needle head at the end of this century. The time period between two new computer types seems to be around six years.

The characterization of a computer as "very large," "large," or "mini" does not refer as much to any computer's actual computing capability than to its size and cost. For example, the size and cost of "micro" computers have changed little since their inception, whereas their computing capability has increased tremendously, creating so-called "supermicros." The cost of microcomputer systems is indicated in Figure 1-1, by a horizontal line. Other computer systems are indicated by horizontal lines on different levels.

The major reason for the rapid increase in computing power at practically constant price and size is the use of the fast-advancing hardware and software technology, which increases the power of computers by around two magnitudes approximately each six years. Each time a new computer type evolved, the computer power increased by about two magnitudes. It follows that microcomputers have approximately the same power as minicomputers had six years ago. Similar relationships hold true for all the other types of computers.

If, on the other hand, one connects the points that correspond to the same power for each type of computer one obtains a slanted line and if one does this for every six years since the inception of each type of computer, one obtains the slanted lines shown in Figure 1-1. As a slanted line indicates a specific amount of computer power necessary for a given application, this figure shows not only the decreasing computer cost for a specific application but also the different types of computers one can choose from as time advances.

As all types of computers use practically the same technology at a given time, one can use this knowledge to determine the age of a given computer.

The major reason that the different types of computers keep their price tag and size but have increasing computing capability lies in improved manufacturing, distribution, and marketing of computers.

1.3 HOW TO SELECT A COMPUTER SYSTEM

1.3.1 Suitability of a Computer System

When selecting a computer system for a specific application, such as for the control of a laboratory heating and cooling system or for data collection, we must first determine if computers can be used for this application. If they can, we must then perform a thorough analysis of this application so that we can select the most appropriate computer system. A well-selected computer system should make the overall operation: (1) less expensive, (2) faster, and (3) more precise.

1.3.2 Selection of the Type of Computer System

Once it has been decided that computers can be used for a given application, and the necessary computer power is determined, the type of computer can be selected from the slanted lines in Figure 1-1. The intersection point of the slanted line corresponding to the necessary computer power for the selected application with the selected vertical year line indicate the appropriate type of computer (large computer or microcomputer) you should use.

If too little capital is available to purchase the appropriate computer, then the application has to be restricted. If more capital is available, one can buy a computer with higher capability for later expansion.

For example, the computer capacity needed to control a laboratory heating and cooling system is relatively small. The capability required for such applications may correspond to the slanted line *B* in Figure 1-1. Using the year line for 1982, we find, that either a pocket computer or a microcomputer would be adequate. Which of these two computers is better suited for this application? Pocket computers have limitations in interfacing with the outside devices; however, their computational capability is usually large enough for an average laboratory application. Adaptors for pocket computers that can accept single or multiple inputs or outputs are available. If two thermostats can control the temperature of a laboratory experiment, a pocket computer with the necessary interface devices would be adequate.

For the same investment, we can buy a microcomputer system with sixteen Input and/or Output channels. The microcomputer is the better buy in view of its higher flexibility and power as its larger size does not in any way impede its function.

The following sections explain in detail the operation of a computer system to allow a buyer of a microcomputer system to design and build a system. Building one's own system may save money, not only by using one's own labor, but also by using only those parts necessary for the application. It may also contribute to one's satisfaction and education. Commercial systems aim at broad application and capability, much of which may not be needed for the intended application, but add to the initial and maintenance costs. Furthermore, an in-house built system may be the only option, since commercial systems may not be available.

1.4   BASIC COMPONENTS OF A COMPUTER

Highly efficient modern computers have been developed from earlier calculators and counters. This is the major reason why any information such as words or numbers processed in computers is in numerical form. For arithmetic operations such as addition, subtraction, or logic for comparing different values, the computer has a special processing unit called the arithmetic and logic unit (ALU). This is the first basic component of a computer.

The second and third components are the INPUT and the OUTPUT sections which enable the operator to enter numbers into the ALU unit and take out the calculated results.

To carry out mathematical calculations or to store programs, the computer must have a special storage device where the input and output of mathematical calculations, intermediary results, or whole programs can be stored. This storage device, known as the main memory of the computer, is the fourth basic unit of the computer.

The fifth basic unit of the computer, the control unit, organizes the flow of information inside the computer: for example, taking a command or data from the input, sending an intermediary result to the memory and sending the end result to the output unit. The five basic computer units as shown in Figure 1-2,

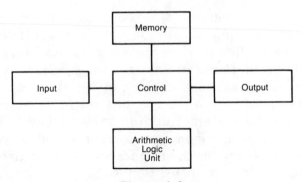

Figure 1-2
Basic Computer Configuration

are as follows: (1) Arithmetic Logic Unit (ALU), (2) Input Unit, (3) Output Unit, (4) Memory or Storage Unit, and (5) Control Unit.

1.5 NUMBER SYSTEMS

1.5.1 Introduction

Laboratory computer inputs and outputs are frequently in the form of analog (continuously varying) data. The most efficient way to process such information in the computer would be in analog form. For this reason, some of the early laboratory computers were of the analog type. Even today, analog computers are sometimes used for handling some very complex mathematical algorithms for clinical purposes where a precision of two (maximum three) digits is adequate. Designing analog computers with a precision greater than three significant digits becomes increasingly expensive because of the sharp increase in cost of high precision parts, power supplies, and amplifiers. Furthermore, storing information in an analog computer is very difficult.

A simple representation of numbers in analog and digital form is given in Figure 1-3, where the number two is represented in analog and digital form. It is basically easier to represent a number by an analog rather than a digital value. For example, two volts may be used to represent the number two and three volts the

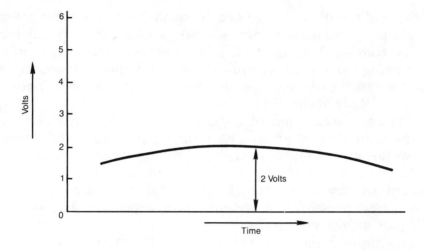

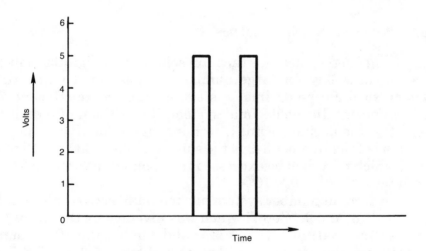

Figure 1-3
Representation of Analog and Digital Numbers

number three. A digital number can be represented by multiple
pulses; two, for example, can be indicated by two five-volt pulses.
   However, a supply voltage variation of ten percent will
change the analog value ten percent (2V to 1.8V), whereas the

digital value will be unchanged, because the number and not the height of the pulses is significant. Stray pulses and other disturbances, coming from internal and external sources, may affect the analog value greatly, while the digital value will remain constant unless the disturbances become so great that they approach the magnitude of the digital pulses.

The representation of a digital number requires more circuitry than that of an analog number, but the cost increases faster for analog numbers than for digital numbers if we go to higher precision numbers, which contain more digits and lower position numbers. Therefore, from a certain precision on, the cost of analog representation becomes more expensive than the cost of digital representation.

As digital circuitry becomes less costly, more of the less precision numbers can be displayed by digital than by analog representation.

1.5.2 Positional Number Systems

Using single pulses for the representation of digital numbers becomes unwieldy for large numbers. A positional numbering system, such as the decimal system, is much more efficient for large numbers. In the decimal system, the location of a digit in respect to the decimal point determines its value. For example, the value of the number 349 is the sum of 3×100 plus 4×10 plus 9×1; which may also be expressed in exponential form as: $349 = 3 \times 10^2 + 4 \times 10^1 + 9 \times 10^0$.

The decimal number system has ten number symbols: 0, 1, 2, 3, 4, 5, 6, 7, 8, and 9. "Zero," which was invented by the Arabs (or Chinese?) several millenia ago, is a valid number; therefore, counting to the number ten requires eleven numbers: 0, 1, 2, 3, 4, 5, 6, 7, 8, 9, and 10. This fact is important to remember in the explanation of the other number systems following.

Although the decimal system is optimal for human use, is it optimal for computers? To find out, we compare several number systems with different numbers of symbols by calculating how many physical representations we need in the computer for the first sixteen numbers. For the decimal system we need twelve representations in the computer for the whole set of numbers from

0 to 15: ten for the least significant digit (0 to 9) and two for the most significant digit (0 and 1). We now compare the decimal system with the duodecimal system.

1.5.2.1 The Duodecimal System

The duodecimal system has twelve basic number symbols against ten of the decimal system as shown in the following table:

Decimal system:	0, 1, 2, 3, 4, 5, 6, 7, 8, 9,
Duodecimal system:	0, 1, 2, 3, 4, 5, 6, 7, 8, 9, A, B,

To represent sixteen numbers in the duodecimal number system we have to write the duodecimal numbers 0_{12} to 13_{12}. (The subscript indicates the number system used.) The numeral 1 in this duodecimal number represents twelve numbers and the numeral 3 in this number, four numbers (10, 11, 12, 13). Together they represent sixteen numbers. To represent the first sixteen numbers in the duodecimal system we need a total of fourteen representations in a computer. Two for the left digit (0 and 1) and twelve for the second digit (0 to B). The duodecimal system is less efficient for the computer than the decimal system, which needs twelve representations. Number systems with a higher number of symbols than the decimal system fare less well with the computer. Consider now a number system with fewer symbols than there are in the decimal system: the *octal* system.

1.5.2.2 The Octal System

The octal system derives its name from the Latin word for eight and it uses only eight number symbols. These are: 0, 1, 2, 3, 4, 5, 6, and 7. The number symbols "8" and "9" are not used. Numbers of equal value in the decimal and octal systems are compared in the following table:

Octal System	Decimal System
0	0
1	1
2	2

Developing a Practical View of the Microprocessor

Octal System	Decimal System
3	3
4	4
5	5
6	6
7	7

We have used up the eight number symbols in our octal number system. We now must enter a new position to the left of the first position. The comparison of the two number systems is shown below:

10	8
11	9
12	10
13	11
14	12
15	13
16	14
17	15

Having run out of number symbols for the octal system we have to increase the digit in the left-hand position by one:

20	16
21	17
22	18
23	19
24	20

This table shows that every time we start with a new position or number in our octal system it is equivalent to a multiple of eight in the decimal system. The octal (base 8) number 24 is equivalent to $8 + 8 + 4 = 20$ in the decimal system.

Which of these two number systems is more efficient for computers? In the octal system we need two representations for the high position (0, and 1), but only eight (0 to 7) for the low position. This only adds up to ten representations. Therefore, the octal system is more efficient in representing numbers than the decimal system. Let us see if number systems with even fewer base numbers will give higher efficiencies.

1.5.2.3 The Binary Number System

In the binary digital number system (base 2) we have only two number symbols "0" and "1." As this system has only two symbols, we run out of number symbols much earlier than in other number systems. A new digital position must be used for the third number, as compared with the ninth number (8) in the octal system and the eleventh number (10) in the decimal system. In the binary system the first place or Least Significant Digit (LSD) has a value of 1, the next position to the left has a value of 2, the next position to the left has a value of 4 increasing by powers of two. In the following table we compare the octal and decimal number systems with the binary system:

Binary System	Octal System	Decimal System
0000	00	00
0001	01	01
0010	02	02
0011	03	03
0100	04	04
0101	05	05
0110	06	06
0111	07	07
1000	10	08
1001	11	09
1010	12	10
1011	13	11
1100	14	12
1101	15	13
1110	16	14
1111	17	15
10000	20	16
10001	21	17

Developing a Practical View of the Microprocessor

In the binary system, as in any other positional system, a new digital position is added as soon as we run out of number symbols in that system. In the first column we run out after two numbers (0 and 1), in the second after four numbers (0, 1, 2, and 3), in the third after eight numbers and so on.

How is the binary system more efficient than other number systems in representing numbers in a computer? Only eight representations—four digital positions with two number symbols in each—are necessary to represent the numbers 0 through 15. Therefore, the binary number system is by far the most efficient number system for this purpose.

The greatest advantage of the binary system becomes apparent when this system is implemented with semiconductor devices. For example, for the representation of the two binary symbols we can select the on and off state of a transistor. These two states are quite insensitive to supply voltage variations, stray electromagnetic fields, or the characteristics of transistors themselves. Great savings can be derived from the acceptability of less demanding standards for the transistors and the use of less costly auxiliary electronic circuitry. The binary digital number system has been adopted by virtually all computer manufacturers because of these tremendous advantages over all other systems.

1.5.2.4   *Character Representation in the Computer*

As the computer uses only the binary number system internally, each character must be translated into a binary number. To find how long this digital number must be, so that all characters can be presented, we must find how many characters there are. There are 26 upper case letters, 26 lower case letters, 10 number symbols, 31 syntax symbols, and about 35 control characters for computer operation. This results in a total of 128 characters. How large must a binary number be so that it can represent 128 characters?

We have already seen that a four-digit binary number can represent up to sixteen numbers (see above table). Adding a fifth position allows thirty-two numbers in a digital number. We see that adding a digital position to a digital number doubles its number capacity. The following table compares binary to decimal equivalents up to eight-digit binary numbers:

Binary Numbers	Equivalent Decimal Numbers
0000 0000	000
0000 0001	001
0000 0010	002
0000 0100	004
0000 1000	008
0001 0000	016
0010 0000	032
0100 0000	064
1000 0000	128

Moving a "1" to the next left binary position of a digital number, otherwise containing zeros, doubles its number value. This is demonstrated in a different way in the following table:

Digital position in binary number	7	6	5	4	3	2	1	0
Binary value of digit	1	1	1	1	1	1	1	1
Decimal value of the above binary digit	128	64	32	16	8	4	2	1

For example, a binary digit with the value 1 in the sixth left position is equivalent to a decimal 64_{10}. An eight-digit binary number can represent up to 256 decimal numbers, from 0 to 255. We obtain the number 255 by adding the decimal values of all the eight binary digits: $1 + 2 + 4 + 8 + 16 + 32 + 64 + 128 = 255$.

1.5.2.5 American Standard Code of Information Interchange (ASCII)

Referring to the question of how many numbers are needed to represent 128 characters, we find that a binary digital number with seven digits is necessary. Seven digits can represent 128 numbers. If we do not need all the control characters or syntax symbols, we can assign the additional characters up to 128 to Greek letters or graphic symbols.

Developing a Practical View of the Microprocessor

HIGH BITS

Bit posit. 1234 / Dec.	Bit Pos. → BIN. / Dec.	567 000 0	567 100 1	567 010 2	567 110 3	567 001 4	567 101 5	567 011 6	567 111 7
0000	0	NUL	DLE	SP	0	@	P	\	p
1000	1	SOH	DC1	!	1	A	Q	a	q
0100	2	STX	DC2	"	2	B	R	b	r
1100	3	ETX	DC3	#	3	C	S	c	s
0010	4	EOT	DC4	$	4	D	T	d	t
1010	5	ENQ	NAK	%	5	E	U	e	u
0110	6	ACK	SYN	&	6	F	V	f	v
1110	7	BEL	ETB	'	7	G	W	g	w
0001	8	BS	CAN	(	8	H	X	h	x
1001	9	HT	EM	)	9	I	Y	i	y
0101	10	LF	SUB	*	:	J	Z	j	z
1101	11	VT	ESC	+	;	K	[	k	{
0011	12	FF	FS	,	<	L	\	l	¦
1011	13	CR	GS	−	=	M	]	m	}
0111	14	SO	RS	.	>	N	^	n	~
1111	15	SI	US	/	?	O	−	o	DEL

LOW BITS

Figure 1-4
ASCII Table

    As these characters are not only sent from a terminal to a computer in the same room but often much farther away, it is necessary to ensure that bits do not change during transmission. We can use an additional bit, the eight bit, for this purpose.

    To recognize the accidental change of a single bit in the code, the transmitting station has a hardware device that automatically puts a "one" or "zero" in the eight position so that the number of "one" bits in the eight-bit number is always even, called even parity, or always odd, called odd parity. The receiving station is advised beforehand in what parity the characters are being sent and can check for the change of a single digit during the transmission. This code will correctly detect all single inversions in the transmitted characters. However, it will detect only a portion of double or triple inversions. For this purpose more sophisticated codes are necessary.

As eight is a multiple of two, it is convenient to handle eight bits together in the computer. Eight bits have been selected as the standard number of bits to represent any character such as A, B, or Z. An eight-bit character is now called a "byte." Even though in previous definitions a "byte" might have been five, six, or seven bits long, a character is always represented by eight bits in present practice even when the eight bit is not used.

The eight-binary-digit character code is now fully accepted internationally. This code is called the ASCII code (American Standard Code for Information Interchange). For your convenience the full code is reprinted in Figure 1-4. The digital binary representations of the different symbols are arranged for easier readability with the least significant bit on the left and the most significant bit on the right. These bits appear the same way on the oscilloscope as shown in Fig. 5-14.

1.5.2.6 *The Hexadecimal Code*

Sometimes it becomes necessary to check to see if a program is properly loaded. As only zeros and ones are in the computer, vast quantities of zeros and ones will appear on the screen or printer representing the area to be checked. For easier recognition of errors, computer designers combine four binary digits and give each of the sixteen combinations of the four digits a single symbol. Because of the sixteen numbers in this system it is called the *hexadecimal* number system, derived from the Greek word for six and the Latin word for ten. Ten decimal number symbols are used for the first ten hexadecimal numbers. The first six letter symbols of the alphabet (A, B, C, D, E, F) are used to provide for the remaining numbers, 10 to 15.

The hexadecimal system, in relation to the other number systems is as follows:

Hexadecimal	Binary	Octal	Decimal
00	0000	000	00
01	0001	001	01
02	0010	002	02
03	0011	003	03

Developing a Practical View of the Microprocessor

Hexadecimal	Binary	Octal	Decimal
04	0100	004	04
05	0101	005	05
06	0100	006	06
07	0111	007	07
08	1000	010	08
09	1001	011	09
0A	1010	012	10
0B	1011	013	11
0C	1100	014	12
0D	1101	015	13
0E	1110	016	14
0F	1111	017	15
10	10000	020	16
11	10001	021	17
12	10010	022	18
13	10011	023	19

1.5.2.7   Conversions Between Number Systems

It can be shown that conversions between hexadecimal and binary numbers can be accomplished very easily. Count four digital positions to the left from the decimal point, and convert these four binary digits to one hexadecimal digit. Similarly, convert the next four binary digits to the left to a hexadecimal digit and continue until all binary digits are converted. If four binary digits for the last hexadecimal number do not remain, fill the remaining binary digits with zeros. Reverse the process to convert hexadecimal numbers to binary numbers. For an illustration, convert the binary number 101000111 to hexadecimal.

Divide the digital number into sections of four digits each, starting from the decimal point. If there is no decimal point to the right of the most right digit, assume that there is.

The four digits of the first section of above digital numbers: 0111
The four digits of the second section: 0100
The four digits of the third section: 0001

Developing a Practical View of the Microprocessor

Zeros are added to the left of the third section to fill in that group. Convert each of the three sections of four digits to the corresponding hexadecimal value using the previous table.

Section	Binary Digital	Hexadecimal
1	0111	7
2	0100	4
3	0001	1

The hexadecimal number equivalent to the binary digital number 101000111 is 147. To convert from hexadecimal to binary, first write the hexadecimal number. Place under it the four-digit binary value for each hexadecimal digit. The combination of ones and zeros as written is the equivalent binary number.

To convert a decimal number to a binary number, the following rule has to be applied. Divide the decimal number continuously by 2 until the number remaining is smaller than 2. Keep the remainders of all divisions. The remainders comprise the binary number starting from the least significant number to the most significant number. Let's show this in an example. We first convert 25 to a binary number.

```
                                        Resulting digital number
                                              ↓
       25 : 2 = 12   Remainder 1 >    1    LSB
       12 : 2 = 6    Remainder 0 >    0
        6 : 2 = 3    Remainder 0 >    0
        3 : 2 = 1    Remainder 1 >    1
        1 : 2 = 0    Remainder 1 >    1    MSB
```

Therefore, the binary digital equivalent of the decimal number 25 is 11001. We can convert the binary number back to the decimal number by using the positional expansion.

The digital number 11001 also can be written

$$1\times2^4 + 1\times2^3 + 0\times2^2 + 0\times2^1 + 1\times2^0$$
$$16 + 8 + 0 + 0 + 1 = 25$$

You can use this technique for all number systems. For example, to convert from the decimal system to the octal system you divide the decimal number by 8 instead of by 2. If you want to convert the decimal number to the hexadecimal system you divide the decimal number by 16, but it is normally much easier to convert the decimal number to a digital number first, and then covert the digital number to an octal or a hexadecimal number.

To convert back to the decimal system, use the positional expansion as shown for the number 25 above.

For fractional numbers a similar rule exists. For example, to convert the decimal number 25.268 to a binary number requires the following procedure. First, convert the number 25 into a binary number. We know that this number is 11001. Next we have to convert the remaining fraction .268 into a binary number. This is done by multiplying it by 2 in the following way:

```
                                              Digital number
                                                    ↓
0.268 X 2 = 0.536 from this number keep the 0    MSB
0.536 X 2 = 1.072 from this number keep the 1
0.072 X 2 = 0.144 from this number keep the 0
0.144 X 2 = 0.288 from this number keep the 0    LSB
```

This process can be continued as long as necessary. As the first zero in this case is the most significant bit, the decimal number 25.268 is converted to a binary number 11001.0100. A similar conversion can be made with any number system. To convert to the hexadecimal system, we multiply the fraction of the decimal number by 16; for a conversion to the octal system, multiply by 8. As mentioned previously, converting to the binary system and then to the octal or hexadecimal system is easier than the direct conversion.

Older instrumentation often used another number system called *binary coded decimal* system (BCD). Each decimal number in this code corresponds to a sequence of four binary digits. As the decimal system has only ten symbols, and four binary digits can represent sixteen symbols, binary equivalents of the numbers 10 to 15 are invalid in a microcomputer. Some microcomputers such as the 6800 (Motorola) have special commands to avoid adding incorrectly BCD numbers.

Summary

The digital binary system is used to increase the efficiency of the computer for all internal operations. For operator ease in following the operation in the computer, the hexadecimal number system is used. The octal system is used in many older machines. All other number systems serve the convenience of the human operator, such as the decimal system, the ASCII, the BCD code, and some other codes as listed below. Older printers and other peripherals may use the 5-bit *Baudot* code. The *Gray* code is especially designed for fast reading of rotary information, as the code changes in only one digital position from one number to the next number.

Decimal	Binary	Hexadecimal	Octal	ASCII	BCD		Baudot	Gray
00	00000	00	000	00110000	0000	0000	10110	0000
01	00001	01	001	00110001		0001	10111	0001
02	00010	02	003	00110010		0010	10011	0011
03	00011	03	003	00110011		0011	00001	0010
04	00100	04	004	00110100		0100	01010	0110
05	00101	05	005	00110101		0101	10000	0111
06	00110	06	006	00110110		0110	10101	0101
07	00111	07	007	00110111		0111	00111	0100
08	01000	08	010	00111000		1000	00110	1100
09	01001	09	011	00111001	0000	1001	11000	1101
10	01010	0A	012	--------	0001	0000	-----	1111
11	01011	0B	013	two	0001	0001	two	1110
12	01100	0C	014	ASCII	0001	0010	Baudot	1010
13	01101	0D	015	numbers	0001	0011	codes	1011
14	01110	0E	016	are used	0001	0100	are	1001
15	01111	0F	017	below	0001	0101	used	1000
16	10000	10	020		0001	0110		
17	10001	11	021		0001	0111		
18	10010	12	022		0001	1000		
19	10011	13	023		0001	1001		
20	10100	14	024		0002	0000		
21	10101	15	025		0002	0001		
22	10110	16	026		0002	0010		
23	10111	17	027		0002	0011		
24	11000	18	030		0002	0100		
25	11001	19	031		0002	0101		
26	11010	1A	032		0002	0110		
27	11011	1B	033		0002	0111		
28	11100	1C	034		0002	1000		
29	11101	1D	035		0002	1001		
30	11110	1E	036		0003	0000		
31	11111	1F	037		0003	0001		

1.6 BASIC MATHEMATICAL COMPUTER OPERATIONS

With the given background in the binary digital system, we can explore how the computer uses this number system to carry out mathematical and logic operations. For maximum efficiency the computer carries out only one operation—mathematical addition. All other mathematical operations such as subtraction, multiplication, division, and all other functions are based on addition.

1.6.1 Addition

Addition in the binary system is really simpler than in the decimal system because only two symbols need to be remembered, 0 and 1. Four addition examples are below:

$$0 + 0 = 0$$
$$0 + 1 = 1$$
$$1 + 0 = 1$$
$$1 + 1 = 10$$

There are only two symbols in this number system. Therefore, we have an overflow or carry when 1 and 1 are added. The carry is added to the next higher position, situated to the left of the old position.

Four-bit binary numbers are added as follows (showing the decimal equivalent for comparison):

	Binary	Decimal		Binary	Decimal
Carry	111		Carry	11	
	0101	5		1011	11
	+ 0011	+ 3		+ 0011	+ 3
	1000	8		1110	14

Eight bit or higher numbers are added similarly:

	Binary		Decimal
Carry	1	11	1
	0101	0011	83
	+ 1001	1011	+ 155
	1110	1110	238

1.6.2   Subtraction

To carry out subtraction by addition, use the complementary number method that is most efficient in the binary digital system. First, review its use in the more familiar decimal system: Add the tens complement of a number to the number being subtracted. For example, if we want to subtract 4 from 8 we first determine what the tens complement of 4 is.

```
  10    Base number of decimal system
- 04    The number for which the complementary number is sought
  06    6 is therefore tens complement of 4.
```

Then we add 8 and 6 to obtain the difference between 8 and 4.

$$
\begin{array}{r}
8 \\
+\,6 \\
\hline
1 \quad 4
\end{array}
$$

Carry (discard)

After the carry is discarded we obtain the correct result, 4. This procedure can be carried out with any number in any number system. For the binary digital system, we first show the conventional subtraction for comparison.

The steps carried out in the binary system are similar to those applied in the decimal system. If there is a "0" in the subtrahend, the digit is brought down from the minuend. A "1" in the subtrahend is deducted from the digit in the minuend. When the digit in the subtrahend is larger than the digit in the minuend, borrow from the next higher digit in the minuend. The four possible situations are:

$$
\begin{array}{l}
00 - 00 = 00 \\
01 - 01 = 00 \\
01 - 00 = 01 \\
10 - 01 = 01
\end{array}
$$

Decimal	*Binary*	
	1	Borrow
10	1010	Minuend
− 04	− 100	Subtrahend
06	0110	Difference

Developing a Practical View of the Microprocessor

Other examples:

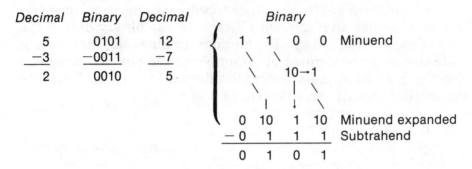

Decimal	Binary	Decimal
5	0101	12
−3	−0011	−7
2	0010	5

Now we calculate the twos complements in the binary system:

The complement of   1 to the base 2 is $10 - 1 = 1$
and the complement of   0 to the base 2 is $10 - 0 = 10$

Examples are as follows:

Example 1 : Normal Subtraction:

$$1 - 1 = 0$$

The same result is obtained by using the twos complement method, adding the twos complement of one to the minuend of one and dropping the carry:

Twos Complement Subtraction:

```
  1 Minuend
+ 1 add twos complement of 1, which is also 1
1   0 thus gives the same result after carry is dismissed.
/
Carry
```

Example 2

Standard Subtraction   *Twos Complement Subtraction*

Decimal   *Binary*   *Calculating the twos complement*

9	1001	10000
− 5	− 0101	− 00101
4	0100	01011 twos complement of 0101 (5)

```
    1001    minuend (9)
  + 1011    add twos complement of 101 (5)
  1  0100   gives the same result 100 (4)
     |
Carry (discard)
```

Example 3

Standard Subtraction   Twos Complement Subtraction

Decimal   Binary   Calculating the twos complement

```
or  12    1100   or  10000
    9   - 1001      - 01001
    3     0011        00111  0111 is the twos complement of 1001 (9).
```

Therefore:

```
    1100    Binary digital for "12"
  + 0111    Twos complement for "9"
  1  0011   The answer is 0011 or 3 to the base ten.
     /
Carry (discard)
```

Calculating the twos complement appears to be quite compli-cated. However, there is a short cut. The twos complement can be found by inverting the binary digital number and adding one to it.
   Thus:

Example 4

Standard Subtraction   Twos Complement Subtraction

```
                         Invert 1001 (9) and
    Decimal    Binary    add one to obtain the

      12        1100     twos complement of 9
    - 9       - 1001            9   1001
      3        0011        inverted   0110
                           add one       1
                                      0111 twos compl. of 9
```

```
Add binary 12 to              1100
twos complement of 9     +    0111
                          1  0011    and obtain 0011 (3)
                          /          the same result as before
                 Carry (discard)    after discarding the carry.
```

It is significant that we can obtain the twos complement by inverting the number and adding one. Inverting a number in the computer can be done very easily with a transistor stage or inverting buffer. The addition of one can be done easily in the ALU. This allows addition and subtraction using the *Add* function only, which speeds up the processing of numbers.

1.6.3 Negative Numbers

From the previous section, the fact that twos complement numbers behave also like negative numbers may be seen. For example:

Example 1

```
a) Decimal    b) Binary    c) Twos Complement Subtraction

     6           0110          5 0101         6              0110
   − 5         − 0101        inv. 1010   twos compl. 5    + 1011
     1           0001      add 1 0001                      1 0001
                          compl. (5) 1011                    /
                                                           Carry
```

Example 2

```
a) Decimal    b) Binary    c) Twos Complement Subtraction

     7           0111          4 0100         7           0111
   − 4         − 0100        inv. 1011   compl. (4)       1100
     3           0011      add 1 0001                    1 0011
                          compl. (4) 1100                  /
                                                         Carry
```

From example 1 we can see that the binary number "−0101" is equivalent to "+ 1011" when the carry is dropped. Example 2 shows that "−0100" gives the same result as "+1100." Negative numbers may be expressed with zeros and ones without using the minus sign. Numbers that start with a zero in the most significant bit (MSB), "0," are positive numbers, whereas binary numbers that start with a one, "1," are negative numbers.

Looking at this in another way, binary numbers that start with a "1," such as "1100," have a dual meaning. As a *signed number,* meaning a number in which the first or the most significant digit indicates the sign of the number, the number "1100" has the value "−4." As an unsigned number, in which all digits count toward the number value, the binary digit number "1100" has the value "12." For positive binary numbers, which start with a "0," the number value, of course, is the same for signed or unsigned numbers.

A number in the accumulator is considered a signed or unsigned number, depending on the instruction used. Even though the ALU always adds up all numbers as unsigned, the ALU always indicates to an instruction if a number can be considered negative or positive.

Because this point is important later for A/D converters the value of signed eight bit binary numbers is calculated below.

(1)	"0"	0000 0000	(2)	"1"	0000 0001
	invert	1111 1111		invert	1111 1110
	add 1	0000 0001		add 1	0000 0001
	" 0"	0000 0000		"−1"	1111 1111

(3)	"+2"	0000 0010	(4)	"+127"	0111 1111
	invert	1111 1101		invert	1000 0000
	add 1	0000 0001		add 1	0000 0001
	"−2"	1111 1110		"−127"	1000 0001

(5)	"+128"	1000 0000
	invert	0111 1111
	add 1	0000 0001
	"−128"	1000 0000

Arranging these values into a table, we obtain:

Developing a Practical View of the Microprocessor

Unsigned Numbers		Signed Binary Numbers	
Binary	*Decimal*	*Binary*	*Decimal*
		Sign bit	
		\	
0000 0000	0	0 000 0000	0
0000 0001	1	0 000 0001	1
0000 0010	2	0 000 0010	2
0111 1111	127	0 111 1111	127
1000 0000	128	1 000 0000	−128
1000 0001	129	1 000 0001	−127
1111 1111	255	1 111 1111	−1

Almost all computers use the twos complement operation internally for signed numbers. It also is used by most I/O devices, such as A/D and D/A converters. Special instructions entered into the computer can interpret any digital number as signed or unsigned. This is important when branching occurs in a program. These special instructions are the BRANCH instructions, which will be discussed in another chapter.

Summary

There are only four numbers systems with which you have to be familiar when working with a computer system:

1. The *binary digital system* which is used primarily inside the computer
2. The *hexadecimal system,* which represents the binary system on the outside of the computer
3. The *ASCII system,* which translates all letter symbols and other symbols into the binary digital system
4. The *decimal system,* which is used exclusively outside the computer

1.7 COMPUTER LOGIC

Logic operations in a computer compare two values to determine if they are equal or if one is larger or smaller. Logic functions are essential for a computer to determine from which of the different program branches to select, based on values calculated in previous program sections. Logic is necessary to carry out mathematical approximation functions or to detect changes in values.

Logic operations are used to direct the flow of information in the computer. For example, the content of the instruction register directs the actions of a logic gate in the computer, carrying out the logic function of a single-pole double-throw switch; at the "one" level the switch directs the information flow in one direction, and at the "zero" level it directs the information in the other direction.

1.7.1 Basic Logic Functions

Only three different logic functions are necessary for any logic expression. All others can be derived from any selected three logic functions. Any logic function can have as many inputs as desired, but only one output. For simplicity, consider systems with only two inputs. The three simplest logic functions are the AND function, the OR function, and the INVERT function.

1.7.1.1 The AND Function

All inputs of the AND function must be high (one) to generate a high output. If any or all of the inputs are low (zero) the output will be low. The possible outputs from two inputs are given in the truth table, Figure 1-5.

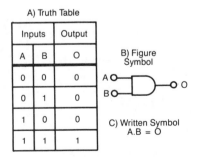

A) Truth Table

Inputs		Output
A	B	O
0	0	0
0	1	0
1	0	0
1	1	1

B) Figure Symbol

C) Written Symbol
A.B = O

Figure 1-5
Truth Table—AND Gate

Developing a Practical View of the Microprocessor

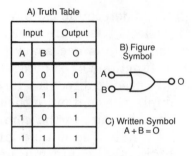

Figure 1-6
Truth Table—OR Gate

1.7.1.2   The OR Function

One or more high inputs will cause a high output with the OR function. All inputs must be zero for the output to be zero. In some ways the function is opposite to the AND function. The truth table for the OR function is shown in Figure 1-6.

The OR function is often used to mix similar, multiple inputs. One multiple input is collected in register A and the other in register B in the following example. Registers or buffers store several bits.

Bit Position	Content of Register A	Apply OR Function	Content of Register B	Result of OR Operation
7	0	+	0	0
6	1	+	1	1
5	1	+	0	1
4	1	+	1	1
3	1	+	0	1
2	0	+	0	0
1	0	+	1	1
0	1	+	1	1

Ones in registers A and/or B show up in the result. The logic OR sign is +. Therefore, A OR B can be written A + B.

1.7.1.3   The INVERT Function

The INVERT function operates as its name implies. Every "one" is inverted into a "zero" and every "zero" into a "one." The TRUTH Table is given in Figure 1-7.

This gate is used to send information from one device with positive logic to one with negative logic. It also is used to complement numbers being used for subtraction.

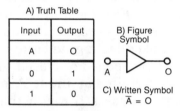

A) Truth Table

Input	Output
A	O
0	1
1	0

B) Figure Symbol

C) Written Symbol
$\overline{A} = O$

Figure 1-7
Truth Table—Inverting Gate

1.7.1.4   The EXCLUSIVE OR Function

The EXCLUSIVE OR function produces an output only if one of its two inputs is "one" and the other is "zero." If both are "one" or both "zero" the output is "zero." The truth table is shown in Figure 1-8.

This function is used frequently in I/O circuitry to detect changes in a variable. Consider a variable that can have only a value "one" or a value "zero" that is being sampled continuously, and the latest sampled value is put to one input of an

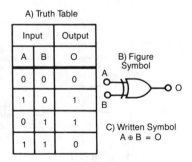

A) Truth Table

Input		Output
A	B	O
0	0	0
1	0	1
0	1	1
1	1	0

B) Figure Symbol

C) Written Symbol
$A \oplus B = O$

Figure 1-8
Truth Table—Exclusive OR Gate

EXCLUSIVE OR device, while the previous value is put on the other input. The output of the device will be "one" if a change occurs in the variable. If no change occurs, the output will be "zero."

Gates

Logic functions can be used as switches to guide information to different locations. For the simple case of the AND function, an integrated circuit representing an AND function is called an AND gate. It is called a gate because it functions like a gate in a fence that can be opened or closed. Assume that binary digital information is arriving at input A or an "AND" gate. Whether the information passes through the gate to appear at the output depends upon the state of the input terminal B. Consider what happens if the input to B is "one."

According to the logic function AND, whenever both inputs are "one" the output is "one" and when the input to one terminal is "zero," the output is "zero." Therefore, as long as the input B is "one" the output shows the same pattern as that arriving at input A. Any information represented by pulses, as is the case in the computer, goes unhindered through the gate. The gate is open. When the input to B is "zero" the truth table shows that the output is always "zero", the gate is closed, and no information may pass. If two of these gates are connected, an information switch results, as shown in Figure 1-9.

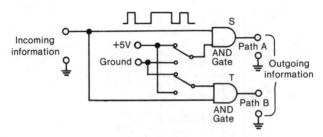

Figure 1-9
Information Channel Switch (See Appendix I for explanation of symbols used.)

Information Switch

The setting of the electronic toggle switch determines whether the AND gate S is open and the AND gate T is closed or vice versa, sending information either to output path A or to path B. "One" or "zero" on the toggle switch determines which path is selected. The "one" or "zero" to operate this dual gate can be supplied by a computer instruction consisting of binary digits directing the information flow in the computer in such a way as to carry out the instruction.

Decoder

The decoder is another important application of logic gates. The decoder, when presented with a bit pattern will set only one specific output wire high for a bit pattern, making a one-to-one relationship between bit pattern and output wire.

The AND gate is the easiest-to-follow building block for a decorder. According to Figure 1-5 the output for this gate goes high only when both inputs are high. Therefore, this gate will respond only to a bit pattern "11." To make it respond to other bit patterns, inverters can be inserted in front of the inputs. If an inverter is put in front of input A and not input B, the output of the AND gate will be high when the whole system is presented with bit pattern "01." Therefore, by putting inverters in front of the AND gate in various ways, it can be made to respond to bit pattern "00," "01," "10," and "11." Each address requires one AND gate and corresponding inverters. If the four inputs to these AND gates are connected to a common input a two-bit decoder results. A schematic for it is shown in Figure 1-10. To decode a 4-bit, 8-bit, or 16-bit address, the number of gates must be correspondingly increased and the inverters so arranged that only one AND gate is set high for one bit pattern.

Summary

Computers usually incorporate only the four logic functions: AND, OR, INVERT, and EXCLUSIVE OR. Any three of these functions can be used to generate the fourth function. Logic gates are the primary means to guide information to the correct locations in the computer.

Developing a Practical View of the Microprocessor

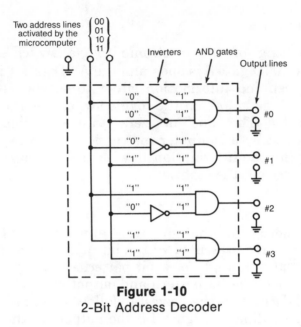

Figure 1-10
2-Bit Address Decoder

1.8 INSTRUCTION DECODER

The instruction decoder is the heart of the controller which is one of the five basic components of the computer. The instruction decoder receives information from the instruction word loaded into the instruction register, and carries out the instruction. First, it compares the bit pattern of the instruction word to a list of instruction words contained in a special ROM in the microprocessor chip. A special microprogram associated only with this instruction word is initiated when a match is found. A microprogram consists of a series of microinstructions. Each microinstruction initiates one or more control signals to set logic switches, decoders, and other devices—for example, to move the content of the program counter into the address register. When all the microinstructions of a microprogram have been sequentially carried out, it tells the program counter to advance so the next instruction can be loaded into the instruction register for execution.

CHAPTER 2

Developing a Practical View of the Microcomputer

2.1 THE COMPUTER WORD

In section 1.5, Chapter 1, we saw that it was best to use eight bits to represent letters, symbols or numbers in the computer. The computer should process these eight bits simultaneously causing all arithmetic, logic, memory, control, input, and output operations to be performed in units of eight bits at a time. These eight bits form a computer word. If a computer is designed to handle sixteen bits simultaneously throughout its operation, then the computer word will be sixteen bits long. Computer words can be any length (number of bits) but are usually factors of 2: 4, 8, 16, 32, 64, or 128 bits long.

In the previous chapter we found that 8 bits can represent up to 256 numbers, a 16-bit number up to 65,536 numbers, a 32-bit number 4.294×10^9. We see that the length of the computer word determines to a great extent the power of a computer. For example, if we compare an 8-bit word computer with a 128-bit word computer, we find that the speed of computing for the 128-bit computer is for this reason bound to be at least sixteen times faster—using data 128 bits long—not considering that the 8-bit computer has to process sequentially through the sixteen sections of 8 bits for a 128-bit number.

The number of bits in a computer word limits the number of instructions a computer can handle. A computer with an 8-bit data word can have only 256 instructions, whereas a computer with a 32-bit word can have up to 4.294×10^9 different instructions, allowing many efficient instructions for specific applications.

The length of the computer word; i.e., the number of binary digits a computer can handle at the same time, makes it possible

33

Developing a Practical View of the Microcomputer

to divide computers into categories of different powers, as shown below:

Computers with a Word Length of:	Correspond to:
1 bit	Hardware logic
4 bits	Microcomputers for control purposes
8 bits	General purpose microcomputer
16 bits	General purpose minicomputer
32 bits	Large computer
64–128 bits	Very large computer

The sophistication and efficiency with which information flows through the computer is another criterion for the capability of the computer. This is determined by the quality of the programs in the computer and the way the computer handles different programs.

2.2 OVERVIEW OF MEMORY SYSTEMS

The memory is an essential part of the computer; it stores the instructions and the data needed to carry out its operations.

For maximum efficiency, the computer has several different types of storage devices. The Arithmetic Logic Unit normally has the highest activity in the computer (40 to 60%). It requires the highest speed of operation and uses the most expensive storage devices: discrete flipflop stages. The high cost of these memory devices can be justified because of the low storage requirements in this section of the computer. Flipflops have an operating speed in the range of nanoseconds (nanosecond $= 1 \times 10^{-9}$ seconds).

The main memory of the computer is less active because for every memory store or read operation there are several ALU operations. Much slower and cheaper memory elements in the computer's main memory may be used. They operate in the order of microseconds (1×10^{-6} seconds). However, the main memory is usually the most expensive component of the computer because of the high number of storage elements in the main memory. This size of the main memory is necessary because it must contain the full length of any application program. If only a portion of a long program is loaded into the memory, the execution of the program is interrupted when the end of the loaded portion is reached. To execute the remainder of the program, it has to be loaded over the first portion of the program into the memory, extending greatly the time of its execution.

Loading an instruction into the main memory from a disk may take 3 to 500 milliseconds, depending upon the device used. The time for sequentially loading a series of instructions or data may be shorter because the number of head movements is reduced. Direct loading of instructions or data from a disk instead of from the main memory into the ALU would tremendously slow down the speed of the computer operation. Disk storage devices are normally used only as banks for programs, data, and sections of very large programs. Common floppy disks have a storage capability from about 80,000 characters for single-sided, single-density 5″ disks to about as much as 1,200,000 bytes for dual-sided, dual-density 8″ disks. Newer 3½″ disks can load up to 1,000,000 bytes because of improved technology.

Hard disks provide much larger storage capabilities than floppy disks. Such disks can store up to a hundred times more information than floppy disks and store and retrieve information nearly one hundred times faster. If still larger amounts of information need to be stored, a digital tape recorder should be used. A digital tape recorder is the best storage device for large amounts of information. However, it may take minutes to load and store information. Figure 2-1 shows the approximate relationship between cost and speed of the most common memory devices.

2.3   BASIC STORAGE ELEMENTS

2.3.1   General

As storing and retrieving of information is one of the basic operations of the computer, a more detailed description follows. The function of a computer storage element is quite similar to that of a household light switch. The "on" position of a switch indicates that the light bulb should be lit. This memory function of the switch is independent from the function of completing the

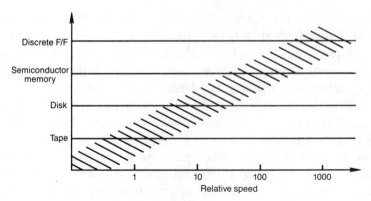

Figure 2-1
Relationship between Memory Device and Speed

electrical circuit to allow current to flow to the light bulb. Similarly, when the light switch is turned off, its new position stores the information that the light bulb should not be lit.

The other function of a light switch is to make or break the light bulb circuit. If the light switch is remotely operated by an electromagnetic actuator, the operation is similar to that of a computer memory element. For example, the position of the light switch can be tested by a short electrical pulse. If the bulb lights briefly, the switch is on; if it does not, the switch is off.

2.3.2   Static Memory Cell

As mentioned above a remotely controlled electric switch (or relay) is fully comparable to a computer storage element. Early computers used relays and switches as storage elements. A mechanical switch is much too bulky, unreliable, and slow for today's high speed computers. A flipflop is a much faster, much smaller, and more reliable electronic equivalent of the memory function of the light switch. For reference, a wiring diagram of the flipflop is shown in Figure 2-2. The flipflop, as its name indicates, has only two stable electronic states, like a light switch. The major components of a basic flipflop are two transistors and four resistors.

The transistor may be considered a control valve for an electronic current, which must be supplied by a battery or power supply. The current through the transistor can be set by a small electric current flowing through the base of the transistor (NPN,

PNP transistors). In a field effect transistor (FET) the amount of current flowing through the transistor is determined by the voltage applied to the base.

Other electronic components in a flipflop are resistors and capacitors. A resistor restricts the flow of an electric current. A capacitor stores electricity, but no direct current can flow through it. To load the capacitor with electricity, electrical current must flow in. To empty the capacitor, electrical current must flow out.

The two transistors of the flipflop are connected to each other in such a way that when one transistor is in the "on" state the other transistor is in the "off" state. To reverse this state a large positive pulse is applied to the base gate of the nonconducting transistor, which makes it conductive and turns the conducting transistor off.

Figure 2-2 shows how the two transistors are connected. The collectors (C1 and C2) of the transistors are connected through two different resistors (RC1 and RC2) to the plus side of the power supply (battery). Whereas, the emitters (E1 and E2) of both transistors are connected to the negative side of the power supply (battery), which is grounded. The base (B1 and B2) of each transistor is connected through separate resistors (RB1, RB2) to the collector of the other transistor. With this arrangement, a low collector voltage on transistor Q1 will result in a low base voltage for transistor Q2. This low voltage will reduce the

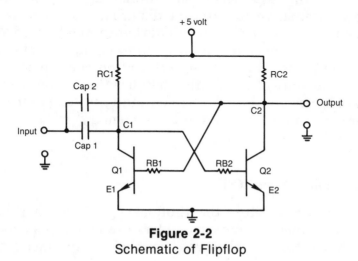

Figure 2-2
Schematic of Flipflop

Developing a Practical View of the Microcomputer

electrical current going into the base of the second transistor Q2 to zero, forcing the main (collector) current through this transistor to zero.

Because effectively no current is flowing through transistor Q2 and the voltage drop across resistor RC2 is zero, the voltage on the collector (C2) of Q2 is the same as the voltage on the plus side of the power supply. This voltage causes a current to flow through resistor RB1 to the base of transistor Q1, allowing current to flow through transistor Q1 and RC1. This current causes a voltage drop across resistor RC1, forcing the voltage of the collector (C1) of transistor Q1 to near ground level. This state of Q1 is the same as we assumed when we started to describe the function of the flipflop. This means that the on state of the first transistor keeps the second transistor in the off state and vice versa. To change the state of the flipflop, a pulse must be applied to the input of the two capacitors. This pulse will momentarily raise the voltage on the base of the nonconducting transistor Q2 through capacitor CAP1, making this transistor conducting. The base voltage on the base B1 of the transistor Q1 will drop after the input pulse has disappeared, turning off transistor Q1. This input pulse has no effect on the already conducting transistor Q1 through capacitor CAP2, because the voltage is already high at the collector C2.

Because of the dual feedback from the collectors of each transistor to the two bases, the flipflop is very stable and extremely insensitive to external disturbances, such as stray pulses or power fluctuations. A disturbance must approach the level of the input pulse for the flipflop to change its state. Similarly, turning the power supply off and on could also cause a change of the state of the flipflop because the feedback voltage, which holds the flipflop in a given state, is temporarily lost. Therefore, a computer loses all its memory when power is switched off.

2.3.3 Dynamic Memory Cell

As mentioned before the flipflop is an expensive storage element. Most modern microcomputers use much less expensive capacitors as storage elements for their main memories. A memory cell using a capacitor as the main storage element is called a dynamic memory cell. A capacitor acts as a storage element in the following manner. When charging a capacitor from a voltage source, voltage builds up between the plates (terminals) of the capacitor as the electrical charge between its plates builds up. When a capacitor is charged with five volts it is said that this capacitor is in the "on" state. When the capacitor is not charged and there is no voltage between its terminals, the capacitor is in the "off" state.

Dynamic memory cells (Figure 2-3) take up less space on the semiconductor surface than static cells because they have fewer components. To reduce the space requirements even further, the capacitance of the connection between the transistor Q1 and Q3 in Figure 2-3 can serve as the storage capacitance of the cell. Transistor Q1 controls the charging and discharging of the capacitor C, whereas the second transistor, Q3, monitors how large the charge of the capacitor is.

Using a small capacitor as a storage element presents a major problem, because a capacitor loses its electrical charge due to internal and external leakage. The tiny storage capacitors formed in the semiconducting body of a memory chip lose their charges rapidly. To minimize additional capacitor charge losses, transistors with very high input impedance, such as field-effect transistors ("FETs"), are used to control and monitor the capacitors (Transistors Q1 and Q2, Figure 2-3).

There are many variations in the basic design of the dynamic memory cell. These are aimed, as in the static cell

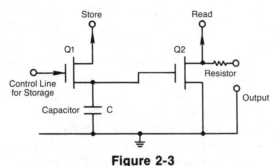

Figure 2-3
Capacitor Storage Element

design, to reduce cost and malfunctions as well as to increase the speed of the cells. The major disadvantage of the dynamic cell at present is the relatively fast discharge of the capacitor requiring a constant recharging of the capacitors about every two milliseconds. Recharging may be accomplished by an electronic circuit on the memory board, the most common practice today. The microprocessor may be set up to recharge the capacitor memory cells every two seconds.

A capacitor memory cell is called "dynamic" because its state is not constant and needs constant recharging. A flipflop memory cell is called "static" because its state does not change as long as it is energized.

2.3.4 Read Only Memory (ROM)

Read Only Memory (ROM) is a common type of memory. Information stored in a ROM is unalterable either by computer or power supply disruptions. A ROM is mostly used for programs needed on powerup of the computer such as monitors, disk loaders, and special interface programs. Information is permanently stored during manufacturing into the ROM by setting each memory location to give an unalterable 5 or 0 V output. A new ROM has to be manufactured to correct an error or make a change.

In the fusible link ROM the designer instead of the manufacturer can set each location to an unalterable "1" or "0." The program then is put into the ROM by a special interface that generates the "0" or "1" by burning fusible links built in at every memory location.

Another more flexible ROM is the Electrically Programmable Read Only Memory (EPROM). It works similarly to the dynamic memory by using capacitors to store information, with the difference that the capacitor charge stays on much longer (over ten years) due to a different, much more expensive, semiconductor design. This memory device may be reprogrammed first by erasing it with ultraviolet light for about ten to fifteen minutes, then it must be programmed with a special interface, which supplies the higher voltage necessary and is able to repeat the program a hundred or more times. The disadvantage of this type of memory is its high cost.

During the design of microcomputer systems, changes must often be made, especially in the monitor programs.

Special versions of single-chip microcomputers exist that contain an EPROM instead of a ROM memory. These EPROM versions cost much more than the usual ROM version of microcomputer chips. However, the savings due to their increased flexibility more than justifies the increased cost.

2.4 ADDRESSING THE MEMORY

The computer uses an identifying number (or address) for each bit of data, program, or program statement it has in a storage device to make possible its recovery. As an example, to store ten consecutive numbers 27, 28, 29, 30, 31, 32, 33, 34, 35, and 36 in the main memory of the computer one can assign the following ten addresses to these points:

ADDRESSES	1	2	3	4	5	6	7	8	9	10
DATA VALUES	27	28	29	30	31	32	33	34	35	36

Assigning a storage element to each of these addresses allows the computer to read and change the data content in any of these addresses.

Storage elements can be arranged randomly without inhibiting the operation of the computer. However, an arrangement with continually increasing numbers is more efficient. Computer memories are pictured with the smallest memory address at the top and the largest address at the bottom. A possible layout of a linear arrangement of memory cells is shown in Figure 2-4. This arrangement is not the best, because the area on the chip is not used very efficiently. Elements are better arranged in a matrix fashion. The time required to reach any specific element in a matrix memory is in this case nearly constant. The distribution of the memory elements is optimal. As each memory element can be reached without any time penalty and can be randomly selected, this type of memory arrangement is called Random Access Memory (RAM).

Figure 2-5 shows the operation of a sixteen-element memory. There are four columns and four rows of elements. An element is

Developing a Practical View of the Microcomputer

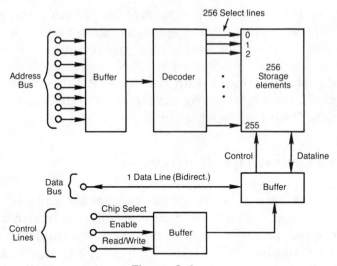

Figure 2-4
Linear Memory Addressing System

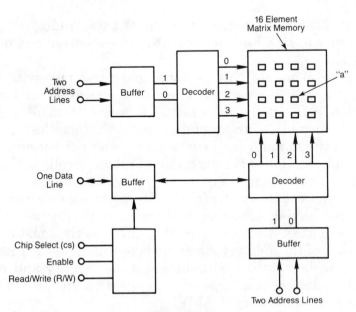

Figure 2-5
Matrix Memory System

energized when the appropriate column and row wires are activated.

The address wires selecting a single memory element are activated by a single address word. For a sixteen-element memory to identify sixteen numbers, the address word must have four bits. Let's take, for example, the address word "1010." As there are four columns, two bits of the address word are assigned to four column address wires. The other two address bits are assigned to the four row wires. A decoder is provided for each of the column and row sides to translate 2 bits to four wires each. The two address bits "10" applied to the four row wires activate the second wire. Similarly, the two address bits "10" for the four column wires will activate the second wire. The address word "1010" activates the element "a" in the sixteen element storage device in Figure 2-5.

The read and write operation is described in more detail in the following section.

2.5   EXPANDED MEMORY CELL CONFIGURATION

2.5.1   Static RAM

Two transistors (Q5, Q6) are added to the original flipflop circuit (Figure 2-2) to make possible the READ and WRITE functions (Figure 2-6). Two other transistors are added to increase the stability of the flipflop. The expanded memory cell works in the following manner: When power is first applied, either Q1 or Q2 may be in the "on" (conductive) state. Assume that Q2 is "on" and node 2 is near ground potential. This state indicates that a "zero" is written into the memory cell.

To write "1" into the memory cell the transistor Q1 must be switched to the "on" state. For this purpose, 5V is applied to the two column select lines in Figure 2-6 and on the row select line, making the two transistors Q5 and Q6 conductive for a short time. The duration of the pulse is designed so that it is present long enough to switch the cell securely on but not long enough to switch it back. During this time a voltage of 5 V is transferred from the left column select line to node 2 and the base of transistor Q1, which were at ground potential, turning transistor Q1 "on." No voltage is transferred to node 1, because both the node

Developing a Practical View of the Microcomputer

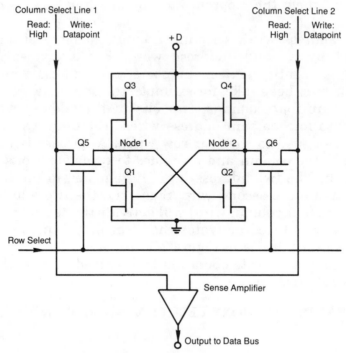

Figure 2-6
Flipflop Memory Cell Expanded

and the column select wire are already at 5 V. Turning transistor
Q1 "on" will turn transistor Q2 "off" because of the double feedback between the transistors Q1 and Q2 (node 2–base Q1, node
1–base Q2). The memory cell is now locked into the "on" state.

To READ the cell, the column select lines are switched off
from their voltage source by a tristate buffer and voltage of 5 V
is applied to the column select lines by the column sense amplifier. A short 5 V pulse applied to the row select line will make
both transistors Q5 and Q6 conductive, but because of the voltage difference between the left column wire node 1 (5 V) and node 2
(0 V), current will flow only in the left column select wire and not in
the right column line, setting the column sense amplifier for an
"on" (5 V) output. The flipflop has not changed state because the
current flowing is too small to effect a change of the transistors.
Many variations of this static memory design cell exist in commercial applications. They are aimed at reducing the area and
increasing the speed and reliability of the memory cell.

2.5.2 Dynamic RAM

A dynamic memory cell (Figure 2-7) is cheaper and more compact than a static memory cell (Figure 2-6).

To write a "1" into a dynamic memory cell, the column write line is raised to 5 volts. Then a short 5 V pulse applied to the row select line, turns on transistor Q1, enabling the capacitor to be changed to 5 V. When the pulse has ended, Q1 and Q3 go into the "off" state essentially disconnecting the capacitor from the row select and column select lines and so locking the "on" condition into the memory cell.

If the selected column write line is at 0 V when the row select pulse is generated, the capacitor will discharge until it reaches 0 V writing an "off" or "0" state into the memory cell.

To read the memory cell the column write line is disconnected from its power source by a tristate buffer. A 5 V pulse is generated on the row select line. If the voltage on the capacitor is 5 V, transistor Q3 will be on and, because of the pulse on the row select line, transistor Q2 is also conducting and a "0" is transferred to the column sense amplifier, which then indicates that the memory cell is in the "on" state. If the voltage of the capacitor is zero, transistor Q2 is nonconducting. The voltage on the column select line is then set approximately to 5 V by a small current bled to the column select line. The column sense amplifier will then indicate an "off" state for the memory cell.

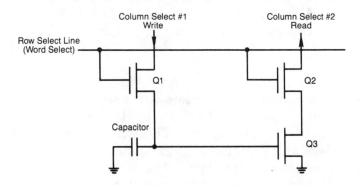

Figure 2-7
Capacitor Memory Cell with Read and Write Capability

2.6 OTHER STORAGE DEVICES

2.6.1 Introduction

A magnetizable film, usually coated with ferric oxide, can be used for information storage in computer systems. This film can be magnetized in specific directions by magnetic fields. A "zero" bit is normally represented by random magnetization. A "one" bit is represented by oriented magnetization. This type of information storage is found with hard disks, floppy disks, and tapes. The major advantage of this technique is that storage of information is independent of power supplies. Its major disadvantage is its relatively slow transfer of information.

2.6.2 Disk Storage

The cost of a single bit for any of the above memories is low—a small fraction of a cent; however, an average-sized memory is still a major portion of the cost in any microcomputer. If one needs to store even larger amounts of information, disk or tape storage should be used. Information is stored in about 40 to 140 circular tracks on the floppy disk. Each track is usually further divided into six or more sectors with 256 or 512 bytes each. One hole in a soft sectored disk signals to the microcomputer the start of the first or other designated sector. To indicate a double-sided disk, the hole in the jacket is moved a little more to the right from that of a single-sided disk. The two outside tracks usually store the directory and other pertinent information for the disk. On a hard sectored disk each sector is signaled by a hole, requiring several holes in a disk.

2.6.3 Tape Storage

Two types of tape recorders are used for microcomputers, audio cassette records, and reel-to-reel tape recorders. The audio cassette recorder is inexpensive. This recorder is not able to store digital pulses and each pulse (digit) must be translated by a special interface into a tone burst. The *Kansas City Standard* has been developed to make this special translation. A "one" is represented by a 2400 Hz tone burst eight cycles long, and a "zero" is represented by a 1200 Hz tone burst four cycles long, making the bit for "one" and for "zero" equally long and conforming to 300 baud or bits per second transmission speed (bps). Cassette recorders are subject to speed fluctuations and a special device in the interface allows speed variations of up to plus or minus 25 percent to occur without any errors. A true clock speed is abstracted from played back characters. This variable clock speed is then used to clock the data correctly into the microprocessor.

Good cassette recorders can store data up to 2400 baud. To store data at much higher rates, DC tape recorders are used. In these tape recorders a special linearizing technique is used to record correctly all frequencies down to DC. Information is recorded on the tape with nine parallel tracks. Eight channels provide for eight bits. The ninth track is used to synchronize the recorded information with the computer. The nine-track DC tape recorder may record one hundred or more times as fast as a cassette recorder because it handles bytes instead of parts of bits. Prices of these recorders are approximately proportional to their speed.

Summary

Digital storage devices can be divided into four major categories:

Device	Speed	Storage Capacity	Major Application
Flipflops	very fast	small	ALU, buffers
RAM	fast	moderate	main memory
Disk	moderate	large	program storage
Tape	slow	very large	long term data storage

2.7 I/O DEVICES FOR USE IN SYSTEMS

The computer system described thus far can function without special input/output devices. The data bus can be connected directly to external digital devices and deliver messages. The address bus can address different external devices. Messages from different external devices can be fed to the computer using a simple polling program. But this leaves the use of the micro-computer somewhat limited.

I/O devices dramatically enhance the capability of the microcomputer. Consider the case of control of the temperature in a laboratory by a computer. Without an I/O device, the computer must compare the actual temperature to the set (reference) temperature continually to avoid missing a change in the temperature.

This is a very inefficient utilization of a microprocessor because of its time spent reading the temperature—maybe more than ten thousand times a second—while no action is required. As room temperatures need to be read only every few minutes, a microcomputer could carry out over ten million calculations between each necessary temperature reading! The computer also could be used simultaneously to balance one's budget or to write a letter. To allow the computer to perform other functions without missing a temperature reading, we could install one of the following arrangements: (1) Get an external clock that alerts the computer every few minutes to take a temperature reading; (2) make a special electronic device, incorporating an EXCLUSIVE OR gate, to alert the computer when the temperature is changing; or (3) use an external device that has its own control signal, which it can send to the computer to read its temperature. Any of these or other similar arrangements would free the computer to perform other functions with very little investment in time, software, or hardware.

2.7.1 External Clock

The external clock provides timing pulses to the computer or other external devices. The frequency of the pulses can be adjusted manually or by computer control from microseconds to hours or days. The external clock can derive its timing from either the AC line frequency, the least expensive way; the computer clock, next in cost; or a dedicated crystal oscillator, the best and most expensive way.

Deriving the timing pulses from the line frequency limits their precision to the order of milliseconds. Deriving timing pulses from the computer clock has the advantage of being highly precise (in the order of microseconds), but the disadvantage is that this clock stops when the computer is switched off. Therefore, times and dates will become incorrect.

The computer clock is a special generator of pulses to carry out the functions in the computer in a synchronized way. The pulse frequency is usually in the order of a million cycles per second and is maintained at a given rate by a highly precise quartz oscillator.

An external timer with its own crystal clock and rechargeable power supply is the most accurate and dependable clock, but is relatively expensive. Such a clock can be set by the software programs residing in the computer.

2.7.2 Interrupt Systems

An interrupt system signals the computer that an important enough event has occurred to justify the jump to a different program to serve the external event. Consider the example of the laboratory temperature control. Suppose the temperature in the laboratory experiment changed while the computer was running an unrelated program.

How is this interruption carried out without disturbing the previous running program? All computers, including microcomputers, have one or more control lines going to the CPU (Central Processing Unit) labeled "Interrupt." When one of those lines is activated, either by going high or low, the computer automatically loads the contents of an address assigned to that interrupt line into the program counter. If the first address of an interrupt service program is entered into this address the computer will execute this interrupt serving program. In the above example, the microcomputer would receive information of a temperature change and issue the necessary control commands to the temperature control system to restore the originally set temperature. The computer would automatically return to the previous running program when it came to the end of the interrupt service program.

To return automatically to the old program, the content of the program counter and the other registers must be stored before the interrupt is carried out. Therefore, when the computer receives an interrupt it first saves the content of the registers before jumping to the address of the interrupt program. When the interrupt program is finished the computer goes back to the program by first restoring the original content of the registers, including the programs counter, and restarting correctly the interrupted program. In Chapter 4, this operation is explained in detail for the four different interrupts of the Motorola 6800.

2.7.3   Parallel I/O Buffers

The main function of I/O buffers is to store external information or to send information to the outside so that it can be picked up or sent by the computer independently of the operation of the outside device. A tremendous amount of computer time is saved because once the computer has prepared the information to be sent out, the information is only on the data bus for a short time. For information to be available for a longer time than a fraction of a microsecond, the computer must be dedicated to sending it continually to the data bus. An I/O buffer frees the computer from that operation and makes the computer available for other service.

When you are using an I/O buffer for sending or receiving information, you also need a system that notifies the outside device or computer that information is available or has been received. This system is called a handshaking system. It coordinates the sending and receiving of signals between the computer and an outside device.

If, for example, the computer is continually sending information to an outside device, it signals to the outside device when the required information is available on the I/O buffer. The computer can now return to another program. The outside device sends a signal to the computer when it has received the information on the I/O buffer and the computer can put the next information on the I/O buffer. The computer interrupts its present program to put the next piece of information on the I/O buffer. In this way, no information is lost. I/O buffers and their ways of operation are explained in more detail in Chapter 4.

2.7.4   Serial I/O Devices

The above-described parallel I/O buffers best serve outside devices that are close to the location of the computer, as is usually the case in a laboratory. Sending information appreciable distances through parallel I/O buffers becomes very costly because of the length and number of wires involved. The information may be sent over only two wires. To send an eight-bit or sixteen-bit word over two wires, the bits must be sent sequentially. This system has been internationally standardized as the RS232 system, described later in Chapter 4, in which all information is sent in groups of eight bits. The information in the eight bits is expressed according to the ASCII code described earlier. Only one character is sent at a time. Bits are added to the ASCII character to signal the start and the end of a character to the receiving side. This allows the sending of the characters at irregular intervals, simplifying greatly the complexity of the transmitting system. The transmitting and receiving side must be set up for the same transmitting speed. Serial transmission is much slower than parallel transmission; but often high speed of transmission is not necessary. Improved technology has increased greatly transmission speed.

To store serial information sent from outside devices, serial I/O buffers are being used by microcomputers. As with the parallel I/O buffers, the serial buffers can generate handshaking signals to control the flow of information so that no byte is lost. More information is given on Asynchronous Communications Interfaces Adapters (serial buffers) (ACIA) in Chapter 4.

Laying wires to send information long distances is often impractical. It would be better to use existing systems such as the telephone system. Unfortunately, the telephone system is designed to transmit the human voice in the frequency range of 300 Hz to 3000 Hz and not the DC component, which is essential for the transmission of electrical pulses. Pulses must be transformed into tone bursts before they go on the telephone line and then they must be reconverted to pulses at the receiving end. The devices that accomplish this are called *Modems* (MOdulator DEModulator). Because a set of additional devices is necessary to send information over the telephone system, additional control signals are necessary, and they also are described in more detail in Chapter 4.

2.7.5 Other I/O Devices

Other I/O devices customarily used in interface systems include Analog to Digital Converters (ADC), Digital to Analog Converters (DAC), Multiplexers, Decoders, and Sample and Hold devices.

A multitude of other I/O devices are used: direct memory access devices, which allow outside information to bypass the CPU and go directly to the memory; memory managing devices to extend the memory range; interrupt controllers to increase the number of available interrupts; power interfaces for motor control; and relays. These devices generally use optical couplers to separate the line from the computer and drive motors. To operate AC motors or other AC operated devices, triacs are normally used. Triacs are semiconductor devices, which can directly control AC currents by small DC voltages.

2.8 PERIPHERALS

2.8.1 General

Peripherals are devices external to the CPU that enhance the operation of the computer. Many peripherals can be connected to microcomputers. Figure 2-8 shows some of the more widely used peripherals in the science and engineering fields; some are described below in more detail.

2.8.2 Terminals

Terminals are used to enter and receive information from the computer. They are equipped with a CRT (Cathode Ray Tube) screen and a keyboard. Most CRT screens display from 16 to 66 lines with 32 to 132 characters. Keyboards are similar to typewriter keyboards, with additional return keys, escape keys,

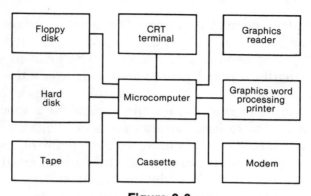

Figure 2-8
Peripherals of Microcomputer System

and break keys; they often have a cursor control pad and a numeric key pad. The cursor indicates where the next character on the CRT screen is being written. Some keyboards have keys to which special functions can be assigned. This is important for special functions in word processor, spreadsheets, and accounting systems. Display speeds range from 110 to over 38,000 baud.

Terminals may have high resolution graphics and disk loadable special character sets available. Some terminals now on the market talk to the operator. Their vocabulary is generally limited to 256 words. One or more lines may be set apart in the CRT display for operator information such as which file is being edited, the character and line position of the cursor, and so on.

2.8.3   Printers

Printers print information from the computer and the terminal keyboard to make permanent hard copy records. There are six basic printer types: character impact printer, matrix impact printer, thermal printer, metal foil printer, inkjet printer, and laser printer.

The character impact printer produces the highest quality printing by using a separate key for each letter as on a typewriter. The images of the letters are mounted on a print wheel, ball, or band for faster print speed and easier exchange if another font is needed. The impact printer is the slowest and one of the most expensive of all printers.

The matrix printer is among the least expensive printers and is at the same time one of the fastest. Each letter is created by the print head using a series of dots. The print head has 7 to over 20 vertically aligned print wires that are activated by an electric coil pressing against an inked ribbon to make dots on the paper. As the head moves in steps across the paper, different wires are activated to form letters, words, and sentences.

Matrix printers can simulate impact printing by printing each line twice or more times at slightly offset positions, thus forming solid lines from dots (dot overprinting).

Further, matrix printers are ideally suited for making high resolution graphics pictures at a relatively high speed. For this purpose the printer should be able to increment the paper advance for each dot forward and backward. For example, with 80 characters per line and with 8 dots assigned for each character, including the space between the characters, a printer has 640 dots per line for high graphics resolution.

The thermal printer is the quietest printer, but is comparatively very slow. Also, the print may fade after some time especially in a warm environment. Thermal printers are usually of the matrix type, where the dots are created by tiny heated spots on the print head. The printing speed is determined by the rate of heating and cooling of the spots on the print head. Such matrix printers, therefore, are usually slow (300 baud).

Metal foil printers compete with thermal printers; they give a more permanent printout and are faster. The copy medium is thin aluminum foil-coated paper. To make a mark, the aluminum foil is evaporated selectively by a small electrical spark from the printing head.

The above printers usually print from 40 to 200 characters per line.

The following printers differ from the printers used with microcomputers because of their higher cost, flexibility, and speed.

Inkjet printers create characters on the paper by pointing a very fine jet stream of ink toward the paper. The capillary from which the ink emerges is vibrated; thus creating tiny ink droplets of uniform size. By electrostatically deflecting the charged droplets, the printer forms letters on the paper. Inkjet printers are fast and are very versatile in printing characters.

Laser printers create letter images on a paper similar to an electron beam in a CRT screen by using a multitude of scans per character line to create all the appropriate images.

A stationary laser beam is deflected by a rotating multi-faced mirror to a rotating drum. The drum is advanced only so much during each scan so that the tiny laser spot is able to cover the whole surface of the drum. To create the images on the drum from the laser beam and transfer them to the paper, a system very similar to that of a xerox copier is used.

The laser printer is without question the most expensive printer discussed here, but it is also the fastest (860 lines per minute) and the most flexible of all the printers. One of its most outstanding qualities is the sharpness of the print.

2.8.4 Modems

Special devices are needed to transmit the information from the computer over telephone circuits. These are called *modems*. Modems are more fully described in Chapter 4.

2.8.5 Other Peripherals

Magnetic tape, cassette, and disk systems have been described in more detail in section 2.6 (Memory Systems) of this chapter.

Other peripherals often used to enter information into a computer system, other than those described in Section 2.6, are: optical character readers (OCR), which are able to read a text into a computer automatically; optical scanners, to read test scores into a computer; graphic tablets to transfer diagrams and maps into a computer; and X-Y printers for printing tables and graphs.

CHAPTER 3

Simplified Guide
to Programming

3.1 INTRODUCTION

Programs are a series of instructions or commands for a computer
to achieve a specific objective. If these instructions are written
in a language made for a specific computer, this computer then
is able to carry out the objective of the program.

There are many different ways to write a program for a specific
objective and many different ways a computer can be designed to
carry out the tasks in a program. Guidelines for computer design
have evolved that make program writing easier. For example,
minimizing the number of basic instruction codes makes writing an
assembly language program much easier. To compensate for the
lower number of instruction codes, the number of modifiers
attached to each instruction code is increased. These modifiers
are called the addressing codes and work in very similar ways for
most instructions in a given computer.

One can see this on the 6800 and its successor chips. Even
though the number of basic instructions decreases from the 6800
to the 6809 and the 68000, the number of addressing modes sharply
increases. The 8080 and its successor chips did not show much
increase in this respect and the 6800 family of microprocessors is
becoming more and more the programmer's choice. This simplifies
the work of the computer programmers who do the majority of work
in setting up computer systems.

There are many other features in a computer that make
programming easier. These are: relocatability, having an adequate
number of registers, easy switching between registers, automatic
error checking, and macrocodes.

The programmer must choose the most efficient language and
computer for a given objective. The language, with the computer

system, must be fast enough to carry out the program. A check must be made to determine if a machine language program is fast enough for the program objective. If it is too fast, the slightly slower, but much easier to write, *assembly language* could be considered. If the speed of the assembly language is not needed, one can choose any one of the higher languages such as: BASIC, FOR-TRAN, PASCAL, ALGOL, ADA, C-Language, LISP. BASIC comes in two versions on home computers: as a compiler and as an interpreter language. BASIC comes usually in the interpreter version, which is much slower than the compiler version, but is, on the other hand, much easier to learn. Each line of program code is separately checked for errors. In the compiler version, the computer checks the program for errors only after the whole program has been entered.

Assembler, compiler, and interpreter are programs that are specific for each computer and that automatically translate the entered source code (program) in the selected language into the machine code, the only language the computer can understand.

Recently, programs have appeared that write programs for the user when given exact information about what they should accomplish. Several of these are now on the market.

BASIC, in its compiler form, has developed to a point where it has become almost as fast, flexible, and adaptable as FORTRAN without FORTRAN's confusion. PASCAL was developed to allow a rigorous application of structured programming, which is a more efficient programming method. Today, it is probably the best language for teaching and science, and it is adequate for engineering applications. FORTH and LISP are relatively recent developments that combine high speed of execution with relative ease of programming, especially for programs that use a high amount of I/O.

Because of the increasing number of microcomputer systems in the United States, prerecorded programs mostly written in BASIC, are now available for many different areas and are quite inexpensive. The probability is high that a program one needs, or at least one close to it, is already available. Such a "canned" program could be easily linked by the programmer into the main application program. Although such a module may require more running time and memory space than that of a dedicated program, its use is justified by the savings in programming effort and by the steadily decreasing cost of memories. One should always remember that if one has to pay for the programming and the hardware development, the average programming costs are eight to nine times higher than the hardware. This is true for practically all types of computer systems.

Another way to save on programming time is to choose the most appropriate operating system. A small microcomputer system only offers the simple elements of an operating system, usually called monitor systems; more sophisticated systems meet the demands for more complex operations. This is true especially for the disk operating systems (DOS) now available for practically all microcomputer systems. One of the finest multiuser operating systems now available on many microcomputers is the UNIX operating system, which was originally designed by Bell Laboratories.

Before we go into more detail about the art of programming, we should like to stress, especially to engineers, the close relationship that exists between hardware design and programming.

3.2 RELATIONSHIP BETWEEN HARDWARE AND SOFTWARE

Software is really just a means to set up hardware for a desired condition. It causes certain voltages to be set at specific points of the computer hardware to obtain the desired outputs. After recognizing the relationship between software and hardware, we think that even a hardware enthusiast will enjoy programming.

Consider first an imaginary Programmable Electronic Processor (PEP). This little device has initially only two modes between the input and the output. In the first mode a "one" on the input will produce an output of "one." In the second mode an input of "one" will produce a "zero" at the output. Figure 3-1 shows how such a device can be built with an EXCLUSIVE OR (XOR) gate and a switch.

According to the truth table in Figure 3-1, a high (1) input at I will produce a high (1) output at F when the control switch is in the lower position (Mode 1), which grounds the input to the control XOR gate. When the switch is in the high position (Mode 2), a high (1) at the input will give a low (0) at the output at F. A bit

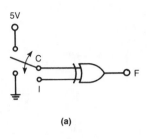

Control	Input	Output
C	I	F
0	0	0
0	1	1
1	0	1
1	1	0

(a)

(b)

Figure 3-1
Exclusive OR Gate

value of "1" corresponds to a nominal voltage of 5 V; a bit value of "0" corresponds to a voltage of 0 V.

Push buttons A and B and an R-S latch can be used instead of the toggle switch C in Figure 3-1. An R-S latch is an electronic device in some way similar in function to the flipflop shown in Figure 3-2. It has two stable states. The main difference is that it has two inputs. Momentarily pressing push button A puts the output Q of the R-S latch into the "on" (5 V) state. Whereas, momentarily pressing push button B puts Q into the "off" (0 V) state. The software of our system contains two programmable instructions to perform the operations as shown in Table I.

The application engineer need not be an expert on the internal workings of the system. He can use the system effectively by considering it to be a device with input and output (I/O) ports, terminals requiring certain applied voltages, a means to enter a program (a keyboard in this case), and a set of instructions (Table I below). In Figure 3-3, the components of Figure 3-2 are divided into two packages. The original components are shown with dotted lines. The new system has two components, as shown in Figure 3-4.

TABLE I. INSTRUCTION SET

Mode	Instruction	Push Button	Operation
1	AA	A	$F = I$
2	BB	B	$F = \overline{I}$

Simplified Guide to Programming

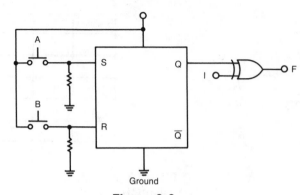

Figure 3-2
Programming with an R-S Latch

The user now has a processor PEP and a keyboard KB. The system can now be set up by connecting the terminals (1), (2), and (3) of the PEP with the corresponding terminals (1), (2), and (3) of the keyboard (KB). Terminal (4) is for the power supply, terminal (5) is the output port, terminal (6) is the input port, and terminal (7) is the ground connection. The application notes to be supplied with this processor provide the *instruction set* (software) for the particular system as shown in Table I.

The software allows us to program the system for either F=I or $F = \bar{I}$ by entering, through the keyboard, either instruction (word) AA or instruction (word) BB. If the system is used for only one application, e.g. F = I, then we can have terminal (2) of the PEP internally connect to terminal (1) and terminal (3) internally to ground. The keyboard (KB) would not be needed.

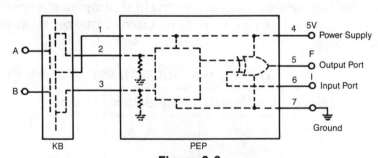

Figure 3-3
Programming an Electronic Processor

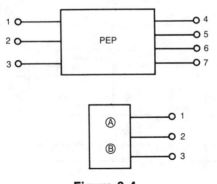

Figure 3-4
System Components

This system can be easily extended. In the above example we stored the program in a latch, which we can designate as *location 1* or *memory with address 1*. In a more complex system we may want to store two instructions at two memory locations with two addresses, 1 and 2. This can be done by first designating the address and then entering the instruction. An example is shown in Figure 3-5.

First, we press key 1 momentarily. This addresses memory location 1 by closing CMOS switches a and b. Second, we enter instruction AA or BB into this address by depressing the appropriate instruction key. Then, after all keys have been released, the system returns to its original state, except that now a "1" or a "0" has been programmed into memory location 1. Finally, we address memory location 2 by depressing key 2, and enter instruction AA or BB into this location.

In this particular example we had two inputs I and $\bar{\text{I}}$. A clock (i.e., a square-wave oscillator) preceding the input terminals of the EXCLUSIVE OR gates by JK flipflops makes possible the entering of input information into the processor at the times prescribed by clock pulses (Figure 3-6).

A sequence of operations may be desired to occur in the system in response to a single input. This can be achieved by using the system of Figure 3-6 with slight modifications. Here, we enter the input at terminal I1 and connect the output of the EXCLUSIVE OR associated with this signal to input terminal I2. Furthermore, an inverter is inserted between the clock output

Simplified Guide to Programming

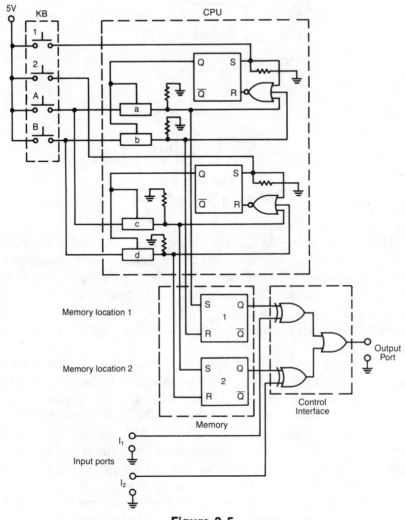

Figure 3-5
System with Two Addresses

and the C terminal of the JK flipflop associated with I2. Instruction 2 will then take effect in sequence after instruction 1.

3.2.1 Process Control

To control the process, the system must be interfaced with a sensor that has a response to the output variable. Suppose

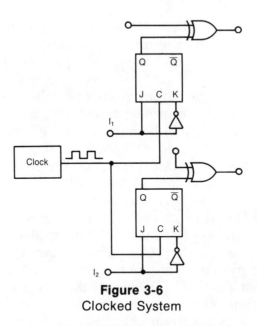

Figure 3-6
Clocked System

we are fabricating a plastic material and the temperature must be maintained at a given value above ambient. We use a resistive heater that is controlled by an *SCR,* and we sense the temperature with a thermistor pair arranged in a bridge. Using the system of Figure 3-4, we built the system as shown in Figure 3-7.

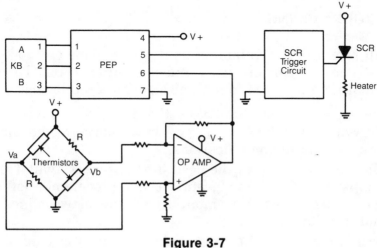

Figure 3-7
Heating System

When the temperature is below the required value, the resistance values of the thermistors (which have negative temperature coefficients of resistance) are greater than the resistances of the resistors R and we have Va less than Vb. This results in zero voltage output from the differential amplifier. Having the PEP processor programmed with instruction BB, the output of the processor will be high (logic "1") which will cause triggering of the SCR, and will energize the heater coil. Conversely, when the temperature reaches the required value, Va greater than Vb, the output of the PEP processor changes to logic "0" and the heater turns off automatically.

To control the temperature to some level below ambient for some other process, use the same PEP controller, except that we program it with instruction AA and we replace the heater with a Peltier cooling system. The controller will produce an output (Va greater than Vb) that will activate the refrigeration unit until Va is smaller than Vb.

The point is that we can use the same hardwired PEP system for different controllers, simply by changing the program. Real life computers are similar with the only difference being that eight programming bits are used in normal microcomputers, instead of one or two programming bits. The eight programming bits comprise the eight-bit word of the instruction code.

3.3 PROGRAMMING GUIDE

We will return to programming as it is now done on most computers. A few important steps and precautions must be taken when writing a program to minimize potential problems.

1. Write clearly and specifically the purpose of the program. Everybody involved in the project should agree on the program and future modifications.
2. Make certain that all the needed hardware is available and compatible with the program. Normal procurement of hardware takes three to nine months lead time between inception and installation.
3. Write clearly how the program is to achieve specific results. For example, if a peak is to be detected, specify what peak detection method is to be used and why. If averaging is to be

used, specify the averaging method (and reference point) to be used and why. At this stage all techniques, methods, and algorithms should be selected and the reasons for particular choices stated.

4. Write an overall flowchart for a program of the complete project. Then, write the flowchart(s) for each section of the program.
5. Decide what languages should be used for the main program and each individual section of the program, and check to see if prepackaged programs are available.
6. After corrections are made and programs are finalized, detailed flowcharts for all programs must be developed and recorded, detailing each separate action of the computer.
7. Each detailed flowchart must be coded with the instruction codes of the selected computer.
8. Errors in instruction codes and flowcharts must be eliminated by running separately the program of each section through the computer.
9. All remaining errors of the complete program must be eliminated by running the whole program through the computer under realistic conditions after each section has been checked separately.
10. Verify the achievement of the goals of the program by demonstrating it on the computer, and obtain the approval of all concerned.

In summary, the major steps of writing a program are:

1. Define objectives.
2. Select principle of carrying out the objectives.
3. Write flow diagram.
4. Code the program.
5. Test the program.

3.4 ELEMENTARY MICROCOMPUTER OPERATION

3.4.1 Introduction

All computers, including microcomputers, follow the basic design of Figure 1-2. Figure 3-8 shows a more detailed view of the

Simplified Guide to Programming

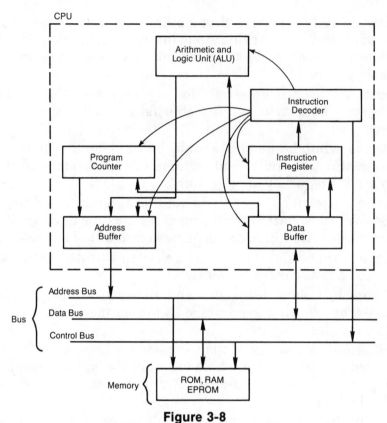

Figure 3-8
Main Interconnections in a CPU

CPU, indicating that most of the control in the computer origi-
nates from the instruction decoder, the special MPU ROM, and
the associated circuitry. By being able to load a wide variety of
instructions and instruction sequences into the decoder, the
computer can respond almost instantly to a wide selection of
commands.

To make the execution of a program more efficient, instructions and data should reside in the same memory area. This concept of storing instructions and data in the same memory area is
called the "Van Neumann Stored Program Concept." This is true
mainly for computers with a single processor. For computers
with multiple processors this arrangement is less desirable.

For a program example, to carry out the mathematical
expression 3 + 4 the following sequence of information and

instructions must be loaded into the main memory in the following order: the number three, the instruction to load this number into the ALU, the number four, the instruction to load this number into the ALU, the instruction to add these two numbers, and finally the instruction to store the sum in a new location. Each time the computer is asked to carry out such a program, the controller goes sequentially through the memory locations of the program selected, starting with the first address and stopping at the last address.

Inserting the two numbers ("3" and "4") of the example into two different places of our program is not very convenient. Grouping all the numbers in one area and the programs into another in the locations near to each other in the RAM memory would be better, especially if one has to process many numbers. One way of doing this would be to put all the numbers in the addressing range 0010 to 0020, while the program to process these numbers would be placed in the addressing range 0000 to 000F. Such a program would be:

Step 1: Locate the first number in the memory.
Step 2: Enter this number in the ALU.
Step 3: Locate the second number in the memory.
Step 4: Enter this number in the ALU.
Step 5: Add these two numbers.
Step 6: Store the result in a designated memory location.

How the computer "executes" the program is shown in detail below.

The computer takes the first instruction and puts it into the instruction register. The instruction decoder connected to the instruction register immediately decodes the instruction and activates the appropriate circuitry. After the execution of the instruction is completed, the program counter is advanced so the next instruction can be fetched. In multiple byte instructions the program counter is advanced during the instruction execution so addresses or data necessary to carry out the instruction can be fetched. This cycle of operation continues until all the instructions in the program have been completed.

An instruction is generally divided into two parts: the opcode (operation code), which tells the computer what to do, and the operand, which is a piece of data or information that the computer processes according to the opcode. The opcode and the operand have eight bits which correspond to the number of bits in the computer word.

The majority of instructions thus have two bytes in a microcomputer. The first byte in any program and in an instruction is always an opcode for positive identification without special key bits. This simplifies, speeds up, and increases the number of possible opcodes and data from 127 to 255 in microcomputers with one-byte computer words.

The program counter is loaded with the address of the first byte (opcode) and then advances to the next higher number after each instruction has been completed until an END instruction is encountered.

3.5 COMPUTER CLOCKS

Decoding and executing the instruction takes several steps in the electronic operation of the computer. To coordinate these steps microcomputers normally have two clocks. One (the first clock) is for the "inside" operations—concerning those for the ALU, controller, or bus—and one (second clock) is for the "outside" operations including memory, and any I/O operation such as disk, terminal, or tape (Figure 3-9).

The clock cycles are arranged so that the rise and fall time for each clock cycle is within the quiet period of the other clock. Only the rise and fall times of each clock cycle activate the microcomputer. The interval between the rise and fall times is used to stabilize any actions that have been initiated. For example, when an address is put on the Address Bus, it takes a certain time for those lines with a "one" to reach the full five volts (Fig-

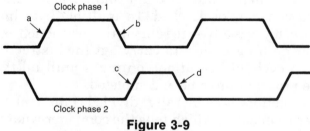

Figure 3-9
Clock Pulses

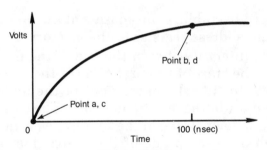

Figure 3-10
Stabilization Time

ure 3-10). The elapsed time between the rise and fall of the clock signal must allow for the voltage rise in the hardware. The shorter the stabilization time, the faster the clock can be and the faster the computer can execute the instruction.

For many computers the clock frequency is around 1 Megahertz (1,000,000 cycles per second). In this case one clock cycle or machine cycle lasts one microsecond. The execution speed of the computer can be increased by using faster semiconductor devices, which result in a higher cost of the computer.

To demonstrate the relationship between the program execution and the clock cycles, we show in detail how the computer loads a number from memory into the accumulator. We use here the opcode 86 of the microprocessor 6809 to load the number 3 into the accumulator. The assembly language representation of an opcode is called the mnemonic of that opcode. "LDA" is the mnemonic for the opcode 86.

The following bytes are loaded into the memory:

Memory		Assembly Language	
Address	Content	Mnemonic	Operand
0000	86	LDA	
0001	03		03

In executing this short program, the following operations occur in the computer. In the first upstroke of the first clock cycle the address (0000) of the LOAD instruction is placed on the address bus. This is an internal operation as the content of the program counter is transferred to the address register. The duration of the first clock is used to stabilize the address at the far end of the long address bus, the address register of the memory.

During the interval between the end of the first cycle of the first clock and the start of the first cycle of the second clock, the content (opcode for LOAD instruction) of the address (0000) is placed on the data buffer by the memory. The interval between the upstroke and downstroke of the first cycle of the second clock is used to stabilize the opcode of the LOAD instruction at the data register. The instruction is immediately transferred to the instruction decoder, where it is decoded. This ends the first machine cycle.

The second machine cycle starts with the upstroke of the second cycle of the first clock when the content of the program counter is transferred to the address register. The program counter has already been advanced (from 0000 to 0001) during the downstroke of the first clock cycle in the previous machine cycle. With the rise of the first clock cycle in the second machine cycle, the address (0001) is placed on the address bus and is stabilized at the fall of this first clock cycle at the address buffer of the memory. The content (3) of the address (0001) is present on the data buffer of the memory at the upstroke of the second clock cycle. At the fall of the second clock cycle, the content of the address 0001, the number "3" has stabilized in the data register and is then transferred to the accumulator. This ends the second machine cycle of loading a number "3" into the accumulator. This instruction is called LOAD IMMEDIATE. The execution of any other instruction can be derived by an expansion or reduction of this sequence of computer operations.

3.6 MICROPROGRAM

Each instruction code placed into the instruction register triggers a specific sequence of unalterable actions in the computer. This sequence is triggered by a microprogram, consisting of a sequence of microinstructions, the microcodes. The microcodes are a series of binary ones and zeros, which are sent to different parts of the computer to actuate specific electronic switches to carry out the instruction. A special ROM on the microprocessor chip translates the opcode into the microprogram codes. All instructions

and their microprograms are stored in this ROM. The microprogram and the microcodes are different for each computer and are
usually unalterable.

A few machines have been built with alterable microprograms. The major advantage of such a machine is that it is possible to replace a time-critical ordinary program section having
several instructions, with a single newly-created instruction. The
speed of writing and execution of a program could be tremendously increased. The disadvantage of such a machine is
that the introduction of microprogrammability increases the
chance of errors because of the much increased complexity in the
computer.

3.7 ASSEMBLY LANGUAGE PROGRAM

Now we can assign specific instruction codes to the six steps of
the program in Section 3.4.1 and see how they function. The 6809
instruction codes and mnemonics are being used here. Notice
that the 6809 instruction codes may combine some of the instruction steps mentioned above. The first two instruction steps
need one 6809 instruction (opcode 96, mnemonic LDA, LOAD
DIRECT) which not only locates the number but also puts it into
the Accumulator. The next three steps need only one 6809
instruction, ADD, which not only locates the second number and
puts it into the accumulator, but also adds the two numbers in
the accumulator.

The LOAD DIRECT instruction is different from the LOAD
IMMEDIATE instruction. The byte following the instruction
code for LOAD IMMEDIATE (86) in the memory is the number
which is loaded into the accumulator. In the LOAD DIRECT
instruction (96) the byte following this opcode is an address
where the number which is to be loaded into the accumulator can
be found.

The sixth step of the previous sequence of instructions corresponds to the third 6809 instruction, which loads the sum into
a new address (0012). A fourth 6809 instruction is necessary to
tell the computer that the program has ended (HALT). Our rudi-
mentary assembly program now becomes:

Simplified Guide to Programming

OPCODE	MNEMONIC	OPERAND
96	LDA	10
9B	ADD	11
97	STA	12
3E	HLT	

Observe that each instruction (except for the last one, 3E) has two bytes (96 and 10; 9B and 11; 97 and 12) and we must reserve two memory locations. We must put into the memory locations 10 and 11 the two numbers 3 and 4, and we must keep the location 12 free for the sum (7) of the two numbers. We obtain the following program:

Memory Address	Machine Language		Assembler Language	
	Opcode	Operand	Mnemonic	Operand
00	96		LDA	
01		10		10
02	9B		ADD	
03		11		11
04	97		STA	
05		12		12
10	3E		HLT	
11		4		4
12		7		7

Details of the Assembly and corresponding Machine language program for the example 3 + 4 are given below. Short explanations are shown in the right-hand column. Further explanations are shown at the end of the program.

Program step	Assembly name (Mnemonic)	Machine code	Machine cycles	Execution sequence
1. Locate 1st number	LDDA	96	(3)	Cycle 1. Take instruction from memory and decode it.
2. Put it into Accumulator	$10 Address of number	10		Cycle 2. Get 2nd byte (the address of number).

				Cycle 3. Put the number (content of the above address) into the Accumulator.
3. Locate 2nd number	ADD	9B	(3)	Cycle 1. Take instruction code from memory and decode it.
4. Put it into Accumulator	$11	11		Cycle 2. Get the next program byte (address of the second number).
5. Add these numbers				Cycle 3. Add the second number (with the help of the above address) to the first number.
6. Store the sum in a different memory location	STAA	97	4	Cycle 1. Get the instruction from program location and decode it.
	$12	12		Cycle 2. Read the content of the next program byte (address where the sum is to be stored).
				Cycle 3. Transfer the sum from the Accumulator to the data register.
				Cycle 4. Transfer the content of the data register to the memory and stores it there.
7. End of program	WAI	3E	9	Cycle 1. Get instruction code and stop program from advancing.

To run the program in the computer, we must load correctly the instruction codes of the program into consecutive memory locations. The location of the program is not important so long as there is RAM memory not in use by other programs such as the monitor or operating system. An error of even one byte in properly locating the first address of a program may cause the computer to interpret a possible address as an opcode and upset the program execution.

According to our program, the first number is in address 0010 and the second number in 0011. The result of the addition is to be put into 0012. All the instructions are loaded into the addressing range 0000 to 000F. The operator sets the program counter at 0000 to instruct the computer to start the program at 0000.

To input the first number (3) into the accumulator we execute the first instruction in the following manner. The address (0000) is automatically transferred to the address register when the program execution is initiated. The address register puts the address on the address bus which transfers it to the input buffer of the memory. After receiving the READ and memory chip select control signal, the memory will put the content of this address (0000) onto its output buffer and onto the data bus.

The content of the first address is processed as an instruction by taking it from the data bus over the data register to the instruction register. After decoding this instruction, the computer has learned that the byte following the instruction byte is an address (10), the content of which is a number (3) which has to be loaded into the Accumulator. This ends the first part of the instruction execution.

The computer has already advanced the program counter to 0001 during the fall of the first clock phrase in the first machine cycle. The address in the program counter (0001) is first sent to the address register, and from there it is sent over the address bus to the memory. After the memory has received the chip select and the "Read" signal, the content (10) of the address (0001) in the memory is put on the data bus and into the data register. Because the data register now contains an address, it must be transferred first to the address register, then over the address bus to the memory. After receiving the proper control signals, the memory puts the content of the address 10, the number 3, on the data bus. The data register picks up this number up and puts it into the Accumulator. This ends the execution of the first instruction sequence.

Completion of the previous instruction sequence tells the computer that the next byte is an instruction. The already advanced address in the address register (0002) is then trans-ferred over the address bus to the memory. With the proper con-trol signals for the memory the content (ADD) of this address (0002) is put on the data bus on to the instruction decoder. Here a similar operation as for the loading of the number 3 is repeated. This finishes the second instruction which stores the number 4 in the Accumulator and adds the two numbers (3 + 4) and stores the sum (07) of the two numbers in the Accumulator.

The next instruction tells the computer to save (STORE) the number in the Accumulator in the specific memory location 0012. The decoding of the instruction STORE is made similarly to the LOAD and ADD instruction.

Next, the controller transfers the updated content of the Program Counter (0005) to the address register and address bus. In response the memory puts the content (12) of the address 0005 on the data bus. As an address it is routed from the DATA bus to the ADDRESS bus and back to the memory. The controller then sends the content of the Accumulator (07) over the data bus to the memory. The memory stores the number on the data bus (07) at the address (12) when the controller has to send a WRITE signal together with the memory select signal. The content of memory location 12 is now "07." Any previous entry at memory location 12 has been destroyed.

The address register is advanced to the address (0006) for the next instruction (HALT) to notify the computer that there are no other instructions to be executed. This is done by stop-ping the advancement of the program counter. This prevents extraneous entries after the end of the program from being interpreted as instructions or data with possible catastrophic consequences for the program.

3.8   FETCH AND EXECUTION PHASES

There are several computer cycles for each instruction in the program or "Fetch." The first brings the cycle instruction from the memory into the processor for decoding. The fetch phase lasts one machine cycle. The "Execution Phase" follows with one or more cycles.

For the instruction sequence LOAD DIRECT, the Fetch and Execution Phase is shown in more detail in Figure 3-11A and B.

The clock phases are on the abscissa and the functions of the computer on the ordinate axes. The computer will load the first byte of the program—into the instruction register. The diagram shows, in detail, the way the fetch and execution cycles in the computer follow each other. This diagram also shows the synchronization of the different actions taken by the computer with the two clock phases.

To summarize, during the fetch phase, the computer locates an instruction code, transfers it to the instruction register, and decodes it. The computer then carries out this instruction during the execution phase.

Here the word "fetching" connotes putting an instruction from memory into the ALU. "Executing" means carrying out an instruction given to the computer. These words are not to be confused with fetching and executing whole programs.

3.9 ADDRESSING MODES

3.9.1 Introduction

The addressing mode is the means by which the instruction byte (opcode) locates the information (operand) to be processed. The address modes, discussed below, follow the usage in the 68XXX computers.

3.9.2 Inherent Addressing

Instructions which do not need an operand to carry out their function or have a fixed operand are called "inherent" instructions. The WAIT instruction is one. Another is the NOP instruction, which only increments the program counter. This is extremely useful in machine language program writing to keep space for additional instructions. Another is the INC instruction, which only increments a register, such as accumulator A (INCA), or accumulator B (INCB), or the index register (INX).

A

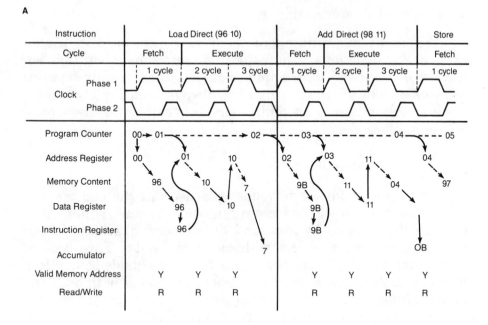

B

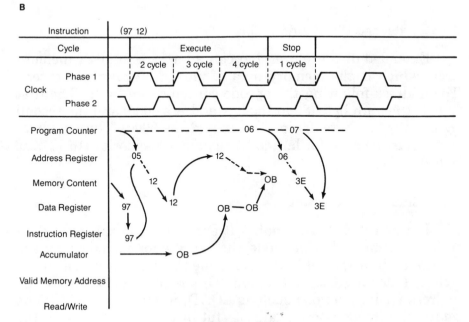

Figure 3-11
Machine Cycles for the Instruction "LOAD ADD,
STORE DIRECT"

3.9.3 Immediate Addressing

When the same numbers, such as II, are used in the sequence of instructions, it is faster and more convenient to insert the letters into the instruction sequence than into a separate table or a location. Such a number always immediately follows the instruction code. This address mode is called the "immediate addressing" mode.

3.9.4 Direct Addressing Modes

The direct addressing mode was used in the sample program. In the direct addressing mode, the instruction code (opcode) is followed by a second byte (operand) which, in our sample program, was the address of the data. This type of instruction is used to transfer data from an outside source to a memory table in the computer. Direct addressing with only one address byte is limited to a memory area of 256 bytes. To reach a greater area we must use "extended direct" addressing.

3.9.5 Extended Direct Addressing

Extended direct addressing can address a full 64K memory area, which is the memory area of most 8-bit microcomputers. The address following the opcode contains two bytes. The first byte is the high byte (80 in the hex address 8000) and the second byte is the low byte (00 in the hex address 8000). Three address bytes must be used for larger 16 Megabyte memories (16,777,216 bytes).

3.9.6 Indexed Addressing

Indexed addressing makes it easier to load tables of data into the memory. In this mode, the address for each data byte is contained in a special buffer (the index register) and not in the byte(s) following the instruction. This register may supply the address for instructions such as LOAD, STORE, and ADD. The addressing mode is especially useful in loading tables into the memory. The indexed addressing shortens the program considerably and saves programmers time, but it increases the time the computer needs to execute the program.

3.9.7   Branching Instructions

The branch instruction is used to prevent the program counter from moving to the next higher number at the end of the last instruction; instead it goes to a specific lower or higher number, so the computer can repeat a certain section of the program or jump over a program section. An instruction—the compare instruction—can be inserted before the branch instruction to tell the computer to ignore the branch instruction. This instruction causes the program to jump to another address *relative* to the original address. The advantage of this "relative addressing mode" is that one can move a whole program from one address area in the memory to another area without any change.

3.9.8   Other Addressing Modes

Other addressing modes are usually extensions or combinations of the ones discussed above. Some of the more useful modes are:

a.   Indirect Addressing

The address following the instruction (opcode) in the indirect addressing mode reaches another address of the information being sought. This ability is useful to redirect the computer to another set of data without changing the program, especially when the data is accessed by several sections of the program (Figure 3-12).

b.   Extended Indirect Addressing

This extends the range of the indirect addressing from 256 bytes in memory space to 64K.

c.   Constant Offset Indexed

In this addressing mode, the computer uses an address by adding the offset to the number stored in the index register. The offset is placed in the byte following the indexed LOAD or STORE instruction.

d.   Constant Offset Indexed Indirect

This adds indirect addressing to the constant offset indexed addressing.

Simplified Guide to Programming

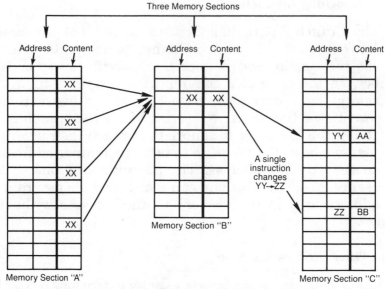

Figure 3-12
Indirect Addressing

e. *Auto Increment*

This addressing mode combines the LOAD or STORE operation in the computer with the automatic incrementing or
decrementing of one or two addressing steps.

3.10 SPECIAL INSTRUCTIONS

3.10.1 General

The most widely used load, store, and branch instructions
are usually supplemented by many other instructions to simplify
arithmetic, logic, and register-to-register operations.

3.10.2 Mathematical and Logic Instructions

Most microcomputers have arithmetic and logic operations
to shift the content of the accumulators either to the left or
right, mostly used in multiplication or division. Depending upon
the instruction used, the bit moving out of the accumulator is

shifted into the carry register or lost. The additional bits moving in can be either zeros or ones.

Other mathematical instructions generally available are addition, subtraction, and multiplication. Some computers such as the 68XXX have a BCD add instruction which correctly adds two BCD numbers.

All logic functions, such as AND, OR, EXCLUSIVE OR, INVERT, are almost always available in the ALU of every computer. These functions can usually be carried out also in the ALU and in the memory.

3.10.3   Compare Instructions

Other instructions include comparing, testing, and clearing of registers and memory locations. Clearing a register or a memory location means setting the content in this location to zero. The comparisons between registers or registers and memory are restricted to indicating that one is larger, smaller, or equal to the other. Carrying out such determination will set the appropriate bits in the condition code register. The conditional branch instruction uses the content of the condition code register to decide if the program should branch or not. The test instruction sets the zero bit if the register to be tested is zero. The negative bit is set in the condition code register, if the highest bit (#7) is one.

3.10.4   Less-Frequently Used Instructions

Often special instructions include: register to register transfer, wait for interrupt, jump to a memory location, jump to a subroutine, return from a subroutine, return from interrupt, and synchronize with interrupt. Most of these are self-explanatory. Returns from interrupt or a subroutine must be included at the end of the service program or subroutine for the program to know where to return. The WAIT instruction stops the processing until the appropriate interrupt occurs to synchronize instructions with external events.

Simplified Guide to Programming

3.11 METHODS FOR SIMPLIFYING PROGRAMMING

a. *Programming Loops*

Programming loops greatly reduce the number of programming steps required and the number of memory locations used. Loops increase the time needed to run a program.

A typical use of a loop would be to load data into a table in the memory from an outside source. Instead of repeating the instruction sequence LOAD, STORE, LOAD, STORE for successive addresses, the index register can follow the constantly changing addresses. While the load instruction uses a constant I/O address, the address the store instruction uses is constantly changing. To automatically change the address it is best to use a loop arrangement, as shown in Figure 3-13, an increment index register instruction—in the loop—constantly updates the

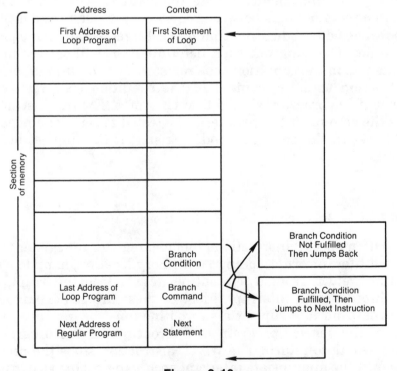

Figure 3-13
Loop Construction in Assembly Language

index register, and thus the address for the next number in the table. To take the program out of the loop, a compare instruction will alert the branch instruction when the table is full.

You can use as many loops in a program as desired so long as the loops are arranged consecutively and are properly nested as shown in Figure 3-14. Nested loops are loops which are located inside each other. Loops arranged in Figure 3-15 are not allowed. The number of nested loops is restricted. Some computers allow seven nested loops, others 128.

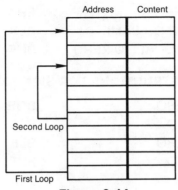

Figure 3-14
Allowed Nested Loops

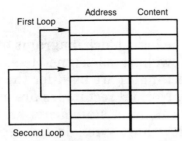

Figure 3-15
Not Allowable Nested Loops

b. *Signed and Unsigned Numbers*

The only group of instructions which can differentiate between signed and unsigned numbers are the branch instructions. Great care must be used in applying them. The branch instructions which can be used for signed or unsigned numbers in the 6800 are shown below.

BRANCH INSTRUCTIONS FOR UNSIGNED NUMBERS

Operations	Mnemonic	Branch Test
BRANCH ALWAYS	BRA	None
BRANCH IF CARRY CLEAR	BCC	C=0
BRANCH IF CARRY SET	BCS	C=1
BRANCH IF = ZERO	BEQ	Z=1
BRANCH IF HIGHER	BHI	C+Z=0
BRANCH IF LOWER OR SAME	BLS	C+Z=1
BRANCH IF NOT EQUAL TO ZERO	BNE	Z=0

BRANCH INSTRUCTIONS FOR SIGNED NUMBERS

BRANCH IF >= ZERO	BGE	B+V=0
BRANCH IF > ZERO	BGT	Z + (B+V)=0
BRANCH IF <= ZERO	BLE	Z + (N+V)=0
BRANCH IF < ZERO	BLT	N+V=0
BRANCH IF MINUS	BMI	N=1
BRANCH IF OVERFLOW CLEAR	BVC	V=0
BRANCH IF OVERFLOW SET	BVS	V=1
BRANCH IF PLUS	BPL	N=0

c. Flowcharts

Flowcharts are the logic block diagrams of the programs. A logic symbol in the flowchart is assigned to each function of the program. Rounded rectangles are used for the start and the end of the flow diagrams. Normal rectangles are used for each function or process and branching statements are indicated by diamonds. Additional flowchart symbols are needed only in more complex applications. Figure 3-16 shows a flowchart designed to collect data from an outside device. The flowchart specifies the actions to be taken by the computer as follows:

1. Collect a data point from the device.
2. Put this data point in the next location of the table into the memory.

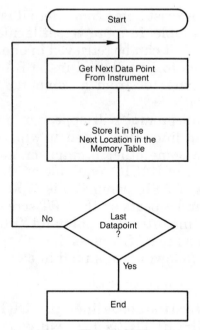

Figure 3-16
General Flow Chart for Data Collection

3. Check to see if the table is full.
4. If it is not, return to step one.
5. If it is, exit the loop and continue the remainder of the program.

d. Algorithm

An algorithm is a procedure (program) which produces a specific outcome for a given task. In the simplest case, an algorithm can be the addition of two numbers. The program outlined above is such an algorithm. More complex algorithms include linear regression analysis, Fast Fourier Transform, and the calculation of the standard deviation.

3.12 GUIDE TO BASIC PROGRAMMING

Before the BASIC language is used on any computer we must be certain that BASIC is "up" on the terminal connected to the computer. On most low-cost home computers it is now on a ROM and immediately available. In more versatile microcomputers, it is on a disk from which it can be retrieved in one or two seconds. A special protocol has to be followed if the BASIC is obtained from a distant computer or from a computer connected to a network.

Usually, a special prompt will appear on the screen when BASIC comes on the line. Most often it will be a crosshatch ("#"). There may be some other prompt, or no prompt at all, depending on the type of BASIC available on the terminal.

The easiest to use BASIC command is "PRINT." In BASIC, the "PRINT" command repeats on the CRT screen what one has written in the same line after the command "PRINT." Try this command and assume the BASIC uses the "#" prompt. After the crosshatch, type the following command line:

#PRINT "HELLO, I AM THE FRIENDLY HOME COMPUTER";

After you have typed the above line on the CRT screen with the keyboard, pushing the RETURN key will cause the following additional line to appear on the screen underneath the command line:

HELLO, I AM THE FRIENDLY HOME COMPUTER

Anything in quotation marks after the PRINT command will be redisplayed unchanged on the CRT screen after pressing RETURN.

3.12.2   Using the Computer as a Calculator

To use the computer as a calculator, write after the prompt "PRINT" and a space, the mathematical equation to be solved. To add 2 and 5, type the following character sequence with the help of the keyboard onto the CRT screen.

#PRINT 2+5

No space is allowed between the prompt "#" and the word "PRINT." A space is to be provided between "PRINT" and the number "2." There is no limit to the number of spaces allowed between the "PRINT" command and the first number as long as it is on the same line. Spaces often are not allowed in mathematical expressions.

The solution to the equation appears on the next line when the return key is pressed, as follows:

#7

The operator must observe specific rules with which to write the mathematical expressions. First the computer examines the mathematical expression to find the highest ranking mathematical operation. This operation is then carried out. The next-higher-ranking mathematical operations are carried out progressively to completion. The order of rank of mathematical operations and their symbols are shown in the following table:

1.	**	Raising a number to a factor
2.	/	Division
3.	*	Multiplication
4.	−	Subtraction
5.	+	Addition

3.12.3   BASIC Functions

BASIC has special commands for the common mathematical functions such as the square root, arctang, sine and cosine. A list of all commands, statements, and functions for ANSI Standard BASIC is found in any BASIC textbook. For example, to calculate the square root of 36, type:

#PRINT SQR(36)

Pressing the return button we obtain:

6

Other mathematical commands can be used in a similar manner. Mathematical expressions frequently used in a program may be given specific names to be used in many BASIC versions together with the other predefined functions.

The result of a mathematical equation may be clarified in the following way:

#PRINT "The square root of 36 is";SQR(36)

Write the sentence "The square root of 36 is" and separate it from the square root expression by a semicolon (";") or comma (","). The comma causes the result "6" to be written in the next six screen fields into which the screen is divided. A semicolon causes the "6" to follow immediately the last information written on the same line. Pressing the return button we obtain:

#The square root of 36 is 6

3.12.4   Data Input

To enter data from the keyboard into a program one can use the INPUT statement. Data from the keyboard must be put into a variable; thus, an input statement takes the form:

#INPUT A

A question mark appears on the screen when the program reaches an input statement that calls for data to be entered from the keyboard. Statements as to what should be entered into the variable may be added to the INPUT command. The instruction given to the computer might be:

#INPUT "ENTER THE RESISTOR VALUE R1",A

When the program comes to this statement the following line will appear on the screen (including the question mark):

#ENTER THE RESISTOR VALUE R1?

Entering here the number 561 assigns that value to the variable A.

3.12.5   Loops

Loops written in assembler language were discussed earlier in this chapter (3.11.1). Loops were shown to be especially useful for reducing the length of a program. Loops in BASIC are normally used for the same reasons—to generate time delays or to fill an array with numbers.

Very often the computer, even when using interpreter BASIC, would collect from a device many more data points than necessary. Commercially available Interpreter BASIC is able to collect approximately one data point every fifty milliseconds.

The best way to make any timing delay is to create a buffer or register and then decrement the number entered in the buffer to zero. The computer takes a specific, even though short, time to carry out one set of the loop instructions. Carrying them out repeatedly one can construct loops with almost any time delay by entering different numbers into the buffer. In BASIC, as in Assembler language, the maximum number in the buffer is limited. Dual timing loops can be constructed, one nested into the other, greatly exceeding the time span to be covered.

Constructing loops with a high level language, such as BASIC, is easy. Use the following sequence:

```
FOR I = 1 TO 3 STEP 1
NEXT I
```

"I" represents the loop counter, which assumes the value 1 (I=1) at start. "STEP" tells the computer to increase I by one every time the computer executes one loop. When I has reached the value three ("TO 3") the computer stops going to the loop and goes to the program statement after the NEXT instruction. Looping to I=3 creates a waiting time three times as long as that of a single loop statement.

We must learn more about the general format of BASIC programs before the loop program can be entered properly into the computer.

3.12.6 Format of BASIC Programs

Most BASIC programs require a separate number for each line after the prompt, which is either typed in by the programmer or generated by the computer. Initially, line numbers should be spaced about ten numbers apart to allow for further additions. BASIC programs must have an "END" statement as the last statement of the program.

There must never be a space between the prompt and the line number. When each line has been typed, it must be terminated by pressing the RETURN key. Pressing the RETURN key puts the line into the computer memory. The cursor is advanced one line and returned to the far left-hand position.

When entering a BASIC program, the interpreter BASIC checks each line for errors as the line is written, but it cannot detect errors which involve more than one line. The first step for finding these types of errors is to list the program by typing

"LIST" after a prompt sign. The computer will write on the CRT screen all entered lines with line numbers.

Once all visible errors have been corrected you can try to execute (or run) the program. This is done by typing a "RUN" command next to a prompt. The computer will indicate any remaining errors such as forgetting the "NEXT I" statement when there is a "FOR I TO 3 STEP 1" statement or the "END."

When no more error messages appear after the program has been run, the program conforms to the rules of the BASIC interpreter used.

Wrong results may still occur if mistakes are made in the logic of the program. To correct these errors you should consult the detailed flow diagram you made before you started coding the program in BASIC.

3.12.7 Examples of BASIC Programs

First, type in the loop program discussed above. After obtaining the BASIC prompt, type in:

```
#10 FOR I = 1 TO 3 STEP 1
#20 NEXT I
#30 END
#
```

Next, list the program by typing in

```
#LIST
```

and pressing the return key. The computer will repeat the entire program for your inspection as follows:

```
#10 FOR I = 1 TO 3 STEP 1
#20 NEXT I
#30 END
#
```

If the program appears to be correct, try to execute it by typing the "RUN" command:

```
#RUN
```

Now press the RETURN key to actuate the "RUN" command. You will see only the prompt sign:

```
#
```

The reason, of course, is that the computer has not been instructed to display messages on the screen in our program.

Messages can be displayed on the screen using the print command. Insert a print line in the loop program stating:

"HELLO, MY LINE IS PRINTED THREE TIMES"

The program will now look like this:

```
#10 FOR 1 TO 3 STEP 1
#15 PRINT "HELLO, MY LINE IS PRINTED THREE TIMES"
#20 NEXT I
#30 END
```

When the "RUN" command is entered, the following display will appear on the screen:

```
HELLO, MY LINE IS PRINTED THREE TIMES
HELLO, MY LINE IS PRINTED THREE TIMES
HELLO, MY LINE IS PRINTED THREE TIMES
```

With this preparation, we can do simple, graphic displays on the screen. Replace the line HELLO, MY LINE IS PRINTED THREE TIMES with just the star ("*") and repeat the loop ten times. The program now looks like this:

```
#10 FOR I = 1 TO 10
#15 PRINT "*"
#20 NEXT I
#30 END
```

When the program is run, the following will result:

```
*
*
*
*
*
*
*
*
*
*
```

This is the start of a Y (ordinate) - AXIS, which may be extended by increasing the number in the FOR TO loop.

To generate an X (abscissa) - AXIS add a ";" to the end of the print statement. This keeps the computer from executing a return each time the print statement is executed. The stars will progress across a horizontal line on the CRT screen as the loop program is executed.

If we increase the number of stars to sixty, the program will change to the following form:

```
#10 FOR I = 1 TO 60
#15 PRINT "*";
#20 NEXT I
#30 END
```

Executing the program results in

```
#*************************************************
```

which is the start of an X-AXIS.

The positive half of a sine curve may be plotted on the CRT screen as long as desired if the X-AXIS is vertical and the Y-AXIS horizontal.

To generate the sine curve on the screen we use the SIN(X) function of BASIC. The program uses two nested loops. The first generates the progression along the vertical X-AXIS (I). The second and inner loop generates the amplitude of the sine curve (K) as a function of I as we progress along the X-AXIS. The program will appear as:

```
#10 FOR I = 1 TO 20
#15 FOR K = 1 TO 40*SIN(3.14*I/20)
#17 PRINT "*";
#20 NEXT K
#25 PRINT
#27 NEXT I
#30 END
```

The execution of the above program is shown in Figure 3-17.

Plotting a sine curve with only one dot for each amplitude requires a new command. The TAB(X) command moves the cursor or the print carriage to a position specified by the number in the parentheses. The number indicates the number of character positions to be moved. The maximum number of characters on a line is usually eighty. The second loop in the program is no longer needed (Figure 3-18).

A full sine curve will be generated in our next example. We add a constant (30) to the expression for A to move the curve to

Simplified Guide to Programming

```
XXXXX
XXXXXXXXXX
XXXXXXXXXXXXXXXX
XXXXXXXXXXXXXXXXXXXX
XXXXXXXXXXXXXXXXXXXXXXXX
XXXXXXXXXXXXXXXXXXXXXXXXXX
XXXXXXXXXXXXXXXXXXXXXXXXXXXXX
XXXXXXXXXXXXXXXXXXXXXXXXXXXXXXX
XXXXXXXXXXXXXXXXXXXXXXXXXXXXXXXX
XXXXXXXXXXXXXXXXXXXXXXXXXXXXXXXX
XXXXXXXXXXXXXXXXXXXXXXXXXXXXXXX
XXXXXXXXXXXXXXXXXXXXXXXXXXXXXX
XXXXXXXXXXXXXXXXXXXXXXXXXXXXX
XXXXXXXXXXXXXXXXXXXXXXXXXX
XXXXXXXXXXXXXXXXXXXXXXX
XXXXXXXXXXXXXXXXXXXX
XXXXXXXXXXXXXXXX
XXXXXXXXXXXX
XXXXX
X
```

Figure 3-17

Computer Printout of Half Sine-Curve, Filled

the right to make room for the second half of the sine curve. To show the full period, we must increase the number of steps from 20 to 40 (from Π to 2Π) (statement line 10). The TAB command is added to the PRINT command to position the "*" at the appropriate spot. To simplify writing the lengthy expression for the sine amplitude we give it the name "A" using the "LET" command.

Figure 3-18

Computer Printout of Half Sine-Curve, Single Points

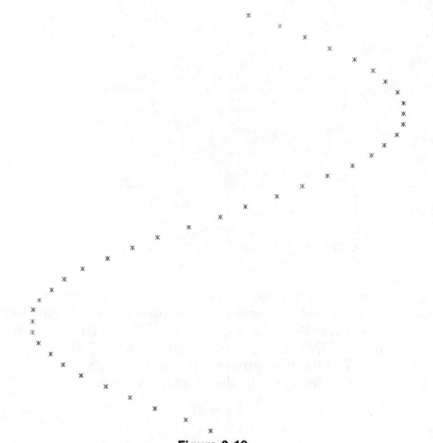

Figure 3-19
Computer Printout of Full Sine-Curve

The program becomes:

```
10 FOR I TO 40
16 LET A = 30 + 30*(SIN(3.14*I/20))
17 PRINT TAB(A);"*"
20 NEXT I
30 END
```

The printout is shown in Figure 3-19.
We now add X and Y axes to this graph. Since the CRT screen and the standard printer are line oriented, every character on the same horizontal line on the graph must be printed

during the same traverse. Once a line is printed it is not possible to add additional characters to it.

The first half-wave of the sine curve is above the X-axis and the second half-wave is below. This means that in the first half of the sine wave the X-axis point is printed before the sine-wave point. In the second half of the sine wave the sine-wave point comes after the X-axis point. The print statement for the sine curve must be divided into two, one for the first half and one for the second half.

An additional decision command selects between the two print statements. The most appropriate command for this purpose is the "IF.....THEN..." command. Type:

```
IF A > 30 THEN PRINT TAB(30); "|"; TAB(A);"*"
IF A < 30 THEN PRINT TAB(A);"*";TAB(30);"|"
```

The "|" is our X-axis character. Adding these two lines instead of line 17 we obtain:

```
10 FOR I = 1 TO 40
16 LET A = 30 + 30*(SIN(3.14*I/20))
18 IF A > 30 THEN PRINT TAB(30); "|"; TAB(A);"*"
20 IF A < 30 THEN PRINT TAB(A);"*";TAB(30);"|"
25 NEXT I
30 END
```

The Y-axis and lettering on it may be added quite easily. Put the lettering on program line number 3. The loop to generate the Y-axis is on line numbers 5, 7, and 8. The print statement of line 9 prevents the Y-axis from interfering with the sine curve generation.

To identify the program, a comment line may be added which will not be executed by the computer when REM is written after the line number. The program now appears as:

```
1 REM GRAPH OF FULL PERIOD OF THE SINE CURVE WITH Y AND X AXIS
3 PRINT "−30";TAB(30);"0";TAB(59);"+30"
5 FOR I = 1 TO 61
7 PRINT "−";
8 NEXT I
9 PRINT
10 FOR I = 1 TO 40
14 LET A = 30 + 30*(SIN(3.14*I/20))
18 IF A > 30 THEN PRINT TAB(30);"|"; TAB(A);"*"
```

```
20 IF A < 30 THEN PRINT TAB(A);"*";TAB(30);"|"
27 NEXT I
30 END
```

The printout is shown in Figure 3-20. Parts of programs that repeat themselves may be written as separate identified sections of the program called subroutines. This can shorten and make a program easier to read.

The subroutine call is exercised in BASIC by the GOSUB ". . . . ." command. The line number, represented by the dots, is the line number where the subroutine starts. The last statement

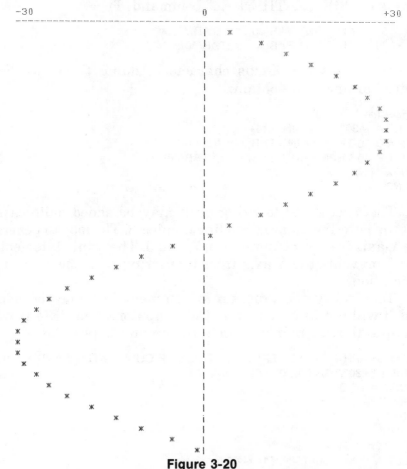

Figure 3-20
Computer Printout of Sine-Curve with Co-ordinate System

of the subroutine is a return command which tells the computer to jump back to the statement following the GOSUB statement. The sine curve program could be rewritten the following way using subroutines:

```
1 REM FULL PERIOD OF A SINE CURVE, WITH X AND Y AXIS, AND GOSUB
3 PRINT "−30";TAB(30);"0";TAB(59);"+30"
5 FOR I = 1 TO 61
7 PRINT "−";
8 NEXT I
9 PRINT
10 GOSUB 100
20 END
100 FOR I = 1 TO 40
110 LET A = 30 + 30*(SIN(3.14*I/20))
120 IF A > 30 THEN PRINT TAB(30);"|";TAB(A);"*"
130 IF A < 30 THEN PRINT TAB(A);"*";TAB(30);"|"
140 NEXT I
150 RETURN
```

This program will give the same curve as the previous program. A sine curve with many periods can be produced just by adding additional GOSUB statements.

Many other commands are available in BASIC. However, this introductory section should give you enough background to write additional programs with the help of available literature.

CHAPTER 4

Understanding the Popular Microcomputer Families

4.1 INTRODUCTION

4.1.1 Overview

In the first three chapters we introduced the different components and functions of an eight-bit microprocessor. In this chapter we will discuss the capabilities and parameters of some of the more popular commercial microprocessors.

Most of the hundreds of different eight-bit microprocessors can be divided into three groups:

1. Those related to the 8008 from Intel
2. Those related to the 6800 from Motorola
3. Others

The Intel 8008 was the first of the successful general-purpose microprocessors available on the market. The 6800 and its successor chips became most successful later because of their versatility and ease of application. Other excellent chips, notably the ones from Texas Instruments and the National Semiconductor became less prominent. Figure 4-1 shows the development of the more prominent microprocessors and how they relate to each other.

This figure shows that newer processors have become more sophisticated (more transistors), and that they have much higher versatility than older ones. The 6800 is a typical example of that versatility. These include a low-current consumption, a self-contained microcomputer including I/O devices such as ADC, and a version with a built-in monitor package.

The major advantages of selecting a standard modification of a popular microprocessor rather than a one-of-a-kind special microprocessor chip are:

98

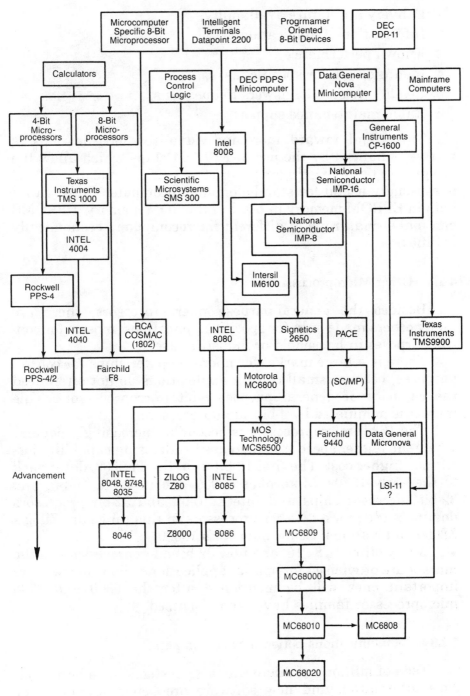

Figure 4-1
A Family of Microprocessors

1. Delivery and future availability,
2. Information of application,
3. Known performance,
4. Identification for specific tasks,
5. Readily available answers to questions,
6. Rapid maintenance support.

This trend toward more individualized modifications is further enhanced by the use of EPROM chips which allow the designer to tailor existing monitors to specific applications. This is especially useful for stand-alone microcomputer chips with a built-in EPROM memory in place of the ROM memory. EPROMS can make small runs of different microcomputers economically justified.

4.1.2   Other Microprocessors

Besides the general-purpose microprocessors, there are many others made only for specific applications, mostly for control purposes in household or industrial use.

There is a large market for microcomputer chips for control purposes, because small control applications do not often need the capacity of general purpose 8-bit microprocessors. This market is dominated by 4-bit microprocessors.

The 16-bit microprocessor is becoming increasingly popular where the higher speed and increased addressing capability justify the higher cost. The first 16-bit unit, the TI 9900, dates back to the early 1970s. Motorola's 68000 and its 8-bit, 16-bit, and 32-bit successor chips and Intel's 16-bit and 32-bit processors dominate the market. Other processors in this range are Zilog's Z8000 and National Semiconductor's 16000.

Many other 4-, 8-, 16- and now 32-bit microprocessors on the market are often used for special applications. Some of the more important ones will be mentioned after the 6800 and 8008 microprocessor families have been discussed.

4.1.3   Communications between Microcomputers

Tens of millions of microcomputer systems have been sold. New information and new software are being developed for many of these systems. Even though not all the owners of these systems want to share the information produced on them, a large number of them would probably like to do so. What would be the best way to share this information?

There are several ways in which software can be distributed. One would be to distribute it like printed material such as books or journals. The advantage here is that the mails and parcel express are well established. The disadvantage of physical transfer is that it is slow. Software which keeps its value for long periods of time such as operating systems, language compilers, and scientific and utility programs can be distributed in this way with high success.

Sometimes data and software are needed at once. This is possible over telecommunication lines, which also allow direct testing of the software without media transfers which could cause additional errors, misunderstanding, lost time, and expense. The major obstacles to electronic distribution are the very high cost of required hardware, the high cost of the network connection time, the slow transmission speed, and the breaking of copyright laws.

Some of these problems may be reduced when the long-heralded "Integrated Services Digital Network" (ISDN) becomes operational. This network will increase the transmission speed of information over 200-fold, making it fast enough to show movies on CRTs. The connection cost will be lower than that of present networks because of the integrated design of the telecommunication devices and computers.

Other problems exist in the distribution of software. One is the lack of standardization in hardware and software systems. Another is the wide diversity of media means used for software communications. Fortunately, more and more software packages and hardware boards are coming onto the market, which allow the automatic translation of the information from one system to that of another.

Standardization would alleviate many of the problems discussed above. Hardware standards now exist which allow a computer to be connected to any other computer in the world. All computer manufacturers seem to follow this standard. But no such standard exists for software. Two computers can be connected and long series of bits can be sent back and forth, but unless the computers match in their software, the result will be gibberish.

The present state of hardware and software development now allows relatively low-cost chips to be made which could be built into any computer. These chips could translate the information in one computer into meaningful information for another computer. Silicon compilers can be helpful in the development of these chips.

4.2   THE 6800 MICROPROCESSOR FAMILY

4.2.1   General

Motorola's model 6800 and its related processors will be discussed in detail because of their popularity and because they are representative of modern microprocessors. The 6800 microprocessor was originally designed to offer a microprocessor easier to use than the 8008. This was accomplished in the hardware by reducing the number of supply voltages from three to one and the number of chips necessary for a complete microcomputer system from five to three. The software was simplified by reducing the number of instructions and increasing the number of addressing modes. As a result the programmer has to memorize fewer instructions without limiting the flexibility of a given instruction.

The speed of execution was increased by simplifying the execution of each instruction by streamlining the machine cycles for each instruction, resulting in an increase in the execution speed of applications programs without increasing the clock speed.

This design philosophy becomes more apparent as one moves to the successor chips of the 6800. The 6809 has fewer instructions than the 6800, and the 68000 has fewer instructions than the 6809. The number of addressing modes is increased. The 56 instructions of the 68000 can be used in almost 1500 different ways. This is only one aspect of Motorola's effort to make the programming of their microprocessors easier. Others will be discussed later.

4.2.2 Motorola's Family of 68XXX Microprocessors

Motorola makes a wide variety of microprocessors ranging from simple, general-purpose units to highly sophisticated single-chip microcomputers. Here is a list of the more important microprocessors:

Microprocessor	Clock Speed	Remarks
6800	1 MHz	
6800A	1.5 MHz	
6800B	2.0 MHz	
6801 to 6808		Different enhancements of the 6800, including one-chip computers (6801/2) and CMOS versions of these (6505/7/8).
6809	1 MHz	Basic enhancement of the 6800. Features more powerful instruction set and about 3 to 4 times the execution speed of the 6800.
68CH10		Single microcomputer with I/O devices built in.
6809A	1.5 MHz	
6809B	2.0 MHz	
6809E		For a multiprocessor system.
68000	8/10/12/14 MHz	16-bit microprocessor.
68008		8-bit version of 68000 runs about 14 times as fast as the 6800 which it replaces.
68010		Virtual memory version of the 68000.
68020		Virtual memory and 32-bit version of the 68000.

Several dozen support chips are now available from Motorola for the microprocessors listed above. Most of these chips can be used with all the above processors. Some of the more important support chips will be discussed in this and the following chapters.

4.3 DESIGN OF THE 6800 MICROPROCESSORS

4.3.1 General

The Motorola 6800 was introduced in 1973 as a more efficient alternative to Intel's 8008. The 6800 microprocessor has the following basic design characteristics.

1. 16-bit address (address range 64K)
2. 8-bit data bidirectional bus
3. Both buses can be operated by external commands (DMA)
4. The input and output port addresses can be located anywhere in the 64K address range. This avoids doubling all load and store instructions into those which go into the memory and those which go into the I/O ports. Setting aside memory locations for I/O operations, without causing trouble to other memory operations, can be achieved by dividing the memory into sections (maybe 4 K) where one section is set aside for I/O, interrupt, and other operations. This section resides on the top of the memory.
5. Simplification in the microcomputer control commands and lines. A whole chip is necessary for this purpose in Intel's 8008, but not in the 6800.
6. The machine and clock cycles are one length in the 6800.
7. The 6800 has fewer instructions but more addressing modes than the 8008.
8. The 6800 registers are assigned to specific tasks. This simplifies the job of the programmer since it is easier to remember the register in which a specific job is always handled. It is a disadvantage if the register needs to be used for other purposes. This difficulty has been almost eliminated by Motorola in the design of the 6809. In the 68000 the 16 general purpose registers have preferable use.
9. Peripheral support devices require a specific synchronization signal E, to insure 100 percent synchronization between

the microcomputer and the peripheral device. This makes it difficult to use the 6800 with non-Motorola peripheral devices. The 68000 series microcomputers do not need this synchronization signal, although they have it available to communicate to 6800 related devices.

10. The Motorola 6800 has only one power supply voltage (5 volt).

11. Practically all microcomputer devices are TTL compatible which makes the interfacing with other devices simpler.

All 6800 microcomputer support devices have, where applicable, versions for 1 MHz, for 1.5 MHz identified by the letter A in the device number, and for 2.0 MHz for which the letter B is attached.

4.3.2 Frequently Used Support Chips

The following lists identifies some of the more important support devices for the 6800. These support chips also can be used with the 6809, and 68000.

1.	The Peripheral Interface Adapter (PIA)	MC6821
2.	Memory Management Unit	MC8629
3.	Programmable Timer Module	MC6840
4.	Direct Memory Access Controller (DMA)	MC6844
5.	Asynchronous Communications Interface (ACIA)	MC6850
6.	Synchronous Serial Data Adapter	MC6852
7.	Clock Generator	MC6875
8.	Two Phase Microprocessor Clock	MC6870
9.	Quad Three State Bus Receiver	MC6880
10.	Priority Interrupt Controller	MC6890
11.	MPU Bus Compatible 8 Bit D/A Converter	MC6890

4.3.3 Detailed Design of the 6800 Microprocessor

In the first chapter we stated that all computers have the following components:

1. Arithmetic Logic Unit (ALU)
2. Memory

3. Controller
4. Input Unit
5. Output Unit

Figure 4-2 shows a block diagram for most microcomputers. The figure shows that the I/O unit, the controller, and the memory always have access to the general bus, whereas the ALU (processor) must be reached through the controller. The general bus typically is located on the "mother board" or backplane of the computer, into which are plugged the controller board (CPU board), the memory board, and the I/O boards.

Figure 4-3 shows a more detailed view of the layout for the 6800 microcomputer. The components are connected to the main "bus," which combines the control, data, and address buses. The controller contains the registers, the instruction decoder (with the ROM), the clock, and the interrupt system. The ALU is connected to the controller but not to the bus.

The memory has full access to the bus with its control, data, and address lines. The keyboard terminal sends information over an I/O board to the bus, whereas the bus sends information over the I/O board to the CRT screen. The printer is connected to the bus through another I/O interface board. A parallel interface is preferable if the I/O bus is located near the bus for a faster transmission speed and better control capability. A serial interface is slower and is better for long distances.

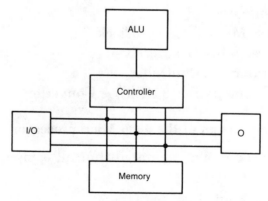

Figure 4-2
General Block Diagram of a Computer

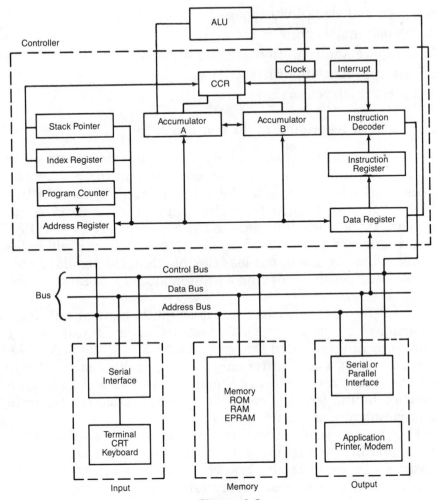

Figure 4-3
Block Diagram of the 6800

4.4 INSTRUCTION SET FOR THE 6800

4.4.1 Overview

The 6800 has a full set of seventy-two instructions. All instruction categories described in Chapter 3 are present. These are:

1. Load and store instructions
2. Arithmetic and logic instructions

3. Index and stack instructions
4. Branch instructions
5. Compare and condition code instructions
6. Interrupt handling instructions
7. Special instructions

4.4.2 Detailed Description of the Instruction Set

The stack in the 6800 differs from those in many other computers in that it can be placed anywhere in the memory by means of a 16-bit address in the stack pointer register. In this way you are not limited to a single unmovable, fixed-length hardware stack since any space in the memory may be specified. The stack pointer can be used as an additional more rapid index register, which is faster, but less flexible than the regular index register because the indexing is automatically coupled to the storage of data.

The 6800 has an extensive set of mathematical and logic instructions, including a DAA instruction to adjust binary numbers to Binary Coded Decimal numbers, and the accumulator can generate a carry after only four digits (half carry). There are two accumulators. Most of the mathematical and logic operations, including test and compare, can be carried out either in the accumulators or anywhere in memory.

Full branch instructions are available for signed and unsigned numbers. Care must be taken to set up the branch instruction properly or the branch may work incorrectly. The most common errors in assembly language programs are usually associated with compare and branch instructions. The next most common errors are those involving mathematical and logic instructions, and the address.

The 6800 has a WAIT instruction, which we have previously explained, to speed up the response to an interrupt.

4.4.3 Application Program

4.4.3.1 Introduction

We will now describe the writing of a data collection program in assembler language. As stated in Chapter 2, the program writing is done best in five steps, beginning with the description of the tasks to be performed.

1. Goal

The program will scan one input port and take data consecutively into a memory table. The scanning of the input ports is continued until all data have been collected.

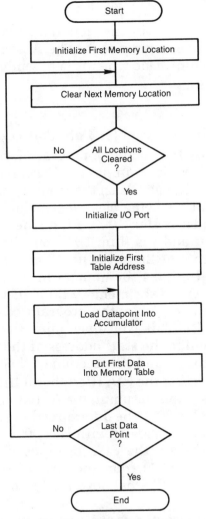

Figure 4-4
Flow Diagram of Data Collection System

2. Means of achieving the goal

    This is done in the following manner. The first loop clears the memory area of the table. The index register directs, consecutively, the different values from the port into a table. This is the second loop.

3. Flowchart

    Make a flow diagram. A flow diagram with two loops is shown in Figure 4-4.

4. Loading

    Code the instructions in the flow diagram. Write the program in Assembler source code. The Assembler then finds the correct machine code when it is assembled (Figure 4-5).

5. Test the program.

4.4.3.2 *Assembly Program for Data Collection*

Figure 4-5 shows the complete program for data collection, which was originally written in assembly source code. We have two loops. In Loop 1 (Label: Clear) the memory area in which we are collecting the data is being cleared. The memory area starts at Hex 500 and ends at Hex 1000. First, the index register is loaded with the last address (line 1). Then, the content of this address is set to zero (line 2). In the next line (3) the index register is decremented. In line 4 the number in the index register is compared with the end of the memory table. If it is not equal to the start of the memory table, the program counter returns to line 3 (label CLEAR). This continues until the number in the index register is equal to the start address of the table (Hex 500); the branch falls through and this section of the program ends.

In the second section the PIA (Peripheral Interface Adapter) is initialized. By clearing accumulator A and storing the information in location Hex 8001 the data direction register of side A is set. Loading the index register with Hex 0004 and storing it in location Hex 8000 will set the PIA for input on the A side and reset the location Hex 8000 from the data direction register to the data register. The PIA is now ready to accept data on the A side.

The third and most important section of the program collects the data from the port and puts them into the memory table. First, the start of the memory table (Hex 0500) is loaded

```
* This program collects data from a port $8000 *
* Program name bopoda01 A.O. Wist 12,25,83 *

Line
  1    0000                                ORG     $0000
  2    0000 8E    1000    START    LDX     #$1000          First
  3    0003 6F    84      CLEAR    CLR     0,X             program
  4    0005 30    1F               DEX                     section
  5    0007 8C    0500             CMPX    #$0500
  6    000A 26    F7               BNE     CLEAR
  7    000C 4F                     CLRA                    Second
  8    000D B7    8001             STA     $8001           program
  9    0010 8E    0004             LDX     #$0004          section
 10    0013 BF    8000             STX     $8000
 11    0016 8E    0500             LDX     #$0500
 12    0019 B6    8000    LOAD     LDA     $8000           Third
 13    001C A7    84               STA     0,X             program
 14    001E 30    01               INX                     section
 14    0020 8C    1000             CMPX    #$1000
 16    0023 26    F4               BNE     LOAD
 17    0025 3F                     SWI
                                   END     START
```

0 ERROR(S) DETECTED
SYMBOL TABLE:
CLEAR   0003   LOAD   0019   START   0000

Figure 4-5
Assembler and Machine Language Program of Data
Collection Program

into the index register. Then, a data value is picked up from the port and put into the accumulator A. An indexed store instruction puts the data value in the first location of the memory table. The index register is incremented and compared with the upper end of the memory table. If it is not equal, the program branches back (Label : LOAD) to the load instruction to pick up another data value. This continues until the index register has reached the upper end of the memory table where the branch falls through, ending the program.

4.5   ADVANTAGES AND DISADVANTAGES OF THE 6800

First, we will list the advantages and disadvantages of the 6800. Then we will discuss the successor chips of the 6800.

1. The 6800 has a single power supply (5 Volt).
2. The I/O addresses are part of the regular memory addresses.
3. Only control signals necessary for I/O devices are available.
4. The machine cycles and the clock cycles have the same duration.
5. Several addressing modes were created to reduce the number of instructions.
6. Most instructions operating on the data in the accumulators can be used in any memory location.
7. The stack pointer can be set to any available memory location and there is no limit to the number of stacks that can be used. The stack also can be used as a second index register.

Disadvantages:

1. It is difficult to transfer data between registers.
2. It is difficult to use other makes of support chips, because it is necessary to have a synchronizing signal E.
3. No direct memory-to-memory transfer instructions.

The difficulty in transferring information between registers and the limited number of registers have been in part remedied in the 6809, and completely eliminated in the 68000 and its successor chips. The use of a synchronizing signal has been eliminated in the 68000. To stay compatible with the 6800 and the 6809, the 68000 can generate the synchronizing signal E. Little effort has been made to truly effect a direct memory-to-memory transfer of data.

An 8-bit page register is included in the 6809, which extends the range of the direct addressing mode to 64K. Besides increasing the number of index registers and stackpointers to two, almost any information can be freely exchanged between all registers, all of which are now 16 bits long except the page and condition code registers. Also there is a hardware multiply capability in this processor.

In the 6809, the number of basic instructions was reduced from 72 to 59 and the number of addressing modes increased to 10.

The 68000 and its successor chips, the 68010 and 68020, have been designed much like large minicomputers. There are 16 general-purpose memory registers—the preferred use for eight of them is for data storage, and seven of them for address storage. It has a 16-bit hardware and divide capability, 128 interrupt locations, and automatic error functions to help the programmer. The 6909E and the 68000 also have full multiprocessor capabilities. The 32-bit version of the 68000, the 68020, has full virtual memory capability. It also has a full 32-bit data bus, 32-bit address bus, and therefore can address $4,29.10^9$ bytes of memory.

4.6 THE 8008 MICROPROCESSOR FAMILY

The original microprocessor, the 8008, was developed by Intel in order to increase the operating and efficiency and reduce the cost of a Datapoint terminal by greatly reducing the number of chips and making the terminal much more adaptable.

Success in developing the 8008 and its modifications stimulated the development of similar chips: the 8080, 8085, Z80, 8086, 8088 and others in this series. We will describe the 8080 instead of the 8008 in the following section because it gives a better base for the explanation of the follow-up chips.

4.7 DESIGN OF THE 8080 MICROPROCESSOR

Figure 4-6 shows the basic design (architecture) of the 8080 microprocessor. It has a 16-bit address bus, an 8-bit bidirectional data bus, and control lines for the bus, I/O, and interrupts. The figure shows the basic connections for the ALU, the program counter, control register and decoder, and a stack pointer. Six additional general-purpose registers are provided. Three basic chips are necessary for its operation: the 8080 microprocessor, the clock chip, and the system controller. These three chips are functionally similar to the 6800 microprocessor chip. In the following discussion these three chips are considered as a unit which is shown in Figure 4-7.

The 8080 differs from the 6800 in many significant details even though they are similar in basic design. A somewhat

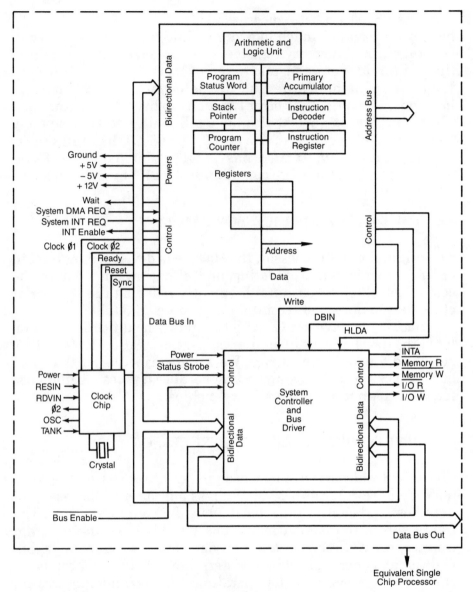

Figure 4-6
8008 Basic System

Machine Cycles

MC1					MC2			MC3			MC4			MC5		
CLP 1	CLP 2	CLP 3	CLP 4	CLP 5	CLP 1	CLP 2	CLP 3	CLP 1	CLP 2	CLP 3	CLP 1	CLP 2	CLP 3	CLP 1	CLP 2	CLP 3

Clock Periods

Figure 4-7
Organization of Machine Cycles

higher flexibility of the 8080 is due to a greater complexity, at the expense of some loss in efficiency in a usual application.

The system controller and the clock driver create control signals for the READ and WRITE commands, used mostly for the memory, the I/O, the interrupts (MEMR, MEMW, I/OR, I/OW, INTA), and a set of bidirectional bus drivers.

A closer look at the design of the machine cycles in the 8080 will show how the functions are created. An 8080 instruction may have from one to five machine cycles and a machine cycle may have from three to five clock periods as shown in Figure 4-8.

Each instruction for the 8080 has, as in the 6800, a fetch period and an execution period. The 8080 differs from the 6800 in that it puts a special data word on the data bus at the beginning of each machine cycle to indicate the kind of operation to follow. The 8080 provides for twelve such operations. Each operation has an eight-bit code, as shown in Figure 4-9. After the 8080 has recognized the code word for a specific operation at the start of the machine cycle, this operation is executed.

The beginning of the first machine cycle is marked by a special synchronization signal. The first machine cycle, is always used for the fetch period. The operation for the second, third, and following machine cycles is determined by the fetched instruction. Let's take, for example, the NOP instruction, which only advances the program counter. The first machine cycle fetches the instruction from memory and puts it into the instruction register to decode it. As this instruction only affects the program counter, no further action is necessary on the data or address buses, and no further machine cycles are used for this inherent instruction.

The LOAD DIRECT instruction for the 8080, corresponding to a LOAD EXTENDED instruction in the 6800, uses four

Status	Data Bus Bit	Instruction Fetch	Memory Read	Memory Write	Stack Read	Stack Write	Input Read	Input Write	Interrupt Acknowledge	Halt Acknowledge	Interrupt Acknowledge While Halt
INTA	DO	0	0	0	0	0	0	0	1	0	1
$\overline{WO}$	D1	1	1	0	1	0	1	0	1	1	1
STACK	D2	0	0	0	1	1	0	0	0	0	0
HLTA	D3	0	0	0	0	0	0	0	0	1	1
OUT	D4	0	0	0	0	0	0	1	0	0	0
M1	D5	1	0	0	0	0	0	0	1	0	1
INP	D6	0	0	0	0	0	1	0	0	0	0
MEMR	D7	1	1	0	0	0	0	0	0	1	0

Figure 4-8
Data Bus Status Information

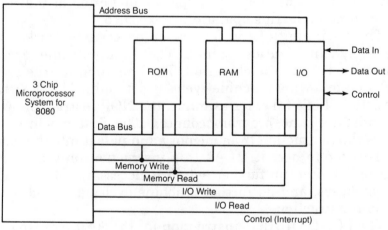

Figure 4-9
8080 Computer System

machine cycles. In the first machine cycle, the load instruction is fetched from the memory, and put into the instruction register for decoding. In the second and third machine cycles, the two address bytes are transferred from memory to the address register and a memory read operation code is put on the data bus at the start of these two machine cycles. In the fourth machine cycle, the new address in the address register is used to transfer the data byte from memory to the data bus and then into the accumulator.

Basically, the executions of the LOAD instructions look very similar in the 6800 and the 8080. Yet in detail the operations are often quite different and more complex in the 8080. The machine cycles are unequal in length, much higher frequency clock cycles are necessary, and the type of operation to be executed is read from the data bus.

The basic operating principles of the 8080 microcomputer have been used in all of the successor chips. Certain improvements have been added, especially in the model 8085, which has some of the features promoted by the 6800.

The hardware of the 8080 requires three power supply voltages: +50V, −5V, and +12V. There are three chips in the basic microprocessor system: the 8080 microprocessor, the clock driver, and the system's controller.

The clock driver supplies two clock phases, one set for the microprocessor, and set in TTL for the other devices. It provides three clock-referenced control signals: the RESET signal, the READY signal, and the SYNC (STSTB) signal. The clock driver has connections for a crystal and for an overtone filter.

The system's controller buffers the eight bidirectional data lines. It generates the two sets of READ and WRITE lines for the memory and the I/O and interrupt acknowledgement. It receives five control signals, status strobe, bus enable, write, data input strobe (DBIN), and hold acknowledge (HLDA) among its functions.

The interrupt system uses the following lines: interrupt request (INT), interrupt enable (INTE), and interrupt acknowledge (INTA). Other lines serving the interrupt system are RESET, HOLD (DMA request), WAIT, bus enable (BUSEN), reset logic input (RESET), and ready logic input (RDYIN).

4.8 INSTRUCTION SET FOR THE 8008 MICROPROCESSORS

The instruction set for the 8080 is quite similar to that of the 6800 microprocessor except for the additional I/O instructions and the lack of an index register. Certain instruction sequences have to be written in a slightly different way because of the unspecificity of the register/accumulators. Assembler programs written in both microcomputers look quite similar, especially if the instruction for any function is written with the same name in both microprocessors.

4.9 ADVANTAGES AND DISADVANTAGES

One advantage of the 8080 microprocessor is the large number of support devices, which are sometimes more sophisticated and can be used for more—even seldom-used—applications. The 8080 has also been on the market longer than the 6800 and more knowledge to use it has been accumulated.

Disadvantages include the somewhat overcomplicated operation, which is unnecessary for the vast majority of applications and slows down the execution of programs. Improvements have been made in successor chips of the 8080. Another disadvantage is the need for three power supplies and three chips instead of one in the 6800.

4.10 TEXAS INSTRUMENTS MICROPROCESSORS

Texas Instruments brought out early microprocessors of very advanced designs. These were designed to meet the needs of telecommunication systems, for which Texas Instruments is a supplier. The almost complete lack of the standard set of registers is the most interesting feature of these designs. They incorporate only a program counter, workspace register, and status register. The first and last registers are self-explanatory and are used in all computers. The workspace register substitutes for the other registers usually provided and creates sixteen registers in the memory for general purposes such as accumulators and stacks index registers.

A major feature is the ability to create as many sets of registers as needed or as memory space allows. If a new set of program counter, status register, and workspace register is generated, the addresses of the old ones are saved in the last three registers of the new workspace register. This allows the creation or recall of as many new sets as necessary.

The flexibility of this design is very useful for message-switching centers and similar applications. It could be adapted with special software to most applications on hand. The series 9900 has a good interrupt-handling system and the serial-to-parallel conversion logic needed in message-switching systems. Initially, however, it had no I/O port interface logic. The higher complexity and the lack of support made these advanced TI microprocessors less popular than other microprocessors.

4.11   OTHER MICROCOMPUTER FAMILIES

4.11.1   Overview

Several other important microcomputer families shown in Figure 4-1 are available in addition to the dominant Intel and Motorola microcomputer families. These serve more special applications, as will be discussed below.

4.11.2   Other Microprocessors

The 6500 series is a modification of the 6800 from Motorola but is not compatible with it. It is used in the Apple and Commodore computers, and in the KIM kit. There are only one 8-bit accumulator, two 8-bit index registers, one 8-bit stack pointer, and one 8-bit status register. The program counter is 16 bits. There is a definite lack of control signals. It is ideally suited for interactive applications using high-resolution graphics, such as needed for home and school.

4.11.3   RCA COSMAC

The RCA Cosmac microprocessor had an advantage over other microcomputers. It used high-impedance CMOS technology, which lowered the total power consumption—an important factor in portable devices, especially in biomedical applications. The COSMAC is well designed but it has, like most other processors, certain design compromises. The timing delays may differ significantly with power variations. The COSMAC may draw as much current as other well-designed non-CMOS microprocessors in certain applications. The introduction of CMOS microprocessors by the two top manufacturers diminished sharply the importance of the CMOS series.

4.11.4   National Semiconductor Microprocessors

National Semiconductor was one of the pioneers of the single-chip microcomputer for control purposes. One of these was the SC/MP, which has special pins to receive and put out logic and serial information directly. The chip also has the necessary control signals to cooperate with several other processors. The availability of similar, but much more powerful, microprocessors from competing manufacturers diminished the demand for this pioneering design and for other very good 8-bit and 16-bit microprocessors from National Semiconductor.

4.11.5   Microprocessors Used in Popular Microcomputers

The list below shows that the more powerful and faster 16-bit microprocessors such as the 8086 or 68000 are preferred for the newer microcomputer designs. Notice that almost all of these microcomputers listed use microprocessors related to either the 8008 or 6800.

Microcomputer	Processor
TRS 80	Z 80
Apple	6502
IBM (WP)	8086
IBM (LAB)	68xxx
Commodore	6502
Kim	6502
Sinclair	Z80
NEC	Z80
SWTPC	6809

Microcomputer	Processor
Radio Shack Color	6809
Radio Shack 16	68000
HP 9825	In house design (16 bit)
Atari	6502
TI Microcomputer	TI 99/4
Apple Lisa	68000
Macintosh	68000
Executive (Sinclair)	68000
ATT	Own design (16 bit)

CHAPTER 5

Interfacing Microcomputers

5.1 INTRODUCTION

Concepts, functions, and components of microcomputers have been presented. This chapter will show how microprocessors are connected to devices or systems such as temperature controls, scientific instruments, and laboratory experiments.

Interface systems and their components must be selected for excellent functionality, high economy, and efficiency to meet the requirements for specific applications.

Highest quality is necessary for the interface systems, as the whole system is only as good as its weakest link. Dependability can be increased by using a fail-safe design. In this case at least two paths for information flow exist between computers and device, a high-quality one and a lower-grade emergency one. When the higher quality fails, the lower quality is automatically switched in.

5.2 BASIC INTERFACE OPERATION

An interface connects the microcomputer system to the application system. The language in the microcomputer, using the digital binary system, must be translated to the specific code recognized by the application devices, and vice versa. Specifically, the interface system must do the following:

1. Translate the information coming from the application devices into the digital binary system used by the microcomputer system.
2. Translate the information coming from the application system to the special language(s) used by the microcomputer.
3. Limit the voltage going into the microcomputer to the voltage range 0-5V.

4. Synchronize the information from the devices with the operation of the microcomputer in such a way so that no information is lost.

5. Insure that all information coming from the microcomputer conforms to the needs of the application devices, just as information from the application devices must conform to the needs of the microcomputers.

6. Be certain that the interface system is efficient, economical, and reliable.

An interface system includes hardware and software. When the functions of the interface have been determined, it is necessary to decide which functions can be carried out best by hardware and which by software.

This decision can influence greatly the efficiency, cost, and reliability of the entire system. Designing to increase the use of hardware to save software is desirable if only one or a few systems are to be made. Hardware is usually cheaper than software for a specific function, especially when labor is considered. Hardware also normally has an advantage over software for a function that is repeated frequently, executed at high speed, and is fully automatic. Software may be comparatively cheaper in applications for which microcomputers are in quantity production because one set of software may be reproduced easily, while a hardware device must be built unit by unit.

The basic components of an interface system are represented in Figure 5-1. One section of the interface translates information coming from the microcomputer to the application system. The other section translates the information coming from the device to the microcomputer. Also, information may be exchanged between the two sections of the interface system.

A simple example of one interface for a pH meter will be used to explain the basic operation of an interface system. Consider the functions of a pH meter measuring the pH value or the Hydrogen Ion concentration of a fluid. The pH value for water is 7.00 and for vinegar 4.00. A change of 1 pH value corresponds to about 62 millivolts. In modern pH meters, this voltage may often be available in digital form.

Even though the output from the pH meter may be in digital form, connecting the pH meter directly to the microprocessor

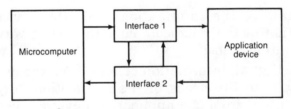

Figure 5-1A
Block Diagram of Interface System

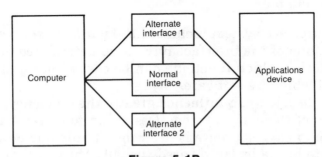

Figure 5-1B
Block Diagram of a Failsoft System

may not be possible. The output of the pH meter must be first checked to see if it is in serial or parallel form before selecting the appropriate input to the microcomputer. If it is serial, the output from the pH meter must conform to RS232 and the ASCII standard. The baud rate of the pH meter and the computer must agree. Check to see if the stop bits and the parity have been set appropriately and that all the proper control signals are available. Serial interconnections will be discussed in greater detail at the end of this chapter.

If the connection is parallel, as is usually the case, check the pH meter for the use of the "two complement" version of the binary digital system. Be certain that the binary output is in the 4- to 5-volt range. Too high a voltage may damage the computer and too low a voltage may not properly activate the computer. Usually, the output of the pH meter has a buffer to maintain compatible voltage under normal circumstances.

If the output of the pH meter is parallel, if it uses the two complement version of the binary digital system, and if it is close enough to 5.0V, the microcomputer will be able to pick up a pH value from the pH meter every ten to twenty-five micro-seconds. This frequent pickup of information is not necessary as the pH value changes slowly compared to this computer reading frequency. In this case the microcomputer would collect a tre-mendous amount of useless data which, in addition, would very soon overload the memory of a microcomputer.

This problem may be avoided by inserting a timing loop into the program to extend the time intervals between data point col-lection to, perhaps per second or longer intervals. Another way to collect the data points at long intervals is to use the interrupt system explained later in this chapter.

We can expand our laboratory system to two pH control sys-tems, as shown in Figure 5-2. Two values are received from two different pH electrodes and buffers. They are sent over a multi-plexor, sample and hold, ADC, and PIA, into the microprocessor, where they are stored in two different memory locations.

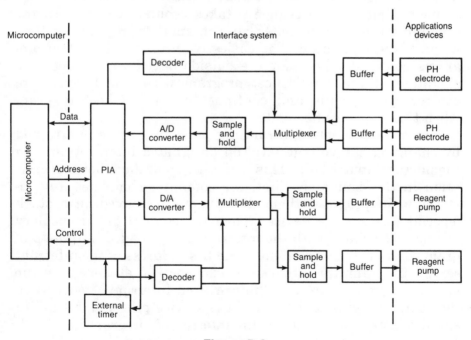

Figure 5-2
General Laboratory System for the Control of Two pH Systems

To maintain a pH value or to change it according to a program loaded into the microprocessor, the microprocessor can give commands over a different pathway to the PIA, DAC, another multiplexor, sample and holds, and buffer to a reagent pump. The control of pump 1 and pump 2 are completely independent of each other because different memory areas are assigned to system 1 and system 2. Specific examples of laboratory systems will be discussed in later chapters.

5.3 INTERRUPT SYSTEM

5.3.1 General

A computer in a laboratory or business can be used profitably between data readings for many other uses during the same time period. For example, a microcomputer controls the temperature of a device by checking the temperature and readjusting, if necessary, the amount of heat supplied every five seconds. This control sequence takes around 100 μsec. In the remaining time the computer can run another program, such as a spreadsheet program. The easiest way to run these two programs consecutively is for the outside device to interrupt the operation of the spreadsheet program when the temperature control cycle begins and continue the spreadsheet program when this sequence has ended.

In most computers, a running program can be interrupted by changing the voltage level on designated interrupt pins on the microcomputer chip. This action triggers the following operation in the computer. First, the computer completes any instruction in progress, then all registers are saved on a stack (special fast storage device). Then the content of the memory location associated with the interrupt pin is loaded into the program counter. If this content is the first address of the interrupt service program, this program is executed. If, at the end of the service program there is a "return from interrupt" instruction, the computer will, at the end of the service program, reload all saved registers and continue the interrupted program.

Typically, microcomputers have at least four different interrupts:

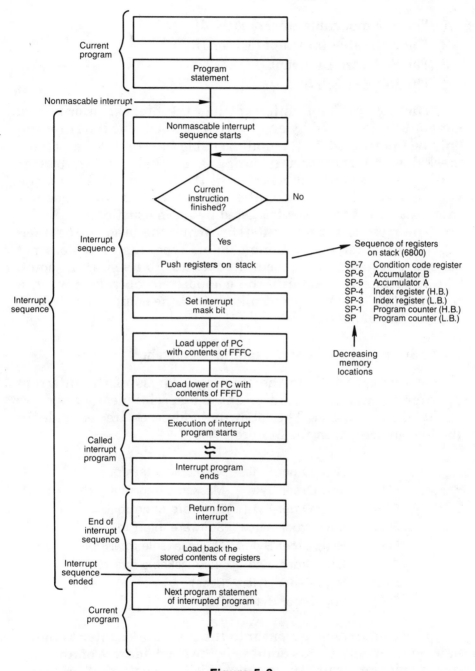

Figure 5-3
Interrupt Sequence

1. The Nonmaskable Interrupt (NMI)
2. The Maskable Interrupt (MI, or IRQ)
3. The Software Interrupt (SI)
4. The Reset (RESET)

The non-maskable interrupt has the highest priority and cannot be interrupted by any other. The maskable interrupt can only be interrupted by the nonmaskable interrupt. When a non-maskable interrupt occurs during a maskable interrupt, the maskable interrupt is stopped until the nonmaskable interrupt is completed. The software interrupt is similar to the maskable interrupt except that it is triggered by an instruction.

The reset is entirely different. While the other three interrupts are similar to the nonmaskable type, the reset does not save any registers and resets the monitor to its starting point. The reset interrupt returns the computer to operation when a program has become uncontrollable and the computer is inoperable at that moment.

5.3.2 Starting Address of the Interrupt Program

The computer finds the starting address of the interrupt program by linking each interrupt to a special memory address in the microcomputer. The following addresses are set aside for the four interrupts in the Motorola 6800:

FFF8	High Order Byte	Maskable Interrupt
FFF9	Low Order Byte	Maskable Interrupt
FFFA	High Order Byte	Software Interrupt
FFFB	Low Order Byte	Software Interrupt
FFFC	High Order Byte	Nonmaskable Interrupt
FFFD	Low Order Byte	Nonmaskable Interrupt
FFFE	High Order Byte	Reset
FFFF	Low Order Byte	Reset

These addresses are put into the program counter to designate an interrupt. If this address is the start address of an interrupt service program, the computer will execute that program. For example, if the content of FFFC is 10 and of FFFD is 00, and the non-maskable pin of the 6800 is set from high to low by an external device, the 6800 will execute the interrupt service program at location HEX 1000. Special chips are available to extend the number of interrupts, such as the priority interrupt controller MC6828 which accepts up to eight external interrupt requests for the 6800.

5.4 MICROCOMPUTER I/O BUFFERS (PIA)

When the computer sends out a data value, this data value is up on the data bus only for a very short time. An outside device must respond quickly to the control signals the computer sends out.

The I/O buffers were developed to simplify the exchange of information between computers and their peripherals, which do not have the necessary logic available. The previously mentioned PIA (Peripheral Interface Adapter) MC6821 is a good example.

Assigning a specific address to the PIA assures that only the data values destined to go to a specific external device will be picked up by this buffer. This buffer can be placed in any location in the memory but is usually placed in the 8000 plus Hex addresses in the 6800 systems and in the E000 plus Hex addresses in the 6809. Four addresses must be assigned for it, one each for the data and control register for the A side and one each for the data and control register for the B side (Figure 5-4).

To set the PIA up for communication with an outside device the following steps should be observed:

1. Set control register bit 2 of the selected output side to "zero."
2. Set input or output data register bits by loading the corresponding data direction register appropriately with zeros and ones.
3. Set control register bit 2 to the value "1".
4. Start sending data through data register to application device.

This sequence of instructions is the same for the A and B sides. Now, we can write a program to set up the PIA with

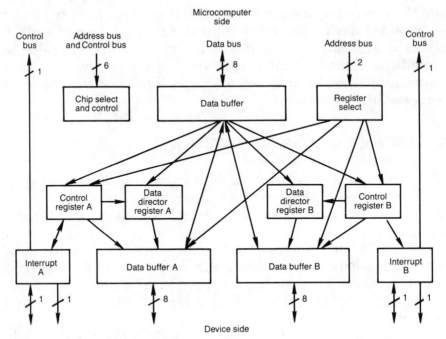

Figure 5-4
Block Diagram for a Parallel I/O Buffer

instructions already learned. If the program starts at memory location 0, the assembly language source program will look like this for the side A:

Assembly program listing	Remarks
ORG $0000	This locates the start of the program.
	Loads the Accumulator with 00.
LDA #$00	Sends the zeros to the A side control register.
STA $8001	
LDA #$0F	Loads the Accumulator A with "1" for bits 0 to 3 and with "0" for the bits 4 to 7.
STA $8000	Loads the data direction register of side A with 0F. Bits 0 to 3 are set for output and bits 4 to 7 for input.
LDA $04	Loads Accumulator A with a "1" in bit 2.
STA $8001	Loads a "1" into control register bit 2 of side A, to direct all information in location $8000 to the data register in side A.

The PIA can now send data out on bits 0 to 3, and receive information from bits 4 to 7 on the A side.

A similar program can be set up for side B. If we set up side B for input only then the following program output results when the source code is executed with an assembler. In the following, we see not only the assembly source code with the memory addresses but also the machine language program.

Machine Language			Assembler Language		
Assembly Address	Machine Address	Machine Code	Assembly Op Code	Operand	Remarks
00001			NAM	PIA-INIT	
00002			OPT	NOP	
00003			ORG	$0000	Start of machine program
00004		* PIA INITIALIZATION			
		* SETUP OF A SIDE			
00005	0000	86	LDA		Set bit 2 of control register to "0"
	0001	00		#$00	
00006	0002	B7	STA		
	0003	80		$80	
	0004	01		01	
00007	0005	86	LDA		Load direction register with "0F"
	0006	0F		$0F	
00008	0007	B7	STA		
	0008	80		$80	
	0009	00		00	
00009	000A	86	LDA		Set control register bit 2 to "1"
	0009	04		$04	
	0B	B7	STA		
	0C	80		$80	
	0D	01		01	
0000A		* SET UP OF B SIDE			
0000B	000E	86	LDA		
	000F	00		#$00	
0000C	00010	B7	STA		
	00011	80		$80	
	00012	02		02	
0000D	00013	86	LDA		
	0014	00		#$00	

A SIDE INITIALIZATION

B SIDE INITIALIZATION

	Machine Language			Assembler Language	
Assembly Address	Machine Address	Machine Code	Assembly Op Code	Operand	Remarks
0000E	0015	B7	STA		
	0016	80		$80	
	0017	02		02	
0000F	0018	86	LDA		
	0019	04		$04	
00010	0020	B7	STA		
	0021	80		$80	
	0022	03		03	

A shortcut is available by writing a PIA initialization program using the index register. When data in the index register are stored in a memory location, the first eight bits are stored in the indicated address and the second eight bits are stored automatically in the next higher memory location. This simplifies our PIA program. If the computer was reset before the program was started (control register bit 2 is "0") the following program would result:

Assembly Address	Machine Address	Machine Code	Assembly Code		Remarks
00001			NAM PIA2-SETUP		
00002			ORG $0000		
00003			* PIA2 INITIALIZATION PROGRAM		
00004	0000	CE	LDX		
	0001	0F		#$0F	
	0002	04		#$04	
00005	0003	FF	STX		A Side
	0004	80		$80	
	0005	00		00	
00006	0006	CE	LDX		
	0007	00		#$00	
	0008	04		#$04	
00007	0009	FF	STX		B Side
	000A	00		$00	
	000B	04		02	

After the above initialization of the PIA instructions LDA $8000 and LDB $8002 (96 8000, 96 8002) will bring a data value of twelve bits into the computer. Four bits can be used for control purposes.

The setup of Figure 5-5 may be used to send information from a digital voltmeter to a microcomputer. Bits 0 to 3 may be assigned to control the digital voltmeter. The remaining twelve bits—four from side A and eight from side B—may be used to transmit the output voltage of the meter to the microcomputer. A number value with the precision of three and a half (decimal) digits can be sent to the microcomputer, because twelve binary digits correspond to a decimal value of 4096. The first three digits of this number may have values from 0 to 9, but the most significant digit can only assume the values 0 to 4.

5.5   INTERFACING ANALOG INFORMATION

The microcomputer and PIA can only accept and transmit binary digital information at a voltage of 5V. An Analog to Digital Converter (ADC or A/D) is necessary for the microprocessor to accept information from and send it to an electrical thermometer, pressure gauge, or other analog output devices.

5.5.1   Digital to Analog Converters

First the DAC will be considered as it is the easiest to explain. The DAC converts a binary digital number into an analog

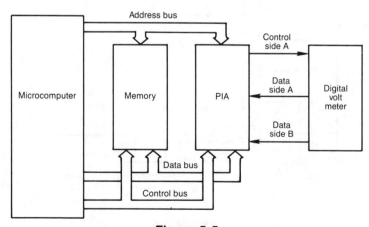

Figure 5-5
Block Diagram of the Interface for a Digital Voltmeter

signal. Each bit is assigned according to its position (MSB to LSB), a voltage, or a current. For example, the most significant bit (MSB) in an 8-bit number (1000 0000) is assigned 128 times the current of the least significant bit (LSB : 0000 0001). The sum of all the currents from all the "ON" bits is added and converted to a proportional voltage signal. Figure 5-6 shows the block diagram for such a converter.

The signals from the data bus are on the left side. These go to the gates of field effect transistors (FETs). On one side these FETs are connected to a reference power supply. The other side ("drain") of these transistors is connected through different resistors to a current summation point. The resistor values are

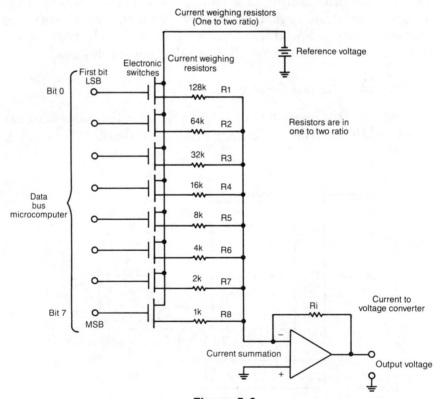

Figure 5-6
Basic Digital to Analog Converter

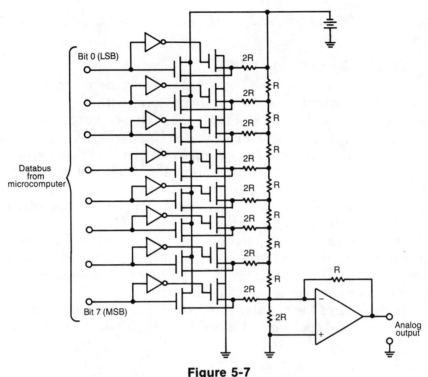

Figure 5-7
DAC with Resistor Ladder

selected in such a way that the current from each bit corresponds to the value of that bit. Often the much easier to manufacture resistor ladder shown in Figure 5-7 is used in place of the
more complex resistor network in Figure 5-6. All DACs use the
same general principle of operation, even though they may
achieve it in different ways.

5.5.2 Analog to Digital Converters

5.5.2.1 *General*

The four basic types of ADC are: successive approximation
ADC, integration type ADC, counter type ADC, and parallel type
ADC. The counter type will be described in detail and the basic

functions, advantages, and disadvantages given for the other types.

5.5.2.2 Counter Type ADC

The counter type ADC generates a series of increasing binary digital numbers, starting from zero, with the help of a digital counter and a clock (Figure 5-8). These digital numbers are converted by a DAC to an analog voltage which is compared with the analog value to be measured. When these two analog voltages are equal, a comparator stops the clock and the further generation of higher digital values. The number present at the digital counter when the clock was stopped is the digital equivalent of the analog number.

The counter type is not the most popular ADC, because of its rather slow conversion speed. A 1 MHz clock and a 10 bit resolution give the converter a 1 millisecond response time, which is slow compared to other ADCs.

Variations of the counter ADC are useful for other purposes. If the directional counter in Figure 5-8 is replaced with a bidirec-

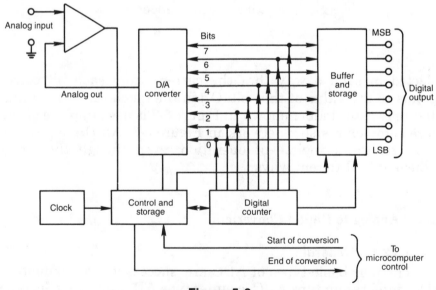

Figure 5-8
Basic Analog to Digital Converter

tional counter. This modified ADC can be used to compare close rotary positions fast and economically.

The counter ADC can also be used as a rather fast-acting and very stable Sample and Hold circuit. For this purpose we need only to change the logic of operation so that the counter, instead of starting to count from zero for every new AD conversion, continues to count from where it previously stopped. An outside logic gate stops the operation when the Sample and Hold circuit is triggered to store the last analog voltage. This Sample and Hold circuit, using a capacitor, will hold the analog voltage indefinitely, unlike the regular type using a capacitor which loses its charge with time.

5.5.2.3 Successive Approximation ADC

The successive approximation ADC is the most popular type. In this ADC, each digital bit starting from the most significant bit (MSB) is in analog form compared to the analog input voltage. If the analog voltage of this bit is less than the incoming analog voltage, this bit value is retained for the digital output and added to the previous one. Otherwise, it is discarded. The conversion ends when the least significant bits (LSB) have been compared. Figure 5-8 can be used also as a schematic diagram for a successive approximation ADC, as the general layout is the same and only the operational logic is different from the counter type.

Figure 5-9 shows the output in the counter type ADC. There can be as many comparisons as there are digital steps between the zero bit value and the end value. This is a maximum of 256 steps for an 8-bit converter. In comparison, the output of a successive approximation ADC only takes eight steps to complete each conversion. The successive approximation converter is usually the much faster type. If the counter ADC uses seven or less steps to complete the conversion of a small analog value, the counter type will be the faster type.

5.5.2.4 Integration ADC

The integration ADC is less popular then the successive approximation type ADC because of its slowness. It is used mostly in digital meters or in similar applications because of its

Interfacing Microcomputers

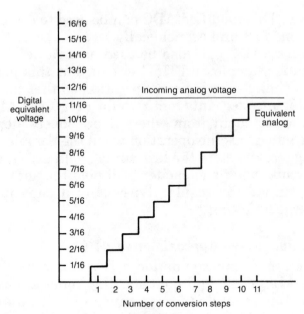

Figure 5-9

Output of Counter Analog to Digital Converter (4 Bits)

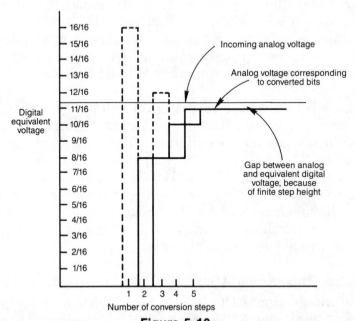

Figure 5-10

Output of Succession Approximation Digital Analog Converter
(4 Bits)

low cost and because it is somewhat less sensitive to noise than the other ADCs.

Only the dual conversion type integration ADC, most suitable to the types of applications considered in this book, are discussed here. This ADC uses an indirect conversion of the analog value. For a fixed amount of time (T) the analog input voltage is connected to an integrating amplifier charging its feedback capacitor. At the end of that time, the integrating amplifier is connected to an internal reverse polarity reference voltage and a counter is started. When the output of the integrating amplifier reaches zero, the counter is stopped. The count is proportional to the incoming voltage, which is displayed as a digital value.

The independence of the dual conversion ADC from the value of a capacitor and the clock frequency are advantages over the simple conversion ADC. The integration reduces disturbing high frequency noises and makes possible the complete removal of frequencies which are multiples of 1/T which would cause problems in other ADCs. For this reason, the dual conversion ADC is ideal for digital meters. Its somewhat slow response, on the order of T/2 is of little consequence when using digital voltmeters.

Figures 5-11 and 5-12 show the block diagram and a plot of the output of the integral ADC. The input voltage, V(in), is accumulated by the integrating amplifier over a fixed time period T. The maximum voltage reached at the output of the amplifier is proportional to V(in) and T. After this period, a negative reference voltage, V(ref), is applied to the input of the integrator, decreasing its output to zero after the time interval T. The input voltage is then proportional to V(ref) X(t/T). T and t are expressed in counts per second and can be calibrated to represent the input voltages.

5.5.2.5   *Parallel Type ADC*

Parallel type ADCs are by far the fastest analog to digital converters but at the same time are the most expensive. Digital logic circuitry is used to calculate a digital output value for each analog input. The speed of calculation depends on the time it takes for signals to travel through the logic gates used. The complexity and resultant cost increases geometrically with the

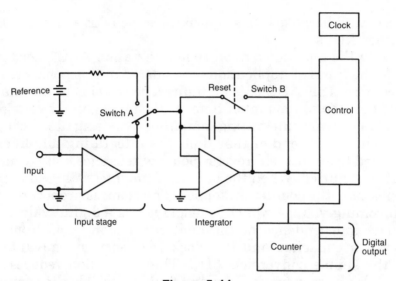

Figure 5-11
Schematic of Integral Analog to Digital Converter

number of bits in the digital output value. For a 3-bit ADC, seven comparators and five 4-input NOR gates are required. For a 4-bit ADC, fifteen comparators and seven 8-input NOR gates are required. This type of ADC could become more practical as the cost of digital chips decreases.

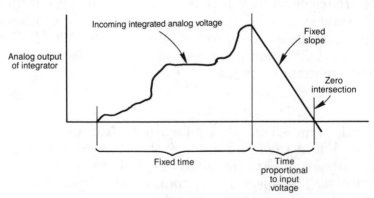

Figure 5-12
Output of Integral Analog to Digital Converter

5.5.3 Application of Interface Systems

Figure 5-13 shows a block diagram of a system for the control of a furnace to demonstrate the application of an interface.

Temperature sensor output potentials range from tens to the hundreds of millivolts. A buffer amplifier is needed to raise the maximum output to five volts for the ADC. The ADC converts the analog input from the buffer to the binary digits necessary for the microprocessor. A PIA is inserted between the microprocessor and the two outside devices to connect the two devices to one single data bus and to store temporarily the incoming and outgoing data.

A program in the microprocessor loads the incoming data into a memory table. The program compares the latest temperature measurement with previous ones together with other factors such as outside temperature, wind speed, and direction. An updated setting for the furnace is sent over the B side of the PIA to the DAC converter. A buffer amplifier raises the control voltage for the furnace to reach the set temperature.

5.6 INTERFACING OVER TELECOMMUNICATION LINES

It is not always possible to locate the microcomputer next to the device which it operates. For example, the microcomputer may have to be some distance from the temperature sensor, the fur-

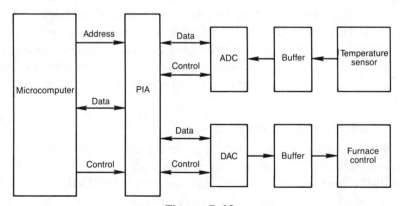

Figure 5-13
Block Diagram for Furnace Control

nace control, or both, as in the case of a central control for several pieces of equipment at different locations.

5.6.1 Wire Connections

The best way to connect a device near a computer is by wiring. Few problems occur when distances are less than 100 feet, especially if ribbon wire cable is used. For longer distances care has to be taken that the capacitance between the wires be kept low and to insure that electromagnetic noise does not interfere with the transmission of signals.

Electromagnetic interferences can be controlled in different ways. In simple cases an electrical shield placed around the wires should solve the problem. This technique may not be adequate, especially for longer cables, which may be thousands of feet long, and double shielding may be necessary. Such shielding is often required in hospital areas, to reduce fire hazards. Care has to be taken to prevent the two shields from contacting each other and that they are grounded separately for maximum effect. Additional protection for special, low-noise applications can be obtained by using optical devices and/or special amplifiers which increase the signal-to-interference ratio.

5.6.1.1 Parallel Wire Connections

Parallel connections are the fastest way to transmit information between a computer and device. Each bit from the transmitting side is sent by a separate wire to the same bit on the receiving side. This is excellent for short connections. For longer distances, parallel wires may become so expensive that the connection could cost more than a good microcomputer system. A very high transmission speed may be necessary sometimes to transfer information between a computer and its devices.

5.6.1.2 Serial Wire Connections

Serial transmission of bits rather than their parallel transmission reduces the cost of the connection tremendously. This is suitable when lower speeds are acceptable. Only two wires instead of nine are needed for sending eight bits because the bits are transmitted through only one pair of wires.

A convention has been adopted to insure that the eight bits sent are transmitted with a minimum of errors. When eight bits are sent as a unit, a header or starting bit is sent first and a closing or stop bit last. The quiet state on the line is indicated by a high state (5 volts). The starting bit changes the high state to a low state, and the stop bit returns the low state to the high state. This convention was introduced some time ago for tele-graph stations located miles apart. A high voltage level from batteries (20 to 60 volts) at the receiving station indicated that the transmitting station and the wire connection in between were up and ready to send signals.

Figure 5-14 gives the convention used to send an eight-bit word. The starting bit drops the voltage from high to low. Then the eight-bit word in ASCII format is sent. After the most signifi-cant and last bit of the eight-bit word has been sent, the stop bit(s) indicate the end of the character by going from low to high. Some slow mechanical devices, such as TTY terminals may need one-and-a-half or two bits for a stop during a continu-ous transmission of characters.

The receiver must not only sense the start and stop bits but also properly sense the state of the bits in between. To accom-plish that, the frequency of the clock in the transmitter and the frequency of the clock in the receiver side must be synchronized within plus or minus 5%. A character of eight bits and the start and stop bits can be sent in irregular intervals (asynchronous operation). The speed with which the characters are sent is called bits per second (bps) or, although less correctly, baud, after Baudot, the inventor of the Baudot code (Chapter 1). The baud speed is measured in pulses per second rather than bits per

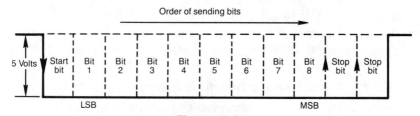

Figure 5-14
Bit Sequence for Sending Asynchronous Information

second. Two consecutive bits that are at the high level may form one pulse. Therefore, the two measures, pulse per second and bits per second, are not identical.

A speed of three hundred bps can send 30 characters of 10 bits per second to the receiver. 110 bps can send only 10 characters per second because 110 is used for TTY terminals, which need two stop bits per character. The speed of many modern terminals has exceeded 38,000 bps and manufacturers are increasing this speed. Higher speed is used primarily for graphics as 9600 bps are needed to fill a standard screen in about one second.

5.6.2 Telephone Communication

For long distances, perhaps a hundred or even a few thousand feet, laying direct wires is impractical. The telephone system is suitable for such service. The telephone is excellent for voice communication system in the 100 to about 3000 Hz frequency range. It is not well suited to the transmission of high frequency pulses which are apt to be badly distorted on standard voice lines.

A pulse is sent over the regular telephone network by translating it into a tone (frequency) burst equal in length to the originating pulse. When the tone burst arrives at the destination, it is retranslated back into a pulse. These translations are done by a modem (MOdulator and DEModulator). A modem for 300 bps, the most common one, sends a tone burst from the transmitting side of 2275 Hz for each ON bit and 2025 Hz for each OFF bit. The ON bit is 1270 Hz and the OFF bit 1070 Hz when sent by the receiving modem. Both units may operate simultaneously because of this frequency difference. The arrangement is shown in Figure 5-15. A line adapter must be used if the modem is not certified for direct use on the telephone lines, to be certain that the telephone system is not disturbed by an unmatched device.

5.6.2.1 *Asynchronous Interface Adapter (ACIA)*

Serial data must be converted to parallel data for use by the computer. Because it takes over 30 milliseconds to receive or transmit a character (byte), valuable computer time is lost when

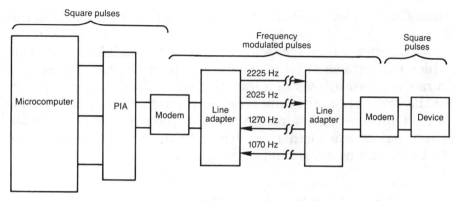

Figure 5-15
Computer Connection over Telephone Lines

the computer receives a character directly. Therefore, a hard-ware device receiving or transmitting data for the computer and making the serial to parallel or parallel to serial conversion of the bytes, must also temporarily store those bytes.

This can be accomplished with special hardware devices such as UART (Universal Asynchronous Receiver and Trans-mitter) or an ACIA (Asynchronous Communications Interface Adapter). The block diagram for an ACIA is shown in Figure 5-16. The ACIA uses double buffering for the receive and trans-mit sides so that it can both receive and transmit data at the same time without waiting for the computer to pick up the last data byte or send a new data byte to the ACIA. The speed with which data is received or transmitted is not always the same because the ACIA can send and receive data at different baud speeds. The status register and the control register in the ACIA allow the computer to monitor continuously the receiving and transmitting of data.

To make sure that the receiving side is up to accept the transmitted data and no data are lost, the ACIA has three con-trol signals available. These are: 1) Request To Send (RTS), which is sent out before the start of the transmission of data to the receiver; 2) Clear To Send (CTS), which is sent back by the receiver to the transmitter in response to the RTS signal to advise that the receiving side is ready to receive data; and 3)

Data Carrier Detect (DCD) indicating that the transmission line is up.

The microcomputer sends data over the ACIA to a modem, which converts each bit of the data into tone bursts. These tone bursts are sent by way of a line adapter to the telephone system. At the destination, they are received through a line adapter, then onto a modem which reconverts the tone bursts into pulses. These pulses are further converted to the parallel form by an ACIA for use at a terminal or a computer.

5.6.2.2   Half Duplex System

In the half duplex system the transmitting unit and the receiving unit take turns sending information to each other. The RTS and CTS signals control this switch.

5.6.2.3   Full Duplex System

In the full duplex system, both sides send and receive simultaneously. Therefore, both RTS and CTS are on all the time.

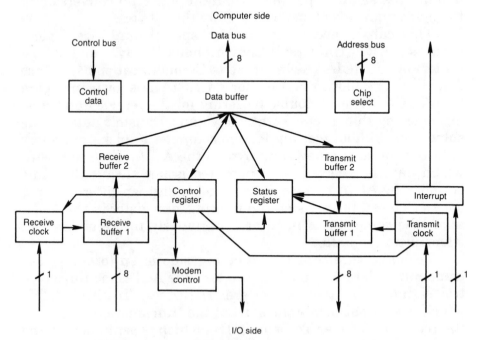

Figure 5-16
Block Diagram of Serial I/O Buffer (ACIA)

This means that the RTS terminal can be connected by a wire to the CTS terminal on the same CRT terminal. A similar connection can be made on the other side. Full duplex transmission of signals over telephone lines requires a sequence of events. After the modem is turned on, the "Data Set Ready" line is set high automatically, indicating to the microprocessor that the modem is ready to transmit and receive. The modem must receive the carrier signal to know that the opposite transmission line and receiving station are up. When the carrier signal is received, it turns on the "Carrier Detect" and the "Clear To Send" signals, which indicate to the microprocessor that the entire transmission system is up and ready for service.

When a carrier frequency signal stops at the end of a message or due to a break, the carrier detect signal will go low. The modem, when properly set up, will automatically stop all further transmissions from both sides so that no information is lost, and will indicate this status at both ends.

In a direct connection without frequency modulation, the RTS signal from one side can be used as the carrier detect signal for the other side. Similarly, the data terminal ready output on one side can be used for the data set ready or ring indicator input on the other side. Figure 5-17 shows the connections between the ACIA and a modem.

5.6.2.4 *International Standard RS232*

The technique described above for handling data transmission is a special case of the International Standard RS232

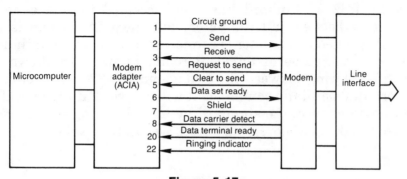

Figure 5-17
Pin Connections on the Modem

Interfacing Microcomputers

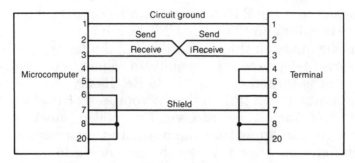

Figure 5-18
Short Distance Connections for RS 232

(updated version is RS440), which specifies the international convention for data handling. It was found when this standard was being developed that the voltage range of 0 to 5 volts was insufficient for a reliable data transmission on lines which might be exposed to wide temperature and humidity changes.

International standard RS232 and the new standard RS440, which is a technical update, specify that an "ON" bit is indicated by a minus voltage, while the "OFF" is indicated by a plus voltage. An "ON" in RS232C would be a voltage from −3 volts to −25 volts in a "positive" logic. Similarly, an "OFF" bit could be from +3 to +25 volts. Therefore, the voltage can vary from +25 to −25 volts on an RS232C channel. The voltage range normally used for computer operation is ±10 volts and must be generated specially. Special chips are available to convert between TTL and RS232C.

The RS232 Standard has been accepted for the external connection between all computer equipment. A modem is not necessary when a computer is connected directly to a terminal or printer in the same or adjacent room. Figure 5-18 shows the simplified wiring between the two 25-pin RS232C connectors of the terminals and the computer. It will not work if the manufacturer deviates from the standard by interchanging pins 2 and 3 to avoid making a more costly crossover in the cable.

CHAPTER 6

A Practical Selection Guide for Microcomputers

6.1 INTRODUCTION

The first step in selecting a computer system for a specific application is to determine as accurately as possible the computational power needed. This approach was described in general terms in Chapter 1. The present chapter is a more detailed guide to selecting the most efficient microprocessor and other components of a microcomputer system best suited to a given application.

Microprocessors and their components may be divided into groups with similar characteristics, as mentioned in Chapter 3. To choose an individual microprocessor, it is best to select the group best-suited, then the unit most suitable from that chosen group.

6.1.1 Selecting the Overall System Design

Planning an overall system is similar to designing a computer program. First, a goal is selected, to be achieved by our application. Next, determine the approach to that goal. A flowchart of the overall system's operation is the next step. When this flowchart shows that a a microcomputer system is beneficial to the application, a microcomputer system, with its hardware and software, will be selected. Thorough testing runs will prove out the completed system, and corrections made as necessary.

6.2 SELECTION OF THE MICROPROCESSOR

Once a determination has been made that a microcomputer is suitable to the task, outline in detail all the steps the computer is to carry out and their time requirements. See the guidelines in Chapter 1 and Figure 1-1. Select the appropriate slanted line corresponding to the computer power needed. If the job is found to be too large or too small for the microcomputer category indicated, either modify the application or choose a different type of computer.

The best microprocessor for the job must be selected after the general type is determined. If a considerable amount of data is exchanged with I/O devices or multiprocessing is of importance, we might select the Motorola 6809. For mathematical processing we might choose the Motorola 68000. For word processing we might select Intel's 8086. For control applications we might select one of TI's or Fairchild's microprocessors. Specific applications for various microprocessors is becoming broader as the two largest and most successful general-purpose microcomputer manufacturers, Intel and Motorola, adapt their microprocessors, with varying degrees of success, to many more applications.

Motorola has chips in the 68000 series which are suitable not only for 8-bit data applications (68008), and 16-bit data applications (68000, 68010), but also for the 32-bit data applications (68020). For smaller applications with very low power drain, the 6805 to 6808 series is excellent. The 6801 (6802) is available with several consumer selectable modes, including some suitable for the auto industry.

6.3 SELECTION OF MICROCOMPUTER COMPONENTS

6.3.1 Introduction

A choice must be made of whether to design the microcomputer system or buy one already in production which uses the microprocessor chip selected. Any one of several commercial microcomputers which uses a fully developed motherboard and bus system is a good choice for an adaptable general-purpose data system. Buying such a unit is usually quicker and cheaper than constructing a system from the beginning. On the other hand, if the microprocessor is to be used for a special laboratory application, such as we discussed in Chapter 7, designing the whole microcomputer system yourself may be necessary.

Many different microcomputer kits are available for people who want to build a very flexible microcomputer but do not want to spend the time it takes to construct an entire system from "the ground-up." Most of these kits include excellent hardware. They provide very useful software such as sophisticated monitors, editors disk operating systems, cassette operating systems, assembler language, BASIC, and PASCAL.

6.3.2   Memory System

The memory system should be tailored to meet the project requirements. Even though the minimum of RAM memory is around 16K for a disk operating system, using 32K would be preferable. Even better is 56K to 64K RAM memory as it will allow you, in addition, to operate a disk system with most higher languages such as PASCAL or FORTRAN. The only exception might be a full UNIX system, for which one needs a minimum amount of 128K memory.

A small ROM memory chip to store a monitor program is important for loading into memory standard programs such as memory test, disk test, computer test, register change and display, debug routines, and a program to load the disk operating system.

If the project involves the continuous operation of a device, and a disk system is not available, an error-free program to operate the device is best put on a ROM chip. This procedure minimizes errors.

While in the intermediate stages of development, it is best to put the program on an EPROM. In the EPROM, the program can be changed many times. Despite claims to the contrary, a program in the EPROM is not as stable as it would be in a ROM. When all desired changes have been made, the program should be transferred to a ROM, and the EPROM used for the next development.

The new electrically alterable memory chips are ideal for program development. They are still quite expensive, and require special voltages to write permanently into their memories.

Bipolar memories offer much higher memory storage and retrieval speeds than other common types of RAMs. But they require an expanded power supply and cost more. For faster and costlier storage capabilities, high speed banks of flipflops can be used.

6.4 SELECTION OF PERIPHERALS

6.4.1 General

The choice of peripherals depends primarily on the intended application for the computer system. Peripherals are unnecessary if a microprocessor chip is built into an instrument, such as for automatic baud speed ranging or a specific algorithm. A good example is the use of a microprocessor for automatic control of liquid delivery (see Chapter 9). Other examples are microprocessors used in washing machines, cars, and furnace controls. A general purpose microcomputer having a full range of peripherals is necessary to develop and test a new application of a microcomputer system.

6.4.2 Terminals

A terminal with a full keyboard and a CRT screen is necessary when changes are made in computer systems. An additional number keypad and/or separate assignable keys for special functions are available for word processors. A screen of 24 lines with 80+ characters per line, perhaps with a 25th command line, is usually adequate. However, 132 or more characters per line are better, for that allows writing in the margins and reduces shifting of the screen for programs such as spread sheets.

A full page display (66 lines) is best for word processing. CRT systems with the necessary resolution are available on more expensive systems. Some systems compromise by having 33 lines or 48 lines available on the screen.

Some of the "intelligent" terminals have two very useful features: A "screen read," which allows the terminal screen content to be read into a printer; a composite video output for projecting the terminal contents on a large video screen, and/or to transfer it to a video recorder.

Terminals with 24 lines of 80+ characters are inadequate for graphics. The graphics representation of such a terminal can be enhanced by a factor of four by rotating the graph 90 degrees. The "horizontal" (X) axis will now be vertical and the "vertical" (Y) axis will be horizontal on the screen. This arrangement is especially useful with a printer because the X-axis is as long as the paper roll. The resolution of a vertical line for graphics on the CRT screen should be at least 190 dots (or pixels, "picture elements") and about 240 pixels horizontally. A graphics resolution of 620 pixels horizontally and 480 vertically is very satisfactory for most life science applications. Up to four separate graphs may be displayed vertically at the same time without reducing the resolution of most of the life science data.

Fine graphics terminals are available. Those by Tektronix are considered to be the best for laboratory and computer graphics displays. Their black and white 4010 display, with 1028 by 779 pixels, offers excellent resolution. Their color terminal, 4027, has a somewhat lower resolution (630 $\times$ 480).

Graphic displays with somewhat less resolution and lower price can be obtained by incorporating special boards which can be built into popular low-cost terminals. One of the most popular high-resolution graphics boards is the one made by Digital Engineering, which can be built into Lear Siegler's terminals, thereby simulating popular graphics terminals. The resulting display resolution is lower because of the limited resolution of the terminal. There is no loss of resolution between this terminal and the host computer because the full high-resolution picture is stored on a memory board. The picture on this memory board is automatically reduced for display to the resolution of the CRT screen.

6.4.3 Permanent Storage Media

Several media exist for the permanent storage of programs. A good cassette system is a reliable and an inexpensive storage system, but it is quite slow. Some higher-speed cassette systems are available, increasing the speed from 300 baud (Kansas City Standard) to 2400 or even 4800 baud. One manufacturer uses a high-speed cassette system in some of their desk-top microcomputers.

Floppy disk systems are necessary for the larger storage capacity required by such programs as PASCAL, FORTRAN, and UNIX. These are excellent time savers. Loading an 8K BASIC system at 300 baud may take over a quarter of an hour with a cassette system. A 16K BASIC program can be loaded from an 8-inch disk in a few seconds. The editing, assembling, and debugging tasks are correspondingly faster.

Five-inch and 3½-inch systems are coming close to the reliability, storage, and speed of 8-inch floppy systems. High transfer speed (4 to 50K bytes/sec), reliability (better than 1 error in 10^8), and storage capability (more than 1 megabyte) are necessary in commercial systems as well as in good laboratory systems.

If higher access speed and more storage space are required, hard disks are indicated. The access speed is about ten to forty times that of floppy disks, and the reliability of accessing is greater. Several first-class Winchester systems offer capacities of 5 megabytes to over 300 megabytes. Some of the hard disk systems have a 5- or 10-megabyte removable hard disk. Prices for the smallest Winchester hard disk systems (5 Megabytes) are in the order of good microcomputer systems.

The advent of large hard disks for microcomputers has introduced a problem. How is a large disk cleared quickly without losing any information of importance? The 9-track tape drive is the answer. There may be 500 to 1000 programs in a large disk system which can be offloaded quickly onto the 9-track tape. A 9-track tape is a must if one has two or more hard disk drives.

6.4.4 Printers

A printer is required if programs are to be developed efficiently to allow the program to be analyzed as a whole rather than by small sections as visible on the screen. Many low-cost printers for the fast printing of computer programs are available. On the other hand, many computer systems have word processing capabilities which require relatively expensive letter-quality printers. A printer with high graphics resolution is necessary to print diagrams, adding to the cost. Fortunately, these three capabilities are available in matrix printers. For memory dumps to the printer, upper-case letters are printed at high-speed. For high quality letter printing, dot overprinting is used, which slows down the printer. These printers have single-sheet friction feeding as well as sprocket advance and are not designed for continuous operation.

For a continuous printing capability, the next higher class of printers is required. These printers have a wider, 16-inch carriage to accept standard computer paper, more fonts, and better printing quality. Special character sets can be loaded automatically from the disk into the printer's memory.

6.4.5 Selection of Transmission Techniques

The most reliable and fastest technique for transmitting information from one location to another is by sending all the bits of the information in parallel and through solid wire connections.

This is the reason many microcomputers are connected to their printers and to their terminals through a parallel connection. This technique speeds up the transmission, increases the reliability, and allows the use of more control signals.

For connections longer than 100 feet away, the cost of the wire itself and the laying of the wire become very expensive. The total cost of the proper wire, professionally laid, may be about $10 per foot. A more economical technique is the sending of information serially using the ASCII code and RS232. The maximum transmission speed is determined by the quality of the cable. The closer together the wires are and the longer the cable is, the higher the capacitance between the wires, which lowers the transmission speed.

The telephone network has the advantage over a privately-laid cable in that it has access to an almost unlimited number of terminals. The usual speed of transmission, 300 to 1200 bps, is lower than in most private cables. This speed can be increased at an increase in cost. The higher cost of a private high-speed telephone line can be justified by heavy use. The telephone service will need to be reevaluated when IDNS is available because it will offer much higher transmission speeds, perhaps at lower cost.

Since the early 1980s, the FCC has allowed the use of ASCII characters in wireless transmissions. It is now easier for licensed operators to send information from one computer to others all over the world. Such operations are further enhanced by the availability of special satellites.

Information may also be transmitted by infrared, light, and sound, although these media are seldom used except under exceptional circumstances. Bell Telephone installed a major telephone trunk line from Boston to Florida using fiberoptics. Such a line not only increases the capacity of the line and lowers its construction cost, but is much less affected by most environmental factors.

6.5 SELECTION OF I/O DEVICES

I/O interfaces should be carefully designed to be efficient, inexpensive, and reliable. Furthermore, they should be failsoft so that when a component fails, the system is able to switch automatically to a different, although perhaps less sophisticated, mode of operation.

An I/O buffer may be necessary to store incoming information or when special handshaking routines are required. An I/O buffer, such as the PIA (6821) described in Chapter 4, can tremendously increase the capacity of the microcomputer. A microcomputer can only send out one character at a time. Low-cost PIAs can store information for later transmission to outside devices while the microprocessor is running another program.

The PIA can be programmed to collect from 1-bit to 16-bit data values. Built-in handshaking routines free the microcomputer for other work and speed up these routines. The PIA also stores interrupt signals to make possible polling line routines.

Analog information must be converted for computers into the digital form by an ADC. The number of bits the ADC should be able to handle depends on the resolution desired. A 0.4% resolution requires 8 bits, and a 0.1% resolution 10 bits. A low-cost counter type ADC may be satisfactory if speed is not important.

If there is noise, and speed is not required, an integration type ADC is probably the best choice. The successive approximation type ADC operates at higher speeds and is most often used in the laboratory.

The fastest of all ADCs, the parallel type, is rarely used because of its high cost.

The DAC is primarily a switching device; most are of one basic design. Fewer differences exist among various DACs than among ADCs, and a DAC costs much less than an ADC having the same speed and bits.

6.6   SELECTION OF PROGRAMMING LANGUAGES

The most efficient software for an application must be carefully chosen. Interpretive BASIC should be considered for most life science applications where speed is not a major factor. It offers most of the capabilities required for biomedical laboratory experiments and of all the high-level languages it is the easiest to learn and write.

Two alternatives exist to obtain higher speed. Compiler BASIC is more than one hundred times faster than the popular interpretive BASIC. Compiler BASIC, on the other hand, does not allow error correcting line-by-line which interpretive BASIC does.

Program execution speed can also be increased by writing the sections of the BASIC as subroutines in assembler or machine language. Most BASIC languages have instructions for switching to and from the assembler language and BASIC. Many life science instruments with built-in computers are using interpreter BASIC with special commands that are written in assembler language to speed up execution time.

An entirely different language, such as FORTRAN, PASCAL, FORTH, C-language, or ADA, offers another choice. FORTRAN has the advantage over other languages in that it is the oldest science-oriented computer language and perhaps the most implemented one. PASCAL is the most structured, logical, and precise of all the high-level languages and is easier to implement and read. PASCAL was originally designed to teach students computer programming and now has developed to the premier language in science and education; it is used almost exclusively in scientific journals.

FORTH was developed especially for ease of data handling in laboratory use. C-language is one of the newer languages which strive to give higher execution speed for general applications. For example, UNIX and most of its derivatives are written in C-language. ADA, the newest international language, is modeled after PASCAL, but was modified to increase the writing and execution speed, and to be more efficient. ADA is now the official language of the DOD and the U.S. Federal Government.

I/O programs are written in assembler or machine language because I/O functions often need a higher speed than the higher language can supply. In addition, the high level language may work only on specific computers. A few versions of high-level languages written for use on specific microcomputers have incorporated commands for the I/O (PEEK and POKE). Even though execution speed of these commands is much faster than in interactive BASIC, writing the I/O program in assembler or machine language further increases the speed of execution.

6.7 HARDWARE/SOFTWARE TRADEOFFS

The question often arises as to whether a function should be implemented in hardware or software. If speed rather than flexibility is necessary for a certain function, hardware is the best choice. Software is preferable for problems in which flexibility has higher priority than speed.

When a microcomputer system is manufactured in high quantities it is better to use software for any function because software needs only to be made once. Hardware must be made for each unit. Hardware becomes the best option when the equipment is made in small quantities. Readily available hardware and software should always be used if possible. Modifications may be considered. A specially made item—hardware or software—is always more expensive than one in production. A special item should be made when there is no other option, no possibility of future production exists, or for educational purposes where there is a personal or a social reward.

6.8 TEMPERATURE CONTROL SYSTEM

A temperature control system may be used as an example to demonstrate the application of microcomputer systems. Such systems may be used in laboratories, houses, or buildings.

6.8.1 Goals

Automatic air conditioning and heating systems regulate temperature and humidity. Each installation must be planned carefully. A house or a laboratory building may be divided into areas each requiring separate controls. The outdoor temperature and humidity, wind direction, speed, and time of day should be taken into consideration. Remote adjustments of the settings may be necessary for some installations. The simple aim is the full automatic control of temperature and humidity in a laboratory building with several rooms.

6.8.2 Principal Ways of Operation

Each room of the laboratory building will need a temperature and humidity sensor and one or more air inlets and outlets. Arrangements should be made so that the temperature and humidity can be set for each hour of the day and week. The outdoor weather condition is measured by sensors on the roof. These sensors gauge the wind direction and its velocity, as well as the outside temperature, humidity, and precipitation. A program must be developed to direct the heating and cooling system to maintain the desired temperature and humidity levels during the entire year.

The thermal energy to be added or removed to heat or cool each area for a different outside condition must be measured to develop inputs for the program. Similar measurements are needed for the humidity. The relationships between the different outside weather conditions and the required inside temperature and humidity can be stored for many different conditions. This information increases tremendously the efficiency of the system. The interrelation between the different areas must be considered if they are to be maintained at different temperatures and/or humidity levels. In developing these relationships one should keep in mind that outside weather conditions, as well as changes in the room temperature, do not change appreciably in a quarter hour or half hour.

6.8.3 Flowchart

Figure 6-1 gives the overall flowchart for this system. Its main purpose is to show how all goals can be achieved with the selected system and that there are no additional functions, components' functions, or components to consider. This system has three main sections. One is the control section of the heating and cooling system, the second is the set value update section, and the third is the error detection section, which verifies all goal settings. Making detailed flowcharts for each of the main sections of the overall flowchart would be the next step. Finally, design the overall block diagram, which will look like that in Figure 6-2.

6.8.4 Selection of the Computer System

The computing power needed for the temperature and humidity control system can be estimated using the above information. Figure 1-1 in Chapter 1 indicates that in 1983 a microcomputer system was best suited for this application.

6.8.4.1 *Selection of the Microprocessor*

The microprocessor must have very good I/O capability to handle the sixteen to twenty I/O channels. It will need fast computational capability to manage the dozen or more control variables from the tables or from the lengthy polynomials as they are received. A good choice would be the Motorola 6809 or Intel's 8085.

6.8.4.2 *Selection of System Components*

Two medium- to high-speed serial ports would be needed for this system—one for the terminal and one for the telephone connection. Fourteen low-speed parallel ports would receive and send information—ten for the temperature and humidity control, four for the weather conditions. The low speed input and output ports could be handled over one multiplexer, thus avoiding a large number of real I/O ports.

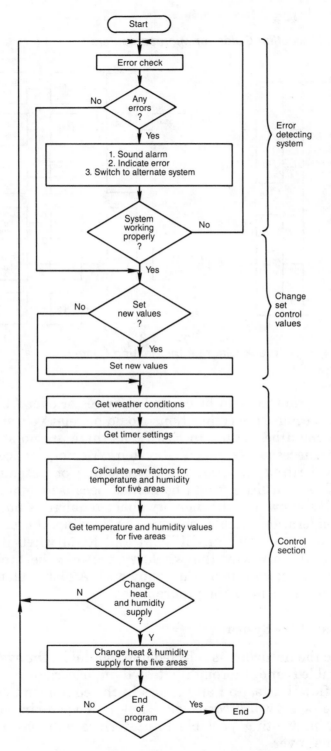

Figure 6-1
Flow Chart for Temperature Control

161

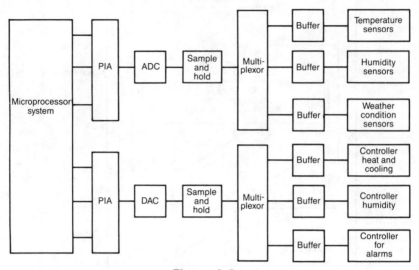

Figure 6-2
Block Diagram for Heating System

All information can be carried on wires or over AC lines in the house because the connections would be relatively short. The software could be written in BASIC as there are no short time responses necessary in such a system. Memory space can be saved by writing the program in machine or assembler language. However, little would be gained because memory prices are relatively low and the memory space required is not large.

Consideration should be given to loading the entire program at one time into an EPROM and ROM when it is fully debugged. In this way the whole system can be brought up without a cassette system or a floppy disk. A disk system is best for the development of the program.

6.8.5 Test of the System

Once the hardware is selected and available, the system will be assembled and thoroughly tested in accordance with the detailed flowcharts, and any errors in the equipment, computer hardware or software corrected. Time now spent in correcting errors or preventing possible future errors will pay for itself many times over.

CHAPTER 7

Increasing the Effectiveness of a System with a Microprocessor

7.1 INTRODUCTION

The choice between using hard-wired, off-the-shelf ICs or a microprocessor system depends upon the component count and/or the flexibility desired. Usually, the microprocessor becomes the better solution as the complexity of the system and/or the desired flexibility increases. Certain flexibility can be obtained with hardwired ICs with potentiometers and/or switches to control parameters.

The microprocessor does not eliminate the need for ICs. The input signals must be conditioned to be acceptable to the microprocessor, and the microprocessor output must be interfaced with displays, relays, and other devices by ICs. Additional memory latches or multiplexers may also be required. A microprocessor-based system including programming can require as much as ten-fold more development time than an equivalent hardwired system. The use of a microprocessor must be justified by higher flexibility, a requirement for smaller space, or large production runs.

We shall demonstrate the improvement in the effectiveness of a system due to the incorporation of a microprocessor by an example for which the component count of the microprocessor-based system and the conventional system are nearly equal. The microprocessor system is shown to be far easier to use and to provide much more valuable information.

Increasing the Effectiveness of a System with a Microprocessor

7.2 SYSTEM DESCRIPTION

We will describe an infusion system which delivers a liquid at a prescribed rate independent of the pressure at the infusion site. A schematic drawing of the system is shown in Figure 7-1. Gas generated by the electrolysis of salt water provides power for the delivery system. The quantity of gas generated is proportional to the electron flux through the electrolysis cell. This gas pressurizes the volume between a rigid housing and a reservoir formed by an impermeable membrane. The liquid stored in the reservoir passes through a submicron filter to one capillary tube for LOW flow condition. A zero displacement valve adds the flow to a

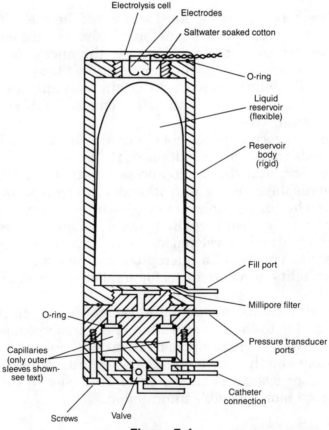

Figure 7-1
Liquid Delivery System

parallel second capillary for HIGH flow. The flow rate is measured and calibrated from the pressure drop across the capillaries, and regulates the electrolysis current for the desired pressure drop. Each capillary consists of a cylinder with a helical, thread-like groove, inserted into a cylindrical sleeve.

Since the system infuses a compressible liquid, errors arise from temperature and pressure variations. These errors may be held within a specified range of ambient conditions by feedback control from the pressure transducer to the electrolytic cell. Under ideal conditions, an alarm system to indicate excessive or insufficient flow could be based on the pressure drop across the capillaries. Ideal conditions do not exist, and additional safety precautions must be taken.

The capillary calibration can change with time. The bore may expand or contract, or a deposit may build up from the liquid passing through the capillary. A leak may bypass liquid around a capillary. Any of these changes would cause an increase or decrease in the current pulse rate which controls the flow. This property is used to activate the alarms. Changes in the back pressure at the delivery site may also affect the current pulse rate. This response is normal while maintaining the correct flow, and must not set off the alarm. A "current window" sets limits for permissible deviations from the nominal value. Time delays must be incorporated into the alarm system to avoid false alarms caused by harmless transients.

7.3   SYSTEM DESIGNED WITH OFF-THE-SHELF INTEGRATED CIRCUITS

7.3.1   Block Diagram

The block diagram of a system built with off-the-shelf integrated circuits that meets the minimum control, monitor, and alarm requirements as described in Section 7.2 is shown in Figures 7-2, and 7-3. Figure 7-2 shows the power supply, the blocked cannula alarm, and the current activation circuits. Figure 7-3 shows the current window alarm circuit, the cumulative flow measurement, and the display circuit. Detailed descriptions are given in the following subsections.

Increasing the Effectiveness of a System with a Microprocessor

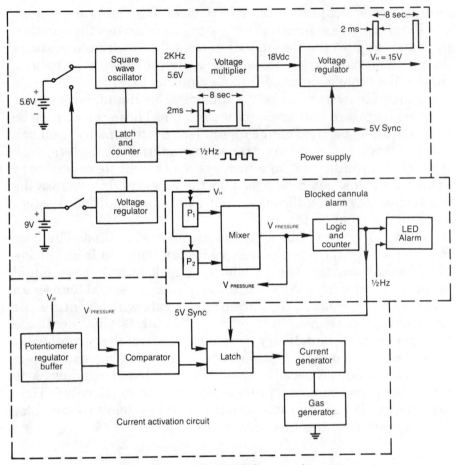

Figure 7-2
Comprehensive Control System (Board 1)

7.3.1.1 *Power Supply (Figure 7-2)*

DC power is supplied either by four 1.4V batteries in series which provide 5.6V, or a 9V battery whose output is regulated to 5.6V. As the pressure transducers require 15V, the 5.6V DC is first converted to a 2kHz square wave. An RC ladder network voltage multiplier raises the 5.6V to 18V. This voltage is then regulated at 15V.

The power supply delivers a current to the system for only 2 milliseconds out of every 8.2 seconds, to conserve battery life.

Consequently, all measurements and monitoring are done on a 250×10^{-6} duty cycle. The duty cycle is controlled by latch and counter circuits which also provide a ½-Hz square wave voltage for use elsewhere in the system.

7.3.1.2 *Current Activation Circuit (Figure 7-2)*

The desired flow is set in terms of a reference voltage across a potentiometer supplied by a 15V pulse from the power supply. The actual flow expressed as a voltage representing the pressure drop across the capillaries is compared to the reference voltage. If it is too low, the comparator applies a voltage to the latch,

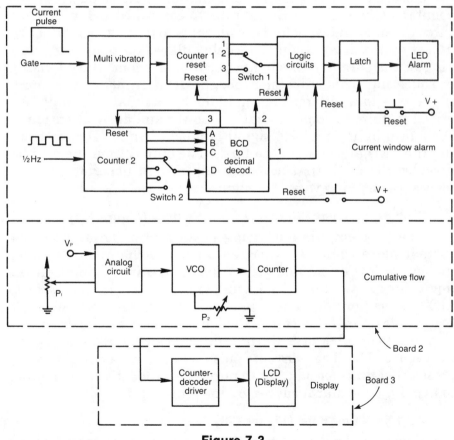

Figure 7-3
Comprehensive Control System (Board 2)

which activates the current generator provided the 2 msec/8.2 sec synchronizing pulse is also present. This current will produce gas from the salt solution.

7.3.1.3 *Blocked Cannula Alarm Circuit (Figure 7-2)*

The differential pressure across the capillaries is measured by the difference (in a mixer) between the output voltages from gauge-pressure transducers at each end of the capillaries. A single differential pressure transducer can be used instead, provided it is immune to the liquids on both sides of its pressure sensitive membrane. The mixer output pulse periodically resets the counter. When the cannula is blocked, there is no flow and therefore no pressure drop. Absence of a reset pulse to the counter activates an LED alarm. A controlled delay of from three to ten minutes, before the alarm is activated, can be set by adjusting the delay count. This delay allows for temporary clogging of the cannula which can occur from momentary kinking or squeezing. This adjustment for the delay is made by connecting a wire to a different terminal, or by manual switching. An added feature, to conserve battery power and draw attention to the alarm light, is a ½Hz signal applied to an AND gate, causing the LED alarm signal to flash. The output from the counter disables the latch that activates the current generator, to prevent a gas buildup when the cannula is clogged.

7.3.1.4 *Current Window Alarm System (Figure 7-3)*

The "current window" triggers an alarm signal when the current pulse count is either too far below the nominal value, indicating low liquid flow, or too far above, indicating that the liquid flow is too high. The window can be set to ±33⅓% or to ±60% of the normal value. Changing the window between these two ranges can be accomplished by moving a wire from one terminal to another or by incorporating a switch SW1, as shown in Figure 7-3. The current pulse count is taken during a preselected time period prior to normal alarm activation in order to avoid a false alarm caused by insignificant transients.

7.3.1.5 *Time Base (Figure 7-3)*

The time base for the control system is established by applying the ½Hz signal, from the power supply, to a binary counter. The output of counter 2 goes to inputs A, B, C, D of a decoder. The D input can be connected with switch SW2 to any of four outputs of counter 2, to generate an output after 9, 18, 36, or 72 minutes on terminal I. Three seconds later, an output voltage act terminal II will be generated, and three seconds after that an output voltage act terminal III of the Decoder will be generated. If, during the chosen time interval, the current pulse is within the specified current window, an output from terminal 2 of counter 1 ($33\frac{1}{3}$% window) or terminal 3 (60% window) allows the system to be reset and the current count restarted.

7.3.1.6   Lower Limit Current Window

The latch (Figure 7-3) activates the LED alarm if the minimum count is not reached before the end of the selected time interval.

7.3.1.7   Upper Limit of Current Window

An output from terminal 1 of counter 1 (Figure 7-3) will activate the LED alarm if the maximum current pulse rate is exceeded before the end of the chosen time interval. The higher the current pulse rate rises above the specified upper limit, the earlier the alarm will be activated.

7.3.1.8   Calibration

The current window alarm may seem overly complex as the current pulses are not counted directly but are used to gate a multivibrator. This method allows the use of different types and sizes of capillaries. The flow calibration for a given capillary is done as follows. The number of current pulses is counted after adjusting the system to the desired nominal flow. The upper limit is determined by adding either $33\frac{1}{3}$% or 60% to the count. The frequency f at the output of the multivibrator is adjusted with the 1 Mohm potentiometer, shown in Figure 7-6, to a value computed by the equation:

$$f = \frac{2^{19}}{P.T} = \frac{524,288}{P.T}$$

f: multivibrator frequency
P: number of pulses per hour
for upper current limit

T: duration of gating pulse
2^{19}: number of pulses required to enter counter 2 (Figure 7-3) to cause one output at terminal 1

For the example illustrated in this chapter the nominal (set) number of pulses is 18 pulses per hour. For a window of $33\frac{1}{3}\%$ the maximum number of pulses is 24 pulses per hour. For $T = 8.2$ seconds, we obtain

$$f = \frac{524{,}288}{24 \times 8.2} = 2{,}664 \text{ Hz.}$$

7.3.1.9 Cumulative Flow (Figure 7-3)

The differential pressure voltage V_p, representing the flow, is added to a voltage set by a potentiometer P1. At zero flow, V_p equals the offset voltage of the pressure transducer. A voltage from P1 is added to V_p to provide the threshold voltage required for triggering the voltage-controlled oscillator. The output from the counter is adjusted by potentiometer P2 to be equal to the cumulative flow for a given flow rate. V_p is not read continuously, but is sampled for 2-millisecond intervals every 8.2 seconds. Therefore, the display is updated every 8.2 seconds. The output pulse count N of the voltage controlled oscillator, which represents the amount of liquid delivered in microliters, is adjusted in the following way:

$$N = \frac{\text{Flow (ml/hr)} \times 1000 \, (\mu l/ml) \times T \, (\text{sec})}{3600 \, (\text{sec/hr})} \times 2.10^n$$

The factor T in the numerator accounts for the intervals between sampling.

Note: The units given in the equation correspond to MKS units as follows:

$1 \, \mu l = 10^{-9} m^3$;
$1 \, ml/hr = 278 \times 10^{-12} m^3/sec$;
$1 \, \mu l/hr = 278 \times 10^{-15} m^3/sec$;

N: pulse count, in pulses per hour

T: Length of gating pulse in seconds (8.2 sec)

2^n: number of pulses that must enter the counter 3 to produce one output pulse at the output terminal of counter 3

7.3.2   Hardware—Circuit Diagram

The circuit diagrams in Figures 7-4 through 7-7 supplement in detail the implementation of the block diagrams in Figures 7-1 and 7-2,

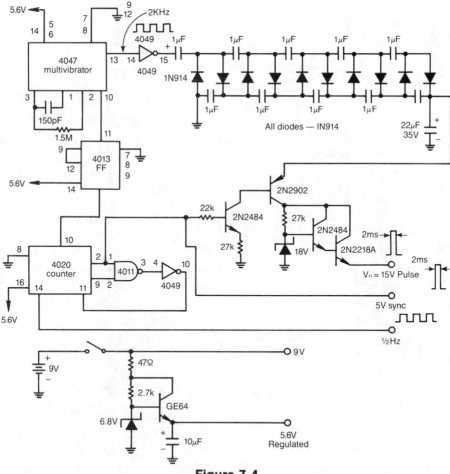

Figure 7-4
Power Supply—Schematic Diagram

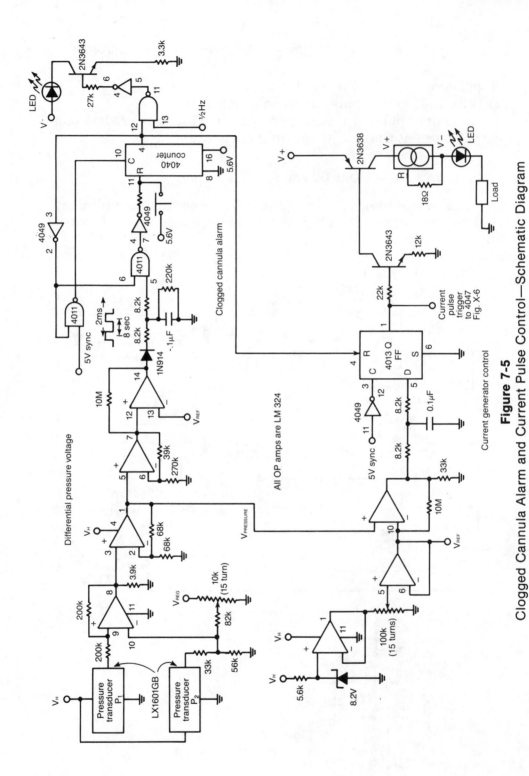

Figure 7-5

Clogged Cannula Alarm and Current Pulse Control—Schematic Diagram

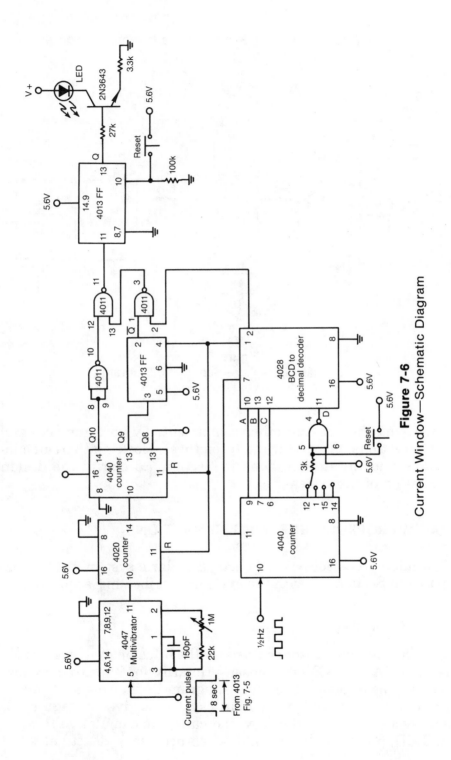

Figure 7-6
Current Window—Schematic Diagram

173

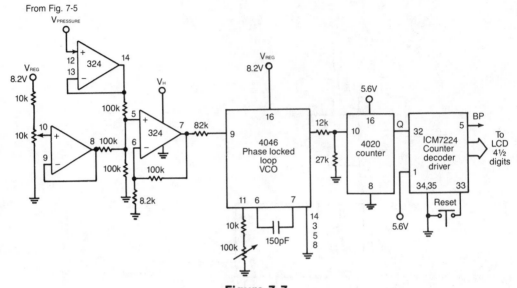

Figure 7-7
Cumulative Display—Schematic Diagram

specifying the ICs and other components by part numbers and pin notations. A careful study of these block and circuit diagrams and the explanations in Section 7.3 clarify the design operation of the system.

7.4 MICROPROCESSOR IMPLEMENTATION

The microprocessor-based control and alarm system will be compared in Section 7.5 with the system described in Section 7.3.

7.4.1 Block Diagram

The microprocessor selected for the infusion system example is the RCA 1802 CMOS, chosen primarily for its extremely low power consumption. The block diagram of the complete microprocessor-based control and alarm system is given in Figure 7-8. The system controls the flow, indicates the cumulative flow on an LCD, provides alarms, and, when necessary, deactivates the

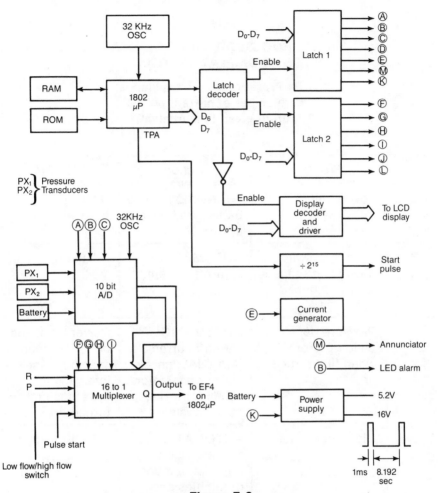

Figure 7-8
Microcomputer-Based Control, Alarm, and Display System
(Block Diagram)

system. In addition to providing alarms, the system also identifies on the LCD any problem causing an alarm. This is accomplished by monitoring the pressure drop across the capillary and
the current pulses. These two variables identify the problem, as
shown in Table 7-1 which presents display, problem, electronic
symptoms, and any actions taken by the control system. For
example, display of the numeral 4 on the LCD indicates that the

Table 7-1

**MICROPROCESSOR CONTROL, ALARM,
AND DISPLAY SYSTEM**

**(ΔP=Pressure across capillaries;
#I=Number of current pulses
during given time interval)**

Display	Problem	Action	Symptom
L	Low battery.	[MANUAL: replace battery and restart system.]	"L" flag up
P	High flow switch does not disengage after prescribed time.	AUTOMATIC: shut-off current.	"P" flat up
1	Pressure does not build up properly when first turned on.	AUTOMATIC: shut off current. [MANUAL: check current generator; check for leaks; restart system.]	Current remains on longer than specified time interval after system is first turned on.
2	Clogged cannula.	AUTOMATIC: activate alarm after set number of minutes and shut-off current.	ΔP=Normal
3	Capillary partially or completely clogged.	[MANUAL: replace capillary.]	ΔP Normal #I Low
4	Leakage around capillary or capillary resistance decreased.	AUTOMATIC: shut-off current.	ΔP Normal #I High
5	Current generator stays on.	AUTOMATIC: shut-off current.	ΔP High #I High

Table 7-1 *continued*

**MICROPROCESSOR CONTROL, ALARM,
AND DISPLAY SYSTEM**

Display	Problem	Action	Symptom
6	Current generator stays off.	[MANUAL: check current generator and electronics.]	ΔP Low #I Low
7	Pressure at infusion site rises abruptly relative to gas generator pressure.	AUTOMATIC: activate alarm after set number of minutes and shut-off current.	ΔP Low #I High
8	Pressure at infusion site drops abruptly relative to gas generator pressure.	AUTOMATIC: activate alarm after specified time interval.	ΔP High #I Low

pumped liquid is leaking around the capillary, or that the capillary resistance has decreased.

Either condition can result in too high a delivery rate and a false cumulative flow reading. The electronic symptoms are: a voltage for a normal pressure drop, V_p, across the capillaries, and too rapid current pulse count. Action taken: current is shut off.

Examine the block diagram of Figure 7-8. The RCA 1802 microprocessor (μP) that controls the operation of the system is in the center. The ROM contains a permanent program that directs the μP to control the system. The RAM holds certain constants which are entered through a detachable keyboard, to update the values of the variables, and to temporarily store data for computations. The constants which are entered into the RAM are: a flow coefficient representing the flow resistance of the LOW flow capillary, the desired flow through only the LOW flow capillary, and the duration of the period of "HIGH flow" when both capillaries are paralleled. The resistance of the second capillary is a known multiple of the first LOW flow capillary.

The time base of the control system is provided by a 32-kHz oscillator.

The TPA output of the microprocessor is divided by the factor 2^{15}, and the resulting pulse is used to initiate monitor cycles for all internal and external (key) inputs to the microprocessor. The datalines transmit information from the μP to Latch 1, Latch 2, and the display decoder and driver. The latch decoder determines which one of these three devices produces an output at any given instant. The A/D converter samples the analog output voltages from the two pressure transducers and the battery, and converts them to digital signals which are transmitted to the μP through the 16 to 1 demultiplexer.

Input signals A, B, and C from Latch 1 determine which of the three analog signals is being sampled at any given time. Signals from the keys R and P, the LOW/HIGH flow switch, and the start pulse are channeled to the μP one at a time, as controlled by the signals F, G, H, and I from Latch 2. The current generator, annunciator, and alarm light are activated respectively by signals E, M, and D, from the latches. Signal K, from Latch 1 causes 16V to appear as pulses, 2 milliseconds on and 8.192 seconds off, to be applied to the two pressure transducers through transistor switches. Signals I and L from latch 2 close the switches that apply the 16V pulses to the pressure transducers. The pulses are applied at different times to the pressure transducer to limit the battery current demand. As a result, it is possible to use a relatively small capacitor at the output of the voltage multiplier which converts the 5.6V battery voltage to the 16V required.

7.4.2 Microprocessor Program

The microprocessor program, written in machine language, is entered through a hexadecimal keyboard into the microprocessor. Initially, the program is evaluated and debugged in a RAM. The final correct program is then entered into a PROM. For high production of the system it would be economical to make a mask to program a ROM. A liberal use of subroutines offers maximum flexibility and ease of debugging. The program

Increasing the Effectiveness of a System with a Microprocessor

is based on the flowchart in Figure 7-9. The main program is given in Table 7-2.

To understand the program in detail, the reader must know the machine code for the RCA 1802 microprocessor. The machine

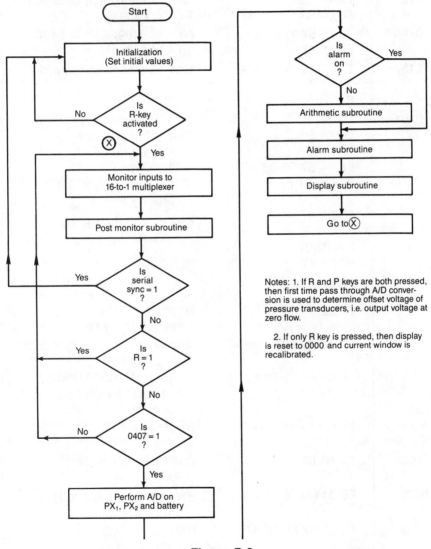

Notes: 1. If R and P keys are both pressed, then first time pass through A/D conversion is used to determine offset voltage of pressure transducers, i.e. output voltage at zero flow.

2. If only R key is pressed, then display is reset to 0000 and current window is recalibrated.

Figure 7-9
Microcomputer-Based System—Program Flowchart

Increasing the Effectiveness of a System with a Microprocessor

Table 7-2

INFUSION SYSTEM-MAIN PROGRAM

Address	Instruction	Comments
01E7	D4 00 3B	Call "Initialization Subroutine"
	F8 04 B7 F8 09 A7	R(7) = 0409
01F0	F8 08 57 17	08→ M(0409) R(7) = 040A
	F8 10 57	10→ M(040A)
0157	D4 00 E2	Call "R-Check Subroutine"
	F8 01 A8 08	} Check to see if R is pressed
	C2 01 F7	
0201	D4 00 5E	Call "Monitor Subroutine"
	D4 01 BB	Call "After Monitor Subroutine"
	F8 04 B7 F8 03 A7	R(7) = 0403
	07 CA 01 F7	M(0403)→ D Go to 01F7 if serial sync = 1
	F8 01 A7 07	} Check R and go to 0201 if R=1
	CA 02 01	
	F8 07 A7	R(7) = 0407 } Check to see if ok for D/A
	07 32 01	M(0407)→ D Go to 0201 if D=0
021E	F8 04 B9 F8 11 A9	R(9)=0411 (points to PX$_1$ data storage)
	F8 08 A7 F8 01 57	R(7)=0408 02→M(0408) (Sets up PX$_1$ with analog switch)
	F8 0D A7 F8 10 57	R(7)=040D 10→M(040D) (Sets up PX$_1$ with Ⓙ)
0230	D4 01 00	Call "A/O Subroutine" for PX$_1$
0233	F8 04 B9 F8 13 A9	R(9)=0413 (points to PX$_2$ data storage)
0239	F8 08 A7 F8 02 57	R(7)=0408 02→ M(0408) (Sets up PX$_2$ with analog switch)

Increasing the Effectiveness of a System with a Microprocessor

Table 7-2 (continued)

INFUSION SYSTEM-MAIN PROGRAM

Address	Instruction	Comments
023F	F8 08 A7 F8 02 57	R(7)=040D 20→ M(040D) (Sets up PX$_2$ with Ⓛ)
0245	D4 01 00	Call "A/D Subroutine" for PX$_2$
0458	F8 04 B9 F8 15 A9	R(9)=0415 (points to power supply data storage)
024E	F8 04 B7 F8 08 A7	R(7)=0408
0254	F8 04 57 F8 0D A7	(Sets up power supply with analog switch) 04→ M(0408)
025A	F8 00 57	R(7)=040D 00→ M(040D)
	D4 01 00	Call "A/D subrouting" for power supply
0260	F8 04 BA F8 09 AA	R(A) = 0409 (if alarm on, skip "Arithmetic Subroutine")
0266	0A 32 6C	
0269	D4 02 89	Call "Arithmetic Subroutine"
026C	D4 07 35	Call "Alarm Subroutine"
026F	D4 06 DA	Call "Display Subroutine"
0272	30 01	Go to 0201 and monitor pushbuttons
0274	00	Extra reserved space

code for the different instructions is supplied by the manufacturer on a hand chart or in a booklet. The present program is supplied only to demonstrate what is involved in designing and building microprocessor based equipment. Studying all the details is not necessary at this time. A general concept can be obtained from the comments column of the program. This column is very important, as it helps the programmer to recall just how a particular problem was solved and to any other programmer who may become involved in the project.

The comments column is written in symbolic language. For clarity, the first few steps of the program are explained in English. Consider the instruction D4 00 3B in Table 7-2 at address 01E7 (Hexadecimal). The notation D4 is the opcode for the machine control instruction which tells the microprocessor to go to the address specified, which is in this case 003B.

The first step of the initialization subroutine is stored at this memory address. The microprocessor will call the initialization routine and execute it when it is first directed to the main address, 01 E7. The end of the initialization subroutine will direct the microprocessor to return to the main program. The second line of the main program instruction column is F8 04 B7 F8 09 A7. The opcode F8 means "LOAD IMMEDIATE"; the microprocessor, loads the immediate following number 04 into the memory location B7. The notation B7 designates the higher section, that is, the upper eight binary digits of the 16-bit Register 7. The remainder of this instruction, F8 09 A7, causes the hexadecimal number 09 to be stored in the lower section of Register 7. In summary, the instruction in the second line of the main program causes the address 0407 to be stored in Register 7.

The next instruction F8 08 57 17, at address 01F0, stores the hexadecimal number 08 at the memory address listed in Register 7 (57). The last opcode in this line (17) causes Register 7 to increment by "1." The hexadecimal number 08 will be stored in memory location 0409, and the new address listed in Register 7 will be 040A. The next instruction, F8 10 57, will store a number 10 at the memory address now listed in Register 7 (now 040A). The first subroutine called for by the main program in the flowchart of Figure 7-10, further illustrates programming for the microprocessor. This corresponds to the program in Table 7-3. The subroutine sets all of the values in memory locations from 0401 through 042A to zero, and turns off the alarm, cuts off the current to the generator, and returns the machine to the main program.

7.4.2.1 Entering Constants into the Program

Three constants B, K, and Th must be entered into the RAM by a keyboard before the pump is started.

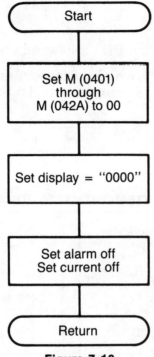

Figure 7-10
The Initialization Subroutine

1. Desired LOW Flow Rate

Let F be the desired flow rate in ml/hr. Enter constant B, which is computed as follows:

$$B = \frac{F \times 1000 \times 8.192}{3600}$$

B: flow rate in nanoliters
$(10^{-12} m^3)$ in 8.192 seconds

The 8.192 second sampling period is determined by dividing the 32 kHz oscillator frequency by the factor 2^{18}.

2. Capillary Constant

Measure the volume of liquid, A in nanoliters, delivered during one sampling period. The constant K is computed as follows:

$$K = \frac{A \times 128}{PD}$$

PD : 2 byte number in memory

Example: If A = 75, which corresponds to a flow of 0.033 ml/hr $(2.55 \times 10^{-15} \text{ m}^3/\text{seconds})$, and PD = 300 then

$$K = \frac{75 \times 128}{300} = 32$$

Table 7-3

INFUSION SYSTEM-INITIALIZATION SUBROUTINE

Address	Instruction	Comments
003B	E7	
003C	F8 04 B7	
003F	F8 2A A7	Sets data in memory locations 0401 through 042A to zero
0042	F8 00 73	
0045	87 3A 42	
0048	30 50	Go to (Branch) 0050
004A	00	Data for latch N2
004B	18	Data for latch N1
004C	00	
004D	10	Data for initial display
004E	20	
004F	30	
0050	E7 F8 00 B7	
	F8 4A A7	Display = "0000" Alarm = 1 off Current = 1 off
	62 61 63 63	
	63 63	
005D	D5	Return

3. High Flow Duration

Enter Th in units of one-half of a sampling period.

Example : Desired HIGH flow duration =15 minutes, then

$$\text{Th} = \frac{15 \times 60}{8.192 \times 2} = 55.$$

7.4.2.2 Current Window Calibration

Since the "normal" number of current pulses varies slightly from pump to pump depending on the capillaries and other components, the microprocessor is designed to calibrate the pump automatically during the first hour of operation under controlled conditions with the flow monitored by means of an electronic balance. This establishes the "normal" current pulse count for that pump. The number of pulses for "too high" and "too low," which establishes the current window is computed and entered by the program into the RAM memory.

7.4.3 Detailed Circuit Diagram and Microprocessor Interfacing Hardware

The microprocessor is a powerful device, but it is useless by itself. An interface must connect the processor to the remainder of the system. Additional hardware is often needed to fulfill special functions. In the infusion example a current generator and alarms must be activated, and information displayed on an LCD. Analog signals from the pressure transducers must enter the microprocessor and voltages from the batteries raised to that necessary for the pressure transducers. Special frequencies must be generated. External control must be provided by analog and digital circuitry, including op amps, latches, counters, and other devices. The circuits are shown in Figures 7-11 through 7-16. Note that the encircled letter symbols in the diagrams represent outputs from latches controlled by the microprocessor. The operation of the complete system becomes clear when these circuits are studied in conjunction with the block diagram in Figure 7-8, and the flowchart in Figure 7-9.

Many of the circuits are similar to those in the conventional IC system discussed in Section 7.3. Certain differences exist which make the circuits particularly compatible with the microprocessor. For example, a 32kHz frequency available from the microprocessor is used to generate the high DC voltage in place of the 2kHz used in the conventional system. The output volt-

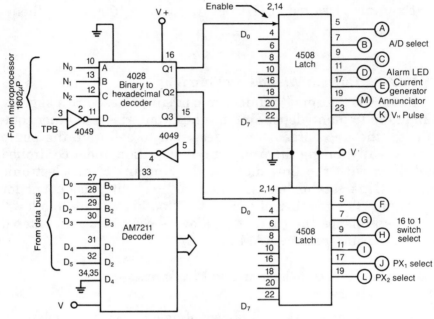

Figure 7-11
Latches and Display

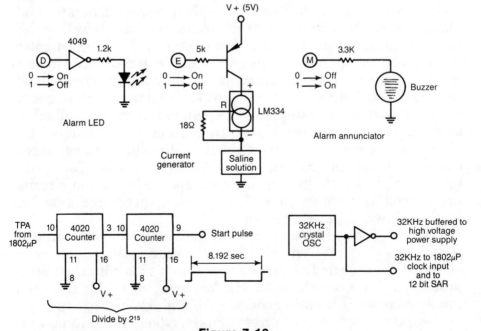

Figure 7-12
Alarms and Controls

Increasing the Effectiveness of a System with a Microprocessor

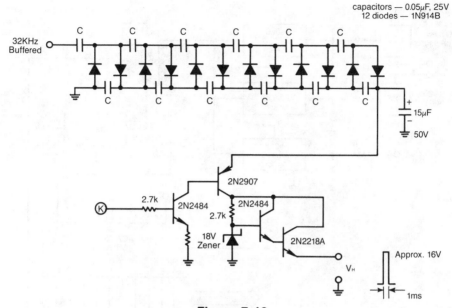

Figure 7-13
High-Voltage Power Supply

ages from the two pressure transducers are subtracted by an operational amplifier in the conventional system. The high voltage pulses are applied to both transducers at the same time, since the output voltages must occur at the same time to be subtracted properly. A heavy instantaneous battery drain results. In the microprocessor-based system, the pressure transducer output voltages are converted to digital numbers, one at a time in close

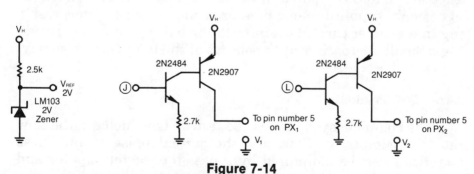

Figure 7-14
Voltage Regulator for A/D Converter and Switches for
Pressure Transducer

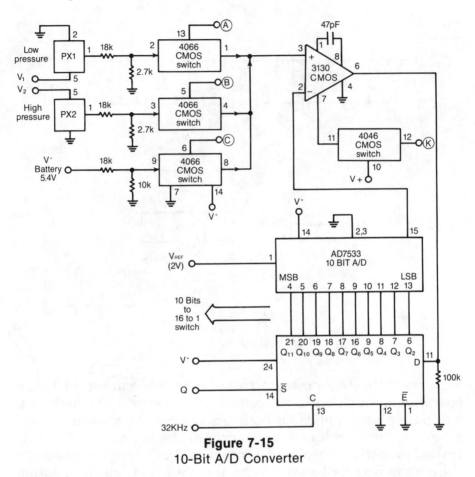

Figure 7-15
10-Bit A/D Converter

succession, and compared in the microprocessor. The high voltage is only supplied to one pressure transducer at a time, resulting in a smaller current drain from the battery, and thus requiring a smaller capacitor at the output of the high-voltage supply.

7.4.4 Test Printout

The complete system must be tested. This includes the flow rate, the cumulative flow, and the current pulse count. These quantities can be monitored by a desk-top microcomputer and printer interfaced with the microcomputer. See Figure 7-17.

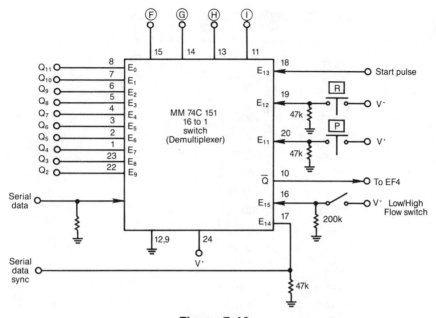

Figure 7-16
16 to 1 Switch

7.5 COMPARISON BETWEEN THE MICROPROCESSOR-BASED SYSTEM AND THE CONVENTIONAL ELECTRONIC SYSTEM

Extensive peripheral circuitry is associated with the power supply, sensors, and display. This circuitry is required whether or not a microprocessor is used. There is little difference in the total component count between the two systems. But the microprocessor-based system is more versatile, more convenient to use, easier to alter, and gives much more information.

The flow rate and duration of the HIGH flow are entered with a keyboard into the microprocessor-based system. These values must be established by tests for the conventional system by using potentiometers. The microprocessor-based system offers a very important feature not available in the conventional system: the automatic calibration for "normal" current pulse count and the current window. The "normal" current pulse count depends upon the individual capillaries. The microprocessor-based system monitors the "normal" pulse count for the first

Increasing the Effectiveness of a System with a Microprocessor

ML USED	FLOW (ML/HR)	PULSE CT*
0	0	*************
.0236	.02355	11
.0475	.02388	16
.0721	.02458	16
.0959	.02377	19
.1197	.02376	17
.1435	.02376	15
.1678	.02425	14
.1923	.02445	14
.2169	.02455	17
.2417	.02475	14
.2669	.02515	14
.2921	.02516	15
.3174	.02526	14
.3424	.02496	16
.3678	.02536	13
.3931	.02526	16
.4183	.02516	16
.4432	.02487	18

Figure 7-17
Microprocessor-Based System: Computer Printout

hour and automatically sets the upper and lower limits according to the percentages listed in the program. Both systems have the same alarm and safety provisions, except for the battery low-voltage test and its indicator, which are only found in the microprocessor-based system. The microprocessor-based system also indentifies the cause of an alarm and displays the alarm code on the LCD, without additional hardware. This is an extremely helpful feature, which is not available in the conventional system.

CHAPTER 8

Application of a Microcomputer in a Medical Laboratory

8.1 INTRODUCTION

Medical laboratories are using increasing numbers of microcomputers for the collection, processing, storing, and display of data. Chapters 7, 8, 9, 10, and 11 show examples of how microcomputers can increase the efficiency, speed, and accuracy of research work and applications, and make it possible to collect data that are more complete and accurate, including data that were not previously obtainable. To achieve this type of performance, careful planning is necessary.

8.2 GOALS FOR A LABORATORY SYSTEM

To illustrate the application of microcomputers, we will describe the selection, design, construction, and testing of a microcomputer system for a medical laboratory to completely and efficiently collect, process, and display data from heart cells.

8.2.1 Preliminary Consideration of this System

A study should start by determining if a computer is advantageous for this laboratory experiment. A description of the system and the results desired is the first step.

8.2.1.1 Description of the System

The system in the example was used to investigate single-skinned cardiac cells. Most of the software and hardware designs discussed can be used for many other medical or non-medical applications.

Single cardiac cells are observed in a special laboratory setup. Two major parameters are monitored: the calcium exchange and the force exerted by the cells on a transducer when they beat. Not only the magnitude and frequency are of interest, but also the shape of the peaks and the time in between them.

This cardiac cell investigation is concerned with the analysis of these variables from different hearts and heart sections and also with the effects of external physical, chemical, or biological agents.

During manual operation the force change and the calcium exchange are recorded in the first two channels of a high speed analog recorder. The third channel is used for the first derivative of the signals in either of the first two channels.

8.2.1.2 Objectives of the Microcomputer System

A set of objectives for the computer system must be established before a system is selected for this application. The system is to be automatic and to take over from and improve upon the manual system. The system should fulfill the following requirements.

1. Record all valid pulses, reject noise pulses.
2. Make a permanent record of the entire pulse, including the pretrigger portions.
3. Use an adjustible threshold level to differentiate between pulses and noise.
4. Record simultaneously pulses from two different sources.
5. Accommodate pulse width variations from 100 milliseconds to 7.5 seconds.
6. Provide for a maximum voltage range from −2.5 volts to +7.5 volts for positive pulses and +2.5 volts to −7.5 volts for negative pulses.
7. Obtain a digital resolution of a full scale (5 volt) pulse to 0.8%.
8. Provide complete remote control of the micrcomputer system.
9. Record all output from the microcomputer and input information from the transducers on an analog computer.
10. Average all pulses during a run and the time between pulses and calculate the standard deviation for each.

11. Calculate the area of the average pulse and of the calibration pulse.
12. Indicate each pulse detected by a small mark on the fourth channel of the analog recorder.
13. Mark the start and the finish of the data collection period with short spikes.
14. Record at the end of each run the area of a calibration pulse as a rectangle with a fixed height but varying length.
15. Show the total number of pulses as short blips after the run.
16. Display without baseline offset the averaged pulses shown on the fourth channel of the analog recorder.

8.3 SELECTION OF A COMPUTER SYSTEM

Next, determine the best way to achieve these goals. Is a computer suitable? The criteria were given in Chapter 1. The first criterion is satisfied by the continual and repetitive collection and processing of data. The second criterion is satisfied because the full automatic collection and processing of data is much faster than manual processing. The third criterion calls for higher precision of the data, which is guaranteed by the uniform handling of data by the computer. The cost per data point will be much lower if the capability for collecting much larger amounts of data is used. The system should pay for itself in a relatively short time.

Now, select the most suitable computer system. Even though the amount of data handled in one day is not very large, some high-speed processing is necessary. Data points are collected every 5 milliseconds and all the data points of a collected pulse must be transferred during this time interval to a buffer. The processing of the collected pulses after the run should not exceed a few seconds.

A suitable computer would conform to line B of Figure 1-1 in Chapter 1. Depending on which year the computer is selected, we may choose a minicomputer, a microcomputer, or a portable computer if we are in the year 1984 or 1985.

Microcomputer systems offer many different capabilities to a wide range of requirements for medical experiments. First, consider the flexibility and adaptability needed. A full-size expandable microcomputer system with adequate memory, off-line storage capability, high level languages, and adequate execution speed is best for many laboratories even though more expensive initially than a smaller unit. Such a system meets unexpected demands, which occur frequently in any research. A low-cost computer system on a single board or a computer on a chip may be adequate if little flexibility is needed for a given application.

A general-purpose in-house computer could only be considered if a noninterruptable high-speed line is always available when needed. Problems may exist with any special language or storage. A dedicated appropriate microcomputer is frequently preferable to an in-house computer for a project such as the cardiac cell study because of its availability and design for the specific purpose. It may be used simultaneously by the in-house computer or later for other work. In-house computer time availability and its suitability must be balanced against the cost of a dedicated unit. Buying a separate computer is not apt to be well-received by the supervision of a computer center if surplus capacity is available.

8.4   DESIGN OF THE SYSTEM

8.4.1   Block Diagram of the System

Figure 8-1 is an overall block diagram of the computer system for the heart cell study. The data inputs from the photometer (calcium concentration) and the force transducer are on the upper left. The control and monitor section with the remote control box and the four-channel analog recorder are on the lower left.

The microcomputer system is on the right. It has a 6809 microcomputer, dual floppy 8-inch disk system, matrix printer, and CRT terminal. The I/O section in the center includes a multiplexer, an ADC, a DAC, buffers, biasing circuits, and power supplies. The left-hand side of the figure presents those com-

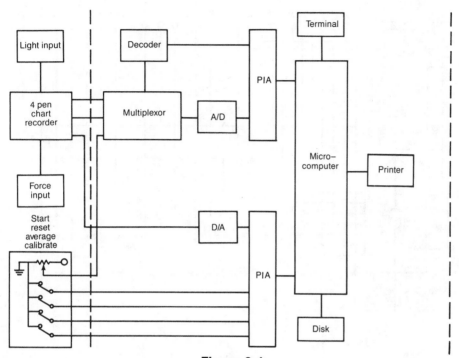

Figure 8-1
Block Diagram for Laboratory Setup

ponents near the experiment. The components on the right can be situated elsewhere in the laboratory.

8.4.2 Data Input to the System

The microcomputer is designed to receive the data from the output stages of analog recorder channels 1 and 2. This has three advantages. First, the laboratory setup can be operated automatically or manually. Second, no preamplification of the signals from the laboratory experiment is necessary, because the output from the recorder channel is at the 0 to 5 volt level required for the microcomputer. Third, all computer inputs and outputs are recorded. A complete record makes it possible to trace a malfunction immediately or check a new feature to determine remedial action. Having the input and output on the same original record is most desirable for production. A schematic diagram of the interface is shown in Figure 8-2.

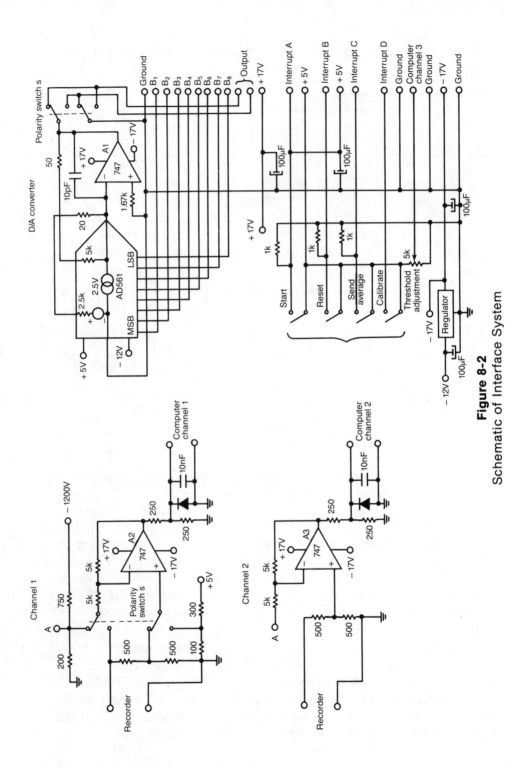

Figure 8-2

Schematic of Interface System

8.4.3 Data Output of the System

The processed data from the microcomputer are displayed on channel 4 of the analog recorder in order to compare the data input and data output on the same graph. The start and finish of the experimental run are indicated on channel 4 by short spikes. An output signal from the computer is indicated on channel 4 as an image proportional in length to the collected pulse. The threshold level can be adjusted with the threshold potentiometer on the remote control box by increasing the voltage from zero until only valid peaks are recorded and noise peaks eliminated. See the schematic diagram of the interface in Figure 8-2.

8.4.4 Automatic Detection of the Peak

The system automatically detects and records random pulses. A preselected threshold level discriminates between valid data and noise. Portions of the pulses below the threshold level would be lost if the computer began to store only the pulses when their voltage reached threshold level. To overcome this problem the computer initially stores all data points in a temporary buffer which has a length equal to the longest pulse. This buffer is circular, meaning that when the buffer is full new data points replace values already in the start of the buffer.

The computer checks each reading to determine if it is above or below the threshold level. If it is above, the computer calculates the time from the last threshold crossing and stores it in a temporary buffer. The computer also checks if the latest data point is higher or lower than the previous point. If it is higher, it is stored in a second temporary buffer. This buffer will contain the highest elevation of the signal, once the signal returns to the threshold line.

If the latest collected data point is below the threshold line and the value in the temporary buffer containing the highest point so far is below the threshold line, the computer goes on to collect the next data point. If the collected data point is below the threshold line, but the value in the temporary buffer for the highest point is above the threshold level, the computer transfers all data points in the temporary signal buffer to a storage buffer, using the highest elevation of the pulse as the reference point for alignment of the pulses in the storage buffer. Once the pulse is transferred, the temporary buffer for the highest point of the signal is cleared. Because the temporary buffer for the whole signal contains the data values of the signal prior to the time the pulse was crossing the threshold line, these data points are collected in this buffer. Specifically, because of the skewness of the pulses, the computer is asked to transfer all points 2.5 seconds before the highest point of the signal and 5 seconds after the highest point into the storage buffer for the whole signal.

The stored maximum value for each signal is also used by the computer to calculate the mean of this value for all signals. Similarly, the time interval between signals, measured between the first crossover points for each signal, is stored in a separate buffer. These values are used to calculate the average time between pulses during a run.

The highest point of the signal is used as the reference point for the mostly triangular-shaped pulses. For different shaped signals a reference point different from the highest point may be selected, such as the threshold crossover point, the half height point, the starting point of the pulse (defined either as the threshold crossing point or the intersection of the baseline with a straight line fitted through the increasing section of the pulse), the midway inflection point, or the midpoint between the start and the end of the pulse. The midpoint is best for rectangular shaped signals. The program can be used for any of these reference points.

The collection time for each pulse can be set from 100 milliseconds to 10 seconds. In the following, assume a collection time of 7.5 seconds.

The computer has a 5 milliseconds data collection cycle. A signal must be transferred from the circular buffer to the storage buffer in the time interval of less than 5 milliseconds. Fortunately, the assembly language used in the 6809 microcomputer is very fast and the 1500 data points of a 7.5 second pulse in channel 1 and the 1500 data points in channel 2 can be transferred in much less than one millisecond.

8.4.5   Time Interval between Peaks

The time interval between two signals is determined by the number of data collections which occur between the first threshold crossover point of the first pulse and the first threshold crossover point of the second pulse. This number is stored in a separate buffer location for later determination of the standard deviation of the pulse intervals.

8.4.6   Special Processing of the Pulse Signals

The computer collects data points in a voltage range from −2.5 volts to +7.5 volts, allowing a 50% overrange of the standard 5 volt range of the recorder. There is no need to record the baseline drift as drift is deducted from the collected pulse data values before they are displayed.

8.4.7   Data Processing Routines Used for the System

8.4.7.1   Averaging

Several mathematical algorithms may be used to process the data output. The simplest is the arithmetic mean of the highest values of all the peaks. This is done by dividing the sum of the peaks in the storage buffer by the number of peaks recorded when the "average" push button has been pressed. The result is returned to the same storage location.

8.4.7.2   Standard Deviation

The standard deviation of the highest elevation of the pulses is calculated by the following formula.

$$sd = (\frac{(xi - x)exp\ (2)}{n - 1})exp\ (1/2)$$

sd Standard deviation

xi Height of individual peak

x   Average of peak height for all peaks
    in a run

n   Number of points

8.4.7.3   Area

The area of a pulse is calculated by adding the data point values in the pulse and multiplying this total by 5 milliseconds. The exact start and end points of the pulse must be known. A special routine was developed to sense the effective start and end of the pulse. Serious errors may result from calculating the area by using the crossover points of the output voltage with the threshold line.

8.4.7.4 Display Routines

Display routines transfer the processed data from a buffer in the computer into the analog recorder. Each data point is delayed in the computer by 5 milliseconds—the time interval between two data readings, before it is sent to the analog recorder. This delay allows the pulse on the recorder paper to be restored to its original shape.

8.4.7.5 Display of the Processed Variables
on the Analog Recorder

The average pulse and average interval between pulses is shown by two marks displaced by the average time. The standard deviation of the pulse height is shown by the vertical deflection of pen 1. The standard deviation of the interval between pulses is shown as horizontal displacement. A rectangle is created when the pen returns to the baseline. The area of the pulse is indicated by a second rectangle of varying width and constant height. The number of pulses is indicated at the end of the display of all the information from both channels by a short pen deflection for each pulse. Every fifth mark is longer to facilitate counting.

8.5 HARDWARE FOR THE SYSTEM

The /09 microcomputer from Southwest Technical Products Corporation (San Antonio, Texas) is used in this example because of its great versatility in laboratory applications. Very little additional expense is required to adapt it to almost any laboratory task. It offers low cost, high speed, and excellent reliability. The /09 uses a 6809 microprocessor with a 64K memory; an 8-inch, dual, floppy-disk drive with 2.5 million bytes of storage capacity; and a CT-82 multifunction terminal. The three input channels required can be provided by a low-cost, 16-channel, 8-bit ADC from JPC (Albuquerque, New Mexico). This ADC has a conversion rate of 3300 per second which can be increased to a maximum of 10,000 conversions per second for single channel use. For higher speed, other I/O cards can be used.

Application of a Microcomputer in a Medical Laboratory

The optical and the force output of the laboratory setup go to the first two inputs of the computer. The third input is for the threshold. Processed digital data is displayed on a 10-bit DAC (#561) analog recorder from Analog Devices (Norwood, Mass.).

Remote control of the computer is provided by a control box which contains four push buttons for: 1) START, 2) AVERAGE (send the collected pulses to the recorder), 3) RESET (clear all buffers for a new run), and 4) CALIBRATE (display the calibration peak). This control box has a reversing switch for negative peaks. It also has a switch to reverse the first and second channels, and an output for a digital meter to monitor the output of the recorder channels.

Two operational amplifiers are used (Figure 8-2) to extend the input voltage range to 10 volts ($-2.5V$ to $+7.5V$) without changing the required output voltage to the computer of 0 to 5 volts. Both amplifiers are similar except that the first channel amplifier has a reversing switch to accept negative input voltages. For positive input and output, the signal is fed to the non-inverting input of the operational amplifier. The negative feedback loop has an amplification factor of two. Both the input and output signals are halved to provide the required overall attenuation of ½.

To invert the incoming signal from negative to positive, it is fed to the inverting input of the operational amplifier. Because in this case the amplification is one, the divider on the input of the operational amplifier is not necessary. The biasing network creates a zero level output voltage when the input voltage is -2.5 volts. The reversing switch allows the computer to accept positive or negative signals.

A buffer amplifier on the output of the 10-bit ADC stabilizes the voltages for a long cable connection between the computer and the analog recorder. Another section of the reversing switch matches the output voltage to that of the input signal.

Each one of the four push buttons on the remote control box starts the execution of a different part of the program in the computer by generating a short pulse. Each push button sets a different control input at a PIA. The program tests continually if any one of the four push buttons has been activated.

Additional stabilization of long power supply lines by electrolytic capacitors and regulators is necessary.

8.6 SOFTWARE FOR THE SYSTEM

First, the language which best fulfills the set goals must be chosen. Speed of execution is one of the main criteria. According to the previous set specifications, the duration of the shortest signal is 100 milliseconds. At least ten points are necessary to adequately represent a signal. To be on the safe side, 20 points were selected for this program. The interval time for collecting data points is 100 (milliseconds) divided by 20 (points) or 5 milliseconds per point. As the interactive BASIC language is much too slow for data collection at this rate, the assembler language was chosen as our software language. A compiler BASIC could have been used instead. A fast and excellent disk macro-assembler from TSC (Technical Systems Consultants, Inc.) is used for this system. This macro-assembler speeds up the coding because of the modular construction of the assembler. Because of the length of the assembler program for this system (twenty-nine pages of sixty lines each), the software program is described only by flowcharts. The full-length assembler program is available on request.

8.7 DATA COLLECTION

8.7.1 General

The design of the overall flow program for the collection, processing, and display of data is described next. This flow diagram (Figures 8-3A and 8-3B) should encompass all goals and principles of operation of the program described so far. There are three main tasks for the data collection section.

The first directs the data received from the recorder to a circular buffer. The second is the program which selects the highest peak of the data points above the threshold. The third searches the circular buffer to see if a peak should be transferred from the circular buffer to the storage buffer.

The following three tasks are used in two separate loops—one of each used for data above the threshold line, the other for those points below the threshold line. Data points must therefore be checked to determine if they are higher or lower than the threshold level for entry into the correct program loop.

Figure 8-3 shows the main flow diagrams for the program. The first page (204) shows the part which initializes the program and first collects data points. It compares the value of the data point in channel 1 to the threshold level.

LOOP 1

When the value is lower, program loop 1 is entered, a zero is sent to the recorder, and a check made to see if the "Start" button or the "Reset" button has been pressed. If the "Start" has been pressed a start spike is sent to the recorder to indicate that the collection of data has begun.

The program then checks for a peak in the circular buffer of channel 1. If a peak is in this buffer, it is added to other peaks already in the storage buffer 1. A peak in channel 2 is at the same time automatically added to storage buffer 2. The time interval between this peak and the previous one is stored in the interval buffer at this time. The program returns to collect the next data point if neither the "Reset" nor the "Output" button has been activated. This is shown in the lower extension of the flow diagram, Figure 8-3B.

LOOP 2

The program enters the program loop 2 when the data point is above the threshold level. A "05" is sent to the recorder and loop 1 is checked to see if the "Start" has been activated and the "Reset" not. If all is well, the program checks whether the latest data point is higher than any previous value. The peak buffer of either channel is updated when a higher value is recorded for the first channel. The buffer pointers and collection counters are advanced and the "Reset" and "Output" checked for activation. The program then loops back for the next data point.

8.7.2   Input Routines

Figure 8-4 shows the three input routines used. The FETCH MACRO routine selects the channel number (1, 2, or 3), sets the gain (1), starts the ADC, and sends the collected data value to the accumulator when the conversion has been completed.

The LOAD MACRO routine uses the FETCH MACRO routine to load the data point from the recorder into the circular buffer. Instructions for maintaining the circular buffer and the

Application of a Microcomputer in a Medical Laboratory

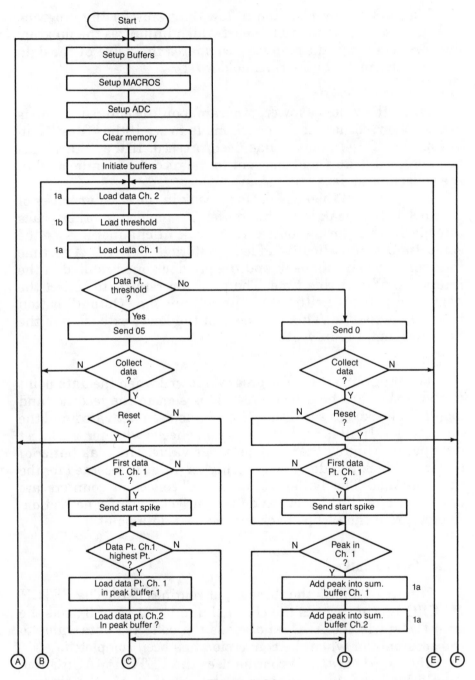

Figure 8-3A
Main Flow Diagram of System

Application of a Microcomputer in a Medical Laboratory

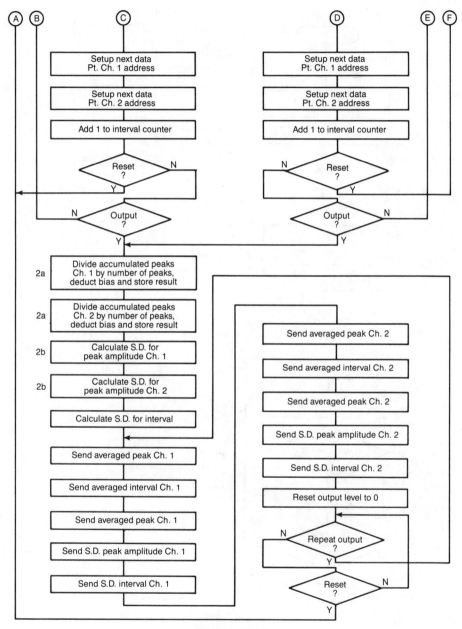

Figure 8-3B
Main Flow Diagram of System

Application of a Microcomputer in a Medical Laboratory

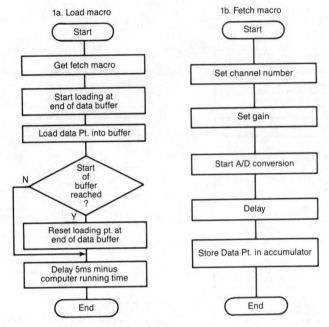

1a. Load macro
- Start
- Get fetch macro
- Start loading at end of data buffer
- Load data Pt. into buffer
- Start of buffer reached ? (N / Y)
- Reset loading pt. at end of data buffer
- Delay 5ms minus computer running time
- End

1b. Fetch macro
- Start
- Set channel number
- Set gain
- Start A/D conversion
- Delay
- Store Data Pt. in accumulator
- End

1c. Load peak into storage buffer

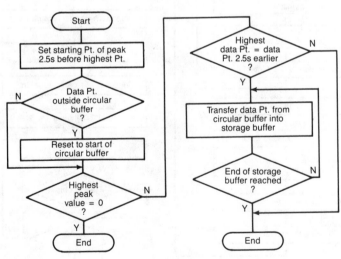

- Start
- Set starting Pt. of peak 2.5s before highest Pt.
- Data Pt. outside circular buffer ? (N / Y)
- Reset to start of circular buffer
- Highest peak value = 0 ? (N / Y)
- End
- Highest data Pt. = data Pt. 2.5s earlier ? (N / Y)
- Transfer data Pt. from circular buffer into storage buffer
- End of storage buffer reached ? (N / Y)
- End

Figure 8-4
Flowcharts of Input Routines

time delay between the collection of data points are also included in this routine.

The LOAD PEAK INTO STORAGE BUFFER routine transfers an entire 7.5 second maximum duration pulse from the circular buffer into the storage buffer if the highest point buffer receives a data point above the threshold level during the preceding 5 seconds. The loading takes place between the collection of two data points.

8.8   DATA PROCESSING AND DISPLAY

8.8.1   Overview

When the operator has collected enough pulses for an experimental run he presses the "Output" button. The program enters section B to calculate the average and the standard deviations of the peak heights and peak intervals for the data from both channels. The calculated values and the number of pulses collected are displayed on the analog recorder.

The display of the calculated values can be repeated as desired by pressing the "Output" button. This feature is useful if the recorder paper is exhausted during a data transfer to the recorder, or if a duplicate copy of the run is needed.

Pressing the "Reset" button to abort a run or start a new run completely clears all buffers and restarts the program.

8.8.2   Data Processing Routines

Short descriptions of the more important data processing routines follow.

8.8.2.1   AVERAGE Routine

The AVERAGE routine uses the storage buffer to average the collected pulses and the interval buffer to average the intervals for display on the analog recorder. These results are used for the standard deviation routine.

The flow diagram for this routine in Figure 8-5 illustrates the procedure. First, the number of peaks is read. Then, the value from the first location, at the high end of the storage buffer, is divided by the number of peaks. As this value is the sum of all

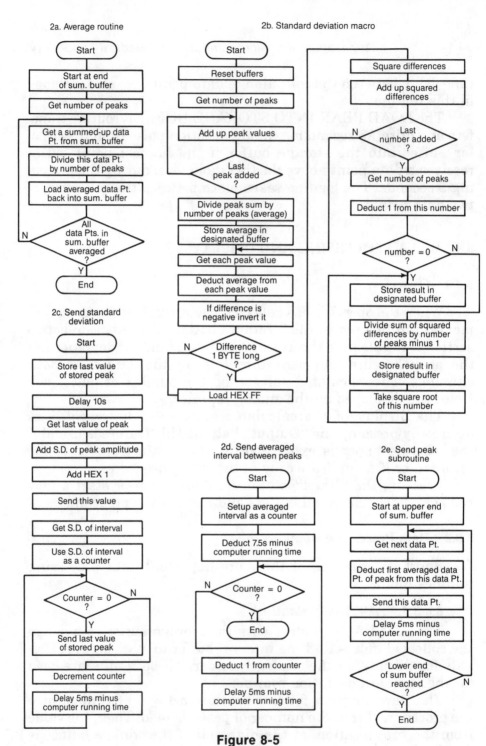

Figure 8-5
Flowcharts of Processing Routines

data points from all the collected pulses at this portion of the pulse, the result of the division is the average of this part of the pulse. This average is returned to the same buffer location. This operation is repeated until all locations in the storage buffer contain average values.

8.8.2.2 DIVIDE Routine

The DIVIDE routine, shown in Figure 8-6, is used several times in the program to divide 16- and 8-bit numbers. The routine may be written in different ways. Any divide algorithm learned in school may be used. Another approach which divides the dividend into two factors will be used here. The first factor determines the magnitude of the dividend and the second its numeric value. This type of division is faster for dividends which include several zeroes.

The routine first checks to see if the divisor is zero. If it is, the routine is aborted. If it is not, the divisor is checked to see if it is 16-bits long (maximum length). If it is not, then the divisor is multiplied by 2 until the divisor has a "1" in the MSB. A counter enumerates the number of multiplications. The dividend is also multiplied by 2 until it has 16 significant bits. The number of times the divisor is multiplied is deducted from the number of times the divisor was multiplied. This number is stored in a temporary buffer.

Next, the divisor is subtracted repeatedly from the dividend until the dividend becomes less than the divisor. The number of subtractions is counted in the quotient. Any remainder is handled as a new divisor after it has been multiplied as often as necessary to make the divisor larger than the dividend. If the multiplication factor in the buffer counter is not large enough to make the divisor larger than the dividend, the division is terminated and the quotient transferred to a permanent buffer.

8.8.2.3 Standard Deviation Routine

The standard deviation routine (Figure 8-5, 2b) calculates the standard deviation of the pulse heights and pulse intervals. The following formula is used for the calculation.

$$ \mathrm{sd} = \left(\frac{(\mathrm{xi} - \bar{\mathrm{x}})^2}{\mathrm{n} - 1} \right)^{1/2} $$

Application of a Microcomputer in a Medical Laboratory

xi variable
$\bar{x}$ average of variable
n number of variables
sd standard deviation

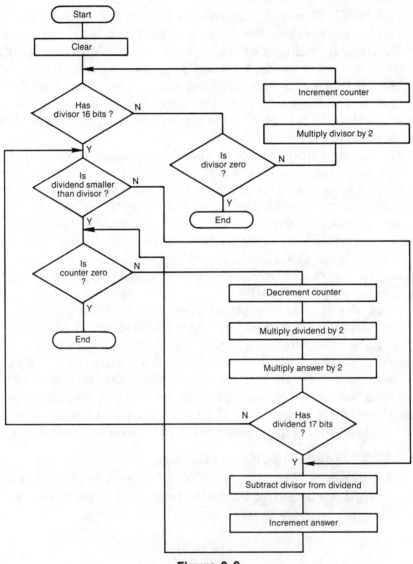

Figure 8-6
Flowchart of Divide Routine

The flow chart for the standard deviation is given in Figure 8-5. After initialization, the average of the variable is calculated. The average is subtracted from each peak variable, the differences squared, and the squares totaled. This sum is divided by the number of peaks minus one. The square root of this result is approximated by the following formula.

$$y(n+1) = (1/2) (y(n) + a/y(n))$$

where:

$y(n)$ nth approximation of square root
$y(n+1)$ $(n+1)$th approximation of square root
a number for which square root is sought

The series of approximations is stopped when the 8-bit numbers $y(n)$ and $y(n+1)$ are equal. The first approximation $y(1)$ is set to

$$y(1) = a/2$$

8.8.3   Display Routines

8.8.3.1   Overview

Different routines are used to display the average peak height, the average interval between the peaks, the standard deviation, and the area and the number of peaks on the analog recorder. These routines set up a counter into which the number of points to be sent out is loaded. This counter is decremented each time a data point is sent out. As the computer can output data points much faster than the recorder can print them, therefore data output must be slowed enough for the sent function to be properly displayed on the recorder trace. The flowcharts for the display routines are shown in Figure 8-7.

The delay time must be equal to the 5 millisecond time interval between the collection of two successive data points in order to reproduce properly the peak on the recorder paper. As the computer required a brief time for processing, the actual delay time must be slightly less than 5 milliseconds so that the total delay time will be 5 milliseconds.

8.8.3.2 Average Pulse Height

Data points are taken from the average peak buffer one by one, each delayed by five milliseconds and sent to the analog recorder. The average is sent twice; the second time it is delayed by the average peak interval.

8.8.3.3 Standard Deviation

The standard deviation of the pulse height and the interval between the pulses form a rectangle on the recorder chart. The standard deviation of the pulse height is set up as a vertical deflection. The standard deviation for the time interval is set up as a horizontal deflection by the help of a counter into which a number proportional to the time interval is loaded. The proportionality factor is set so that without taking excessive space the standard deviation can be read accurately from the chart paper. A CLEAR instruction returns the recorder pen to zero and completes the rectangle.

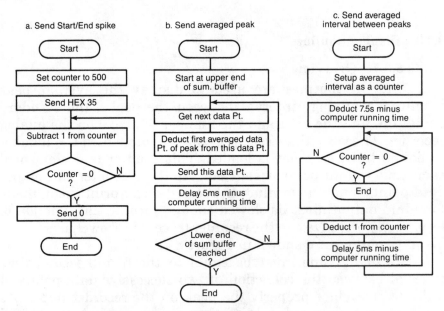

Figure 8-7
Flowchart of Display Routines

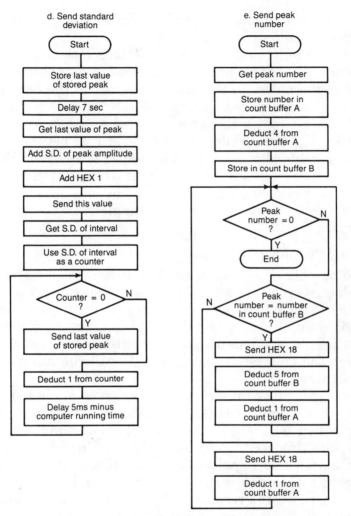

Figure 8-7
Flowchart of Display Routines (part I)

8.8.3.4   Area of a Signal

The area of a signal is determined in the following way. The pulse is indicated on the recorder chart as a series of dots. The area of the pulse may be considered as a number of narrow, long rectangles, with the height of that dot above the baseline. The width is 5 milliseconds, as the dots are separated by a collection interval of 5 milliseconds. To obtain the area, the computer sums up the heights of all dots which represent a signal and multiplies this sum by 5 milliseconds.

Two different methods are available. The location of the maximum value of the pulse may be used to determine the start and end of the pulse. In this case the noise on the baseline will be added to the peak area. The second method uses the threshold method and estimates the area under the threshold by simple arithmetic. The area under the threshold line between the two crossovers is added to a triangular-shaped area before the pulse crosses the threshold line, and a similar triangular area after the pulse again crosses the threshold line. The total area of the peak is displayed on the recorder as a rectangle with uniform height and varying width.

8.8.3.5 *Number of Signals*

The number of signals is the last information displayed on the analog recorder. Small deflections of the recorder pen, equal in number to the pulses in the run, are generated. The number of signals is set up as a counter (Figure 8-8) as in the previous display routines. A small deflection of the recorder pen is generated each time the counter is decremented until the number in the counter is zero.

Each fifth mark on the recorder chart is made longer with the help of a second counter to make the counting easier. A number which is five less than the starting number is loaded initially into this second counter. When the number in the first counter has been decremented by five in single steps, making the numbers in both counters the same, this count is displayed as an elevated mark on the recorder. This procedure is repeated until the number in the first counter reaches zero.

8.9   EXPANDING THE MICROCOMPUTER SYSTEM

8.9.1   Different Uses for the System

The system can be used to reduce the noise on the output because averaging reduces white noise by a factor of $n^{1/2}$, where n is the number of pulses averaged. In Figure 8-9 the amount of noise reduction is shown by comparing the noise in channel 1 to

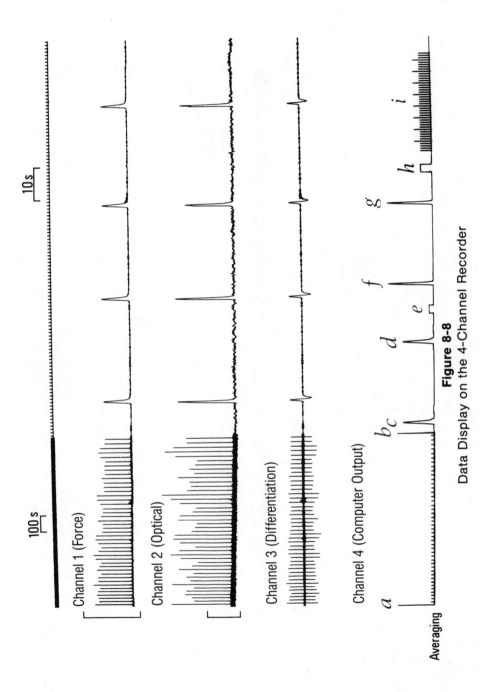

Figure 8-8

Data Display on the 4-Channel Recorder

Application of a Microcomputer in a Medical Laboratory

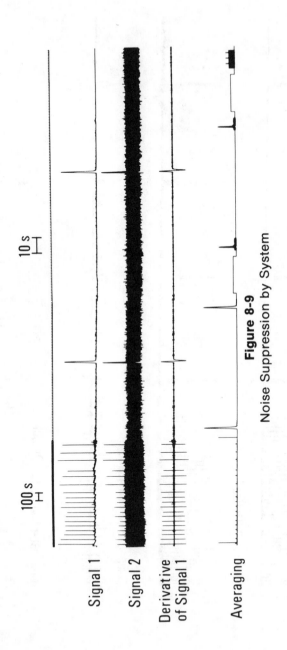

Figure 8-9

Noise Suppression by System

the output in channel 4. The noise reduction shown corresponds exactly to the formula above.

8.9.2 Expanding the System

8.9.2.1 Introduction

The capability of the system described above can be further improved for the application discussed and for others. Some changes which can be made with relatively small efforts are described below.

8.9.2.2 Different-Shaped Signals

The system described can handle many types of signals provided a single reference value can be found for each pulse. If the pulse is different from a triangle-shaped pulse a single reference value can be calculated. The two crossover points of the threshold line by a signal are located by the system and a single reference point calculated for the midpoint between them. The location of the reference point could be located anywhere between these crossover points, to suit a specific application. Any other shaped pulse can be handled in a similar way.

Signals below the threshold line may be considered noise and are ignored by the computer. A new approach must be used to recognize these signals. The rate of change in the rising slope of a signal can separate a signal from noise. Noise signals have usually a much greater slope than data pulses. Any noise which has a slope similar to the data may cause trouble. Perhaps two different criteria could be used simultaneously to recognize specific signals. Possible values to consider include the height, the angle of the initial slope of the signal, and the duration of the signal.

8.9.2.3 Number of Signals

The number of pulses stored can be increased relatively easily as they are not stored individually. Little modification is necessary to increase the storage capacity from 50 pulses to 500 pulses. A maximum number of 128 which can be stored for the representation of the height of one pulse (5 volts) and 50 pulses store only a number value of 6400 in a two-byte buffer (64K).

Additional minor changes make possible storing 2,000 to 3,000 signals. The length of the storage buffer must be increased from two bytes to three bytes to avoid overloading the storage buffer, as up to 384,000 bits may be stored in one location. In addition, all pointers working in the storage buffers must jump three locations instead of two when they go from one storage location to the next.

8.9.2.4   *Time between the Collection of Two Points*

Timing loops built into the collection routines written in assembly language extend the interval between two data points in the above-described system to 5 milliseconds. Therefore, the collection speed could be increased more than five-fold (less than 1 millisecond intervals) if the timing loops were taken out of the collection routines and the clock frequency increased to 2 MHz, a frequency commonly used in SWTPC computers.

8.9.2.5   *Number of Input Channels*

The total number of input channels which can be used with the example depends on the time interval between two consecutive data points. The system can accept the information from at least fifteen channels when the collection time is 5 milliseconds. In case the collection interval is 1 millisecond the system can accept data from 3 channels. A further reduction in collection time is difficult for an ADC because with a conversion time of 300 microseconds it allows only three conversions per 1 millisecond.

Higher collection rates are possible with faster ADCs. Those with a conversion time of 25 microseconds are readily available and the cost—with multiplexers—is less than $100. The speed of collection must be increased correspondingly by rewriting some of the assembler codes. Little increase in the speed of collection is possible if the pulse-detection system is not changed. When the data points are stored in less complicated buffers in the main memory, three points can be stored in 40 microseconds. Allowing for the time delay caused by the ADC, an 80-microsecond data collection interval can be maintained easily. A three-input channel system can collect and store data faster than every 0.1 milliseconds.

This speed of operation probably would not interfere with the operation of any routine in the system. The only routine which might interfere with a 0.1-millisecond data collection speed is the one which transfers a detected signal from the circular buffer to the storage buffer. For data collection speeds in this time range (0.1 milliseconds) or lower, the peak transfer might have to be spread over more than one interval between data collections to avoid any interference.

If one intends to use the above-described system and anticipates even higher data-collecting speeds, it would be better to use the 68008 instead of the 6809. The 68008 microprocessor is about 5 to 6 times faster than the 6809, and is much more adaptable.

8.9.2.6 Permanent Storage of Data

Each data point of the collected signals must be stored separately if the data are to be processed differently later. All collected pulses are stored initially in the main memory, as the time to store one data point on the disk is on the order of 10 to 900 milliseconds. The computer needs 600 locations for a 3-second pulse. Twenty-five signals 3 seconds long require 30,000 bytes storage locations ($600\times25\times2$). After all pulses have been collected, processed, and recorded, they can be sent to the disk for permanent storage without interference with the system's operation.

Each data point can be stored as soon as it is collected if a hard disk is available for the system, because of the high storage speed. Twenty Megabytes, hard disks can store thousands of typical runs.

Cassette tapes are not recommended for this type of data storage in spite of their low price, because of the extreme length of time it takes them to load and feed back data.

8.9.2.7 Use of Different Software

The program described above can be written using a BASIC compiler. The execution speed of the compiler probably would be fast enough to collect all the data with the necessary speed. Other possible choices for the system would be the PASCAL compiler, which in the case of a FLEX system also had commands for collecting data from outside the C-compiler or the FORTH language.

8.9.2.8   Automatic Loading of the System

The following steps must be taken with the /09 system to load the program manually when the system is turned on. First, "D" is pushed, to load the disk operating system. The date must then be provided. Next the selected program is loaded from the disk into memory. Finally, the program is set to the starting position for the program. All further operations of the program are fully controlled from the remote control box located near the investigator.

Hardware and software are available which can fully automate the loading operation of the program. To do this, a hardware date card must be inserted into one of the I/O slots. The date card keeps the correct date, hour, minutes, and seconds even when the power of the computer is turned off. A second hardware device sends a "D" to the monitor when the computer is switched on.

A special software program takes the date from the date card and automatically inserts it into the date slot. A second software program initiates an "exec" program which automatically loads the desired program from the disk and sets the program counter in the right position.

To switch the system off, simply push the "RESET" button and turn off the power switch.

CHAPTER 9

Improving a Laboratory Setup with a Microcomputer Test System

9.1 INTRODUCTION

Microcomputers are used in the laboratory to increase the precision of measurements and to relieve personnel of tedious work. General considerations and procedures for designing an instrumentation system are similar regardless of the particular application. As an example, we will discuss the development and application of a microcomputer-based instrumentation system designed to evaluate a liquid delivery system. The decision process demonstrated here can be adapted well to other applications.

9.2 BASIC DESIGN CONSIDERATIONS

A test setup which will evaluate the performance of a system to deliver a liquid at an adjustable constant rate independent of the discharge pressure is to be designed in detail.

9.2.1 Description of the System to Be Tested

The desired flow of liquid is expressed in terms of a proportional voltage set by a potentiometer. The flow is monitored from the pressure drop across the capillary through which the liquid passes. This pressure drop is converted by a transducer into an electrical voltage, which is compared to the reference voltage set by the potentiometer. When the voltage corresponding to the pressure drop is lower than the voltage set by the potentiometer, indicating insufficient flow, a series of current pulses applied to the system increases the flow. These control pulses continue until the measurement during a later sampling period indicates that the flow rate has increased to the desired level. The current pulses generate gas, which enters a cavity behind a collapsible plastic bag to displace liquid in the bag container. Battery life is extended by monitoring the variables every eight seconds for approximately two milliseconds.

9.2.2 Quantities to Be Measured and Recorded

In order to evaluate the performance of the system, it is necessary to measure and record the reference voltage, flow in terms of the output voltage from the differential pressure transducer across the capillary, presence of control current pulses, room temperature, atmospheric pressure, and pressure inside the cavity containing the gas. The discharge pressure is controlled by adjusting the liquid level, in a cannula connected to the exit port of the delivery system with respect to the liquid level in the plastic liquid reservoir.

For laboratory personnel to measure and record manually all these quantities at one-hour, one-half-hour, or 10-minute intervals over long periods of time—perhaps twenty-four hours, seventy-two hours or a week—is a formidable job. Clearly the answer is an automated, microcomputer-based data collection and recording system.

9.3 SELECTING HARDWARE

9.3.1 Equipment—General Considerations

9.3.1.1 Microprocessor
The system in the example is relatively simple. An 8K-byte, 8-bit microprocessor should be adequate. The capacity required can only be known once the system design is completed, or nearly completed. An estimate on which to base the design must be made at the outset.

9.3.1.2 Peripherals
Interpretive BASIC is selected for the programming language since the test equipment should be easily programmable and a high-speed execution is not required. A full-size keyboard

and a CRT monitor will be used to enter and debug the program. A printer is provided for a hard-copy, permanent record of the data.

9.3.1.3 Sensors and Interface

Temperature, pressures, and the control current pulses are to be measured. Analog signals must be processed and converted into a digital form acceptable by the microprocessor. A budget must be prepared to determine how much may be spent on ready-made equipment and what equipment should be custom-designed and built in the laboratory. A block diagram of the instrument system is shown in Figure 9-1.

9.3.2 Specific Hardware Selection

The Commodore Model 2001 microcomputer with a Commodore Model 4022 printer meets the requirement for a low-cost, general-purpose microcomputer with the necessary peripherals. This computer has an 8-bit, 6502 microprocessor with 8K bytes of memory. It can be programmed in interactive BASIC. The 4022 printer is compatible with this microcomputer and has its own built-in microprocessor. It is capable of graphic and alphanumeric printouts. The program for any particular application can

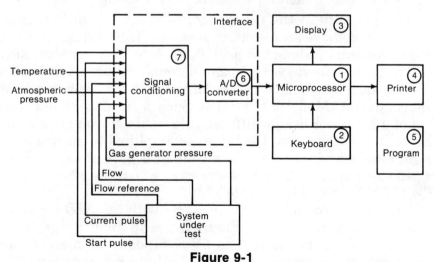

Figure 9-1
Overall Diagram of Instrumentation System

be stored on a magnetic tape cassette, freeing the computer and the printer for other work when they are not needed for the original application. Only a few minutes are required to return the program to the computer memory.

ADAK-1, a low-cost A/D converter compatible with the equipment is commercially available from Technical Hardware, Inc. Purchasing a ready-made A/D converter, like any other general purpose equipment, is justified to expedite the project.

The situation is quite different for the pressure transducers and temperature sensors. These are special-purpose items. With the signal conditioning and processing units, they would be very expensive. Purchasing low-cost transducers that meet the required specifications, and building the required electronic circuitry in the laboratory is advantageous for this application.

9.4 HARDWARE DESIGN

9.4.1 Pressure Measurement

Two pressures are to be recorded: the gauge pressure (above atmosphere) of the gas in the cavity and the atmospheric pressure.

9.4.1.1 Gas Generator Pressure Measurement

The pressure in the gas generator is 1,000 mm H_2O (9797 N/m^2) or less above atmospheric pressure. This corresponds to a gauge pressure of about 1.5 psi (10,342 N/m^2). A suitable, inexpensive (approximately \$75.), small, semiconductor-type gauge pressure transducer is commercially available from National Semiconductor (Model LX1601GB). Such a transducer unit consists of a 4-resistor bridge diffused into a thin silicon membrane. The output voltage from the bridge is amplified by means of an operational amplifier which is an integral part of the pressure transducer package. The pressure range is from −5 to +5 psi (−34,474 N/m^2 to +34,474 N/m^2).

Interfacing the pressure transducer with the A/D converter is considered next. Refer to Figure 9-2. The input range to the ADAK-1 A/D converter is 0 to 5V. Output from the pressure transducer at zero gauge pressure is 7.5V, the offset voltage. The maximum output voltage is 16V. This gives a dynamic range of

8.5V (7.5V to 16V) for a pressure span of 0 to 5 psi (0 to 34,474 N/m^2). The maximum pressure from this setup is 1.5 psi (10,342 N/m^2) corresponding to a 10V output [(8.5/5)×1.5+7.5]. The best way to adapt the pressure transducer output to the A/D converter is to buck the 7.5V offset voltage of the pressure transducer before applying the signal to the A/D converter by subtracting 7.5V, with a circuit such as the one shown in Figure 9-2. The output of this circuit is set to 0 for a 0-psi gauge pressure and to 5V for 1.5psi (10,342 N/m^2). The 8-bit A/D converter (having 2^8=256 levels) gives a resolution of (1.5/256)=0.0059 psi or 5.9 mm H$_2$O (40.679 N/m^2), which is 0.59% of the maximum pressure.

In Figure 9-2 the output from the pressure transducer is buffered by operational amplifier 1 and connected to op amp 2. The bucking voltage is applied by op amp 3, which is driven by the adjustable voltage-dividing network. Input to the A/D converter is adjusted by amplifier 4 to provide the gain for the 0 to 5V dynamic range. Operational amplifiers 1 and 5, which are voltage followers, are desirable to provide isolation. The RC net-

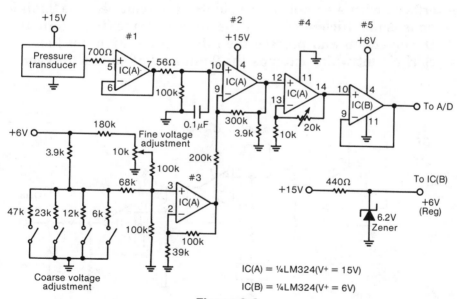

Figure 9-2
Circuit for Reducing Pressure Transducer Offset
Output Voltage

Improving a Laboratory Setup with a Microcomputer Test System

work at the output of op amp 1 filters noise from the output of the pressure transducer. The voltage dividing network is more elaborate than necessary. It is incorporated in the design for versatility, to offer coarse adjustment (switches) and fine adjustment (a potentiometer). A Zener diode regulator provides 6 volts from a 15V power supply.

9.4.1.2 Atmospheric Pressure Measurement

Changes in atmospheric pressure are measured by a pressure transducer and interface circuit identical to that used for the gas container pressure measurement. The port of the transducer open to the atmosphere is closed for reading atmospheric pressure relative to the pressure at the time the port was sealed.

9.4.2 Flow Measurement

System flow is controlled by a voltage proportional to the differential pressure across a capillary. As stated in Section 9.2.1, this voltage is monitored every 8 seconds for approximately 2 milliseconds. The system and the test equipment are interfaced with a sample and hold (S/H) circuit because 2 milliseconds is insufficient time for the microcomputer to perform the A/D conversion and process the information. Figure 9-3 shows an S/H circuit which extends the 2-millisecond pulses to several

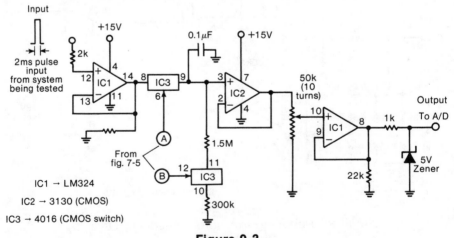

Figure 9-3
SAMPLE/HOLD Circuit to Extend Pulse Duration

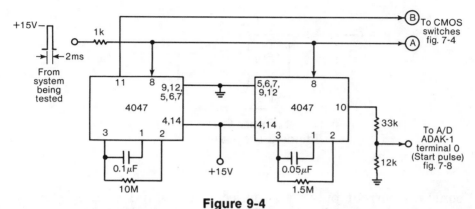

Figure 9-4
Multivibrators to Generate CMOS Switches and A/D
Converter Control Pulses

hundred milliseconds. The circuit samples the signal when CMOS switch A is closed and CMOS switch B is open. Switch A opens at the end of the 2-millisecond input pulse and the circuit stores the information. Switch B closes and the S/H circuit discharges when a pulse is applied to that switch. Switch B opens when pulse B is complete. The S/H circuit accepts new information when switch A closes at the beginning of the next 2-millisecond pulse. The voltage level is adjusted by means of the 50K potentiometer shown in Figure 9-3. The 5V zener diode is installed to protect the A/D converter. The control signal for switch B is generated by a multivibrator shown in Figure 9-4. This figure also shows a second monostable multivibrator which generates a pulse to activate the A/D converter and to start the conversion of the information it receives.

9.4.3   Temperature Measurement

The temperature is measured by means of the leakage current of a temperature sensitive diode. Figure 9-5 shows this circuit. With increasing temperature the leakage current increases, thereby increasing the output voltage. The output voltage V_o is applied to the A/D converter.

9.4.4   Current Pulses

The current pulses in the example are supplied by a constant current source. A voltage pulse is generated whenever the

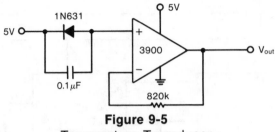

Figure 9-5
Temperature Transducer

constant current pulse is supplied. This signal is interfaced to the A/D converter by the zener diode amplitude-limiting circuit shown in Figure 9-6 to limit the maximum input to 5V.

9.4.5 Flow Reference Voltage

The flow reference voltage is obtained directly from the system under test. The voltage appears as a 2-millisecond pulse. This signal is interfaced to the A/D converter where an S/H circuit extends the length of this pulse to be compatible with the A/D converter, as was done for the voltage representing the actual flow. The circuit is identical to that shown in Figure 9-3.

9.5 DETAILED INTERFACE DIAGRAM

The connections between the system under test and the microcomputer-based instrumentation, shown in blocks 6 and 7 of Figure 9-1, are given in detail in Figure 9-7.

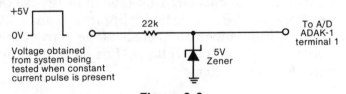

Figure 9-6
Voltage Amplitude Limiting Circuit for "Current Pulse Present" Sensing

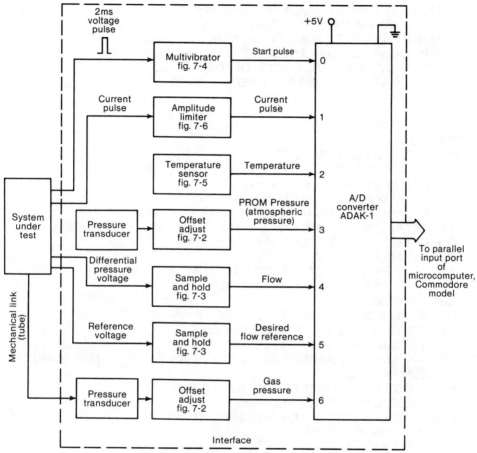

Figure 9-7
Details of Systems Interface

9.6 PROGRAM DESIGN AND DISPLAY

After the hardware is assembled, instructions must be issued to the microcomputer. A BASIC program is written and entered into the microcomputer by means of the keyboard.

9.6.1 Program Description

Figure 9-8 is a program to display data on the video screen and to type a hard-copy graphical record on the printer. A

```
10  PRINT "□";"INSULIN FLOW PARAMETER
         PROGRAM":PRINT:PRINT
12  PRINT"I WILL NEED SOME DATA FROM YOU":PRINT
14  INPUT"GIVE NO-FLOW PRESSURE VOLTAGE";Q1
15  INPUT"GIVE REFERENCE VOLTAGE";Q2
16  INPUT"GIVE FLOW (ML/HR) AT REF VOLTAGE";Q3
100  S6=0:S5=0
860  RESTORE:READS
870  READA:POKES,A:S=S+1:IFA=1THEN900
880  GOTO870
900  IFPEEK(135)<27THENPOKE135,27
1001  DATA826,169,255,141,67,232,169,0,141,75,232,162,8,173
1002  DATA76,232,141,151,3,202,16,7,173,151,3,141,76
1003  DATA232,96,169,193,141,76,232,142,65,232,169,225,141
1004  DATA76,232,169,128,141,150,3,141,65,232,234,234,234
1005  DATA172,65,232,234,234,169,2,45,77,232,240,5,152
1006  DATA77,150,3,168,78,150,3,240,7,152,77,150,3
1007  DATA76,104,3,152,157,152,3,76,76,3,1
1500  PRINT:PRINT"A/D CONVERSION ROUTINE. WAITING
         FOR    START PULSE ON INPUT #0"
2000  GOTO5000
3000  REM**A/D SUBROUTINE
3020  SYS(826):L=PEEK(920):IFL<20THEN3020
3030  SYS(826):L=PEEK(920):IFL>20THEN3030
3040  A=PEEK(921):B=PEEK(922):C=PEEK(923):O=PEEK(924):E=PEEK
         (925):PRINT"□"
3050  PRINT"PULSE";A:PRINT"TEMP";B:PRINT"ROOM
         PRESS";C:PRINT"GAS";PEEK(926)
3060  PRINT"GAS PRESS";O;O*.0313725:PRINT"REF
         VOLTAGE";E;E*.0313725
3070  PRINT:PRINT:PRINT
3080  PRINT"WAITING FOR NEXT MEASUREMENT"
3090  RETURN
5000  OPEN6,4,6:PRINT#6,CHR$(24):CLOSE6
5100  OPEN5,4:PRINT#5," ":PRINT#5," "
5200  PRINT#5,"PULSE  TEMPERATURE  ROOM  PRESS        FLOW
         PRESSURE"
5500  OPEN6,4,6:PRINT#6,CHR$(18):CLOSE6
5600  PRINT#5," ":PRINT#5," "
6000  REM ** GRAPH ROUTINE**
6050  GOSUB3000
6100  PRINT#5,"▦ | | | ▦ | | | | | | | | | | | | ▦ | | | | | | | | | |
      ▦ | | | | | | | | | | | | | | | | | | | | | | | ▦";
6200  PRINT#5,"| | | | | | | | | | | | | _ _ _ _ _ _ _ _ ▦";:PRINT#5,CHR$(141);
6300  A$="■":A1−1:IFA>50THENA$="■"
6400  IFA>50THENA1=3
```

Figure 9-8
BASIC Program (see text section 9.6.1)

```
6500 B$="■":T=INT((B-122)/3):IFT<0THENT=0
6600 IFT>19THENT=19
6700 IFINT(INT(T/2)*2)<TTHENB$="■"
6800 A2=4-A1+INT(T/2)
6900 C$="■":T=INT(C-226) :IFT<0THENT=0
7000 IFT>19THENT=19
7100 IFINT(INT(T/2)*2)<TTHENC$="■"
7200 A3=14-A2+INT(T/2)-A1
7300 REM **E=REF D=GAS PRESSURE
7400 D$="■":T=D-E+50:IFT<0THENT=0
7500 IFT>101THENT=101
7600 IFINT(INT(T/2)*2)<TTHEND$="■"
7700 A4=24-A3+INT(T/2)-A1-A2
7800 PRINT#5,TAB(A1);A$;TAB(A2);B$;TAB(A3);C$;TAB(A4);D$;
     :PRINT#5,CHR$(141);
7850 S1=D*.0313725:S2=S1-Q1:S3=S2*Q3/3600/(Q2-Q1):
     S4=S3*8.189:S5=S5+S4
8000 GOSUB3000
8100 A$="■":A1=1:IFA>50THENA$="■"
8200 IFA>50THENA1=3
8300 B$="■":T=INT((B-122)/3):IFT<0THENT=0
8400 IFT>19THENT=19
8500 IFINT(INT(T/2)*2)<TTHENB$="■"
8600 A2=4-A1+INT(T/2)
8700 C$="■":T=INT(C-226):IFT<0THENT=0
8800 IFT>19THENT=19
8900 IFINT(INT(T/2)*)<TTHENC$="■"
9000 A3=14-A2+INT(T/2)-A1
9100 D$="■":T=D-E+50:IFT<0THENT=0
9200 IFT>101THENT=101
9300 IFINT(INT(T/2)*2)<TTHEND$="■"
9400 A4=24-A3+INT(T/2)-A1-A2
9500 PRINT#5,TAB(A1);A$;TAB(A2);B$;TAB(A3);C$;TAB(A4);D$;:PRINT
     #5,CHR$(141);
9505 L1=PEEK(926)
9510 E1=INT(L1-200):IFE1>70THENE1=70
9515 IFE1<0THENE1=0
9520 PRINT#5,TAB(E1);"*";:PRINT#5,CHR$(141);
9530 S1=0*.0313725:S2=S1-Q1:S3=S2*Q3/3600/(Q2-Q1):S4=S3*
     8.189:S5=S5+S4
9531 S6=S6+1
9540 IFS6>=2THENGOSUB10000
9550 PRINT#5," "
9600 GOTO6000
10000 PRINT#5,TAB(62);S5;:PRINT#5,CHR$(141);:S6=0
10010 RETURN
```

Figure 9-8

(continued)

sample of the hard copy record is shown in Figure 9-9. The graphical display includes the "desired flow" or flow reference setting, the actual flow, room pressure, room temperature, and the control current pulses. The cumulative flow is printed out numerically. The first printout of the cumulative flow must be ignored, as it results from an erratic signal when the system is first turned on.

9.6.2   Analyzing the Computer Printout

Figure 9-9 demonstrates the effectiveness of a microcomputer-based instrumentation system. Once the current which activates the flow is turned on, it remains on until the flow rate reaches the reference value. This transient period lasts 8.5 minutes. The gas pressure and flow increase gradually until they reach their respective steady state values. Note that the graphical presentation of flow is truncated at values considerably below the steady state value.

Once the steady state is reached, the control current pulses occur at intervals of approximately 48 seconds. Next, the following external disturbances are introduced: at instant A in Figure 9-9 the liquid discharge pressure is increased abruptly by 150mm (H_2O ($1,470$ N/m^2) and at instant B, 18 minutes later, the pressure is decreased gradually over a period of 23 minutes until it reaches the original pressure at instant C.

The graphical presentation in Figure 9-9 shows that after the disturbance is introduced at instant A, the current pulse rate increases, causing the gas pressure to increase to a new steady value. The current pulses then settle to a lower rate. Once the discharge pressure begins to decrease at instant B, the time intervals between the current pulses increase while the gas pressure decreases gradually. When the discharge pressure returns to its original value at instant C, the gas pressure stabilizes at its original value and the control current pulses stabilize at their original rate. The flow continues to be essentially constant during the entire time period.

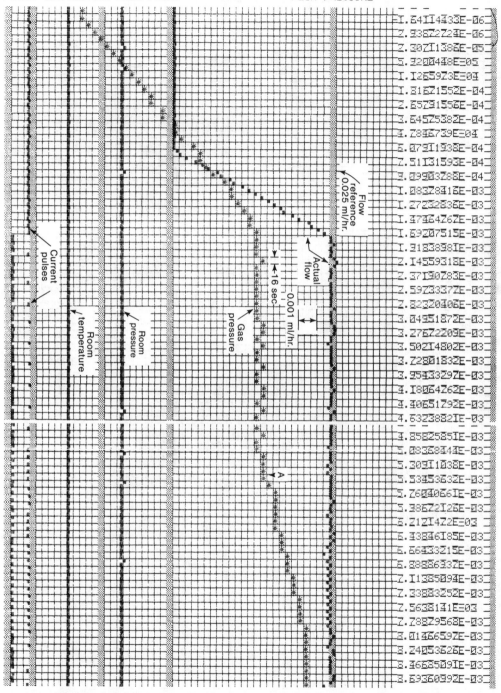

Figure 9-9 Printout Controlled by the Program in Figure 9-8 (Reprinted with permission of National Institutes of Health-NIAMDD, Bethesda, MD)

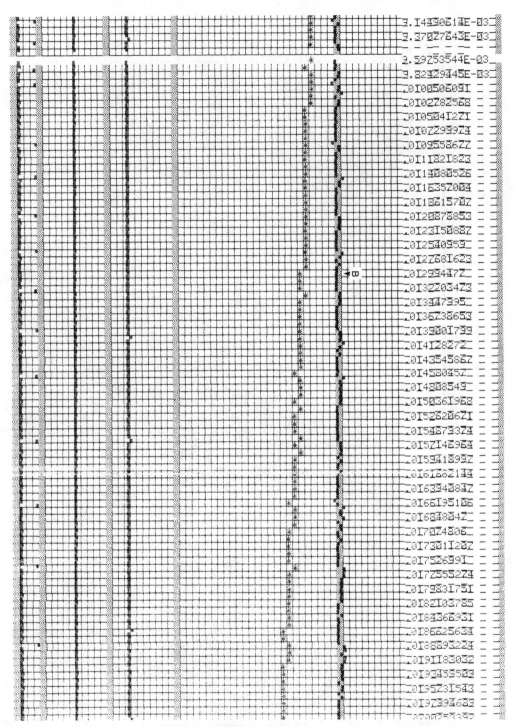

Figure 9-9
(continued)

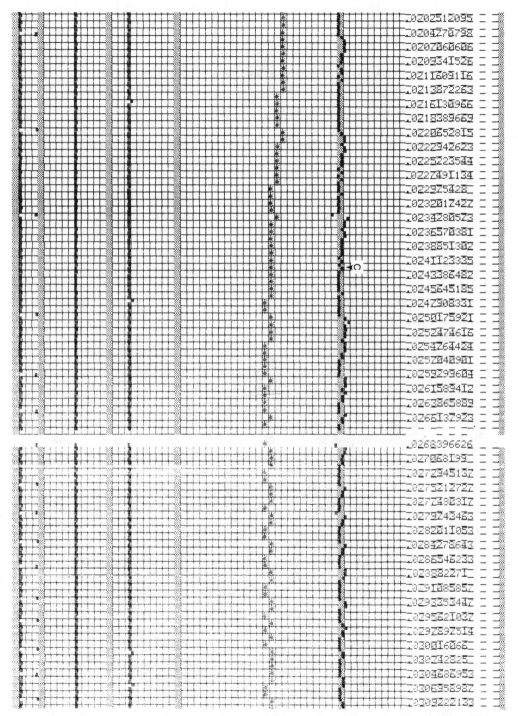

Figure 9-9
(continued)

235

9.7   IMPROVING FLOW MEASUREMENT WITH A DIGITAL MICROBALANCE IN CONJUNCTION WITH THE MICROCOMPUTER

As described so far, the flow is recorded in terms of a variable of the system: a voltage proportional to the differential pressure across a capillary. This reading is only as reliable as the capillary. If the capillary resistance changes due to partial clogging, the flow reading will not be correct. The accuracy of the system can be improved by measuring the flow directly, independent of any part of the system. This can be done by weighing the liquid discharged at the exit port. In principle, this is a simple matter. However, when this technique is integrated with the rest of the system, some new problems arise. The discussion of the solution is of sufficient general nature to be useful in solving similar microprocessor problems.

The discharge flow is weighed by a Mettler Model A30 electronic balance. The microcomputer computes the flow rate by dividing the weight by the duration of that flow. The balance introduces two problems into the instrumentation system: (a) the balance has a current loop which outputs information serially, (b) the balance output is at a much higher rate, 2400 bps, than the microcomputer can accept it (50 bps). The solution is to convert the serial information into parallel information, store it, and feed it to the microcomputer at a suitable lower rate.

A circuit which slows down and transfers this information is shown in Figure 9-10. A RCA 1802 microprocessor, is used for this purpose. Only the first of the two "bursts" of information put out during each output sequence by the balance is accepted by the serial/parallel converter. This information contains 8 bytes: a polarity sign, a decimal point, and 6 numerals. The bits of each byte are outputted in series. They are converted into parallel bits and entered into the RCA 1802 microprocessor during a few milliseconds and stored in the microprocessor RAM locations 041C through 0423 (HEX) shown in Figure 9-11. Next, the information is transferred to locations 04FA through 04FF shown in the same figure. Then, it is transferred to the Commodore 2001 microcomputer through a multiple analog switch during a period of 1.2 seconds.

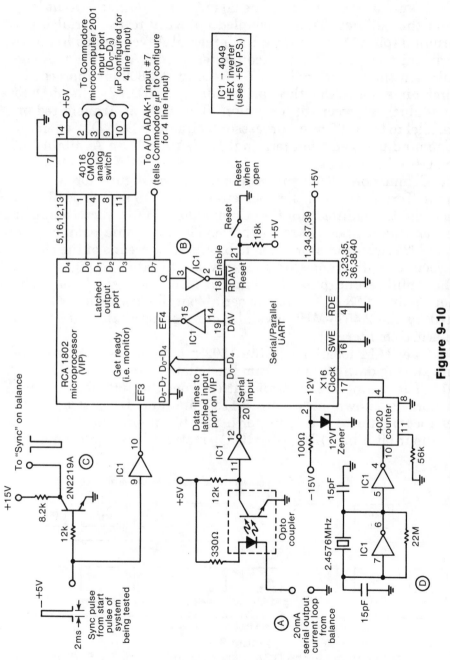

Figure 9-10

Interfacing Electronic Balance with Microcomputer

237

Improving a Laboratory Setup with a Microcomputer Test System

Figure 9-10 shows at A the 20-mA serial output current loop from the balance. This is coupled optically to the serial input terminal (pin 20) of the UART (Universal Asychronous Receiver Transmitter) serial/parallel converter, Model AY5-1013A. A signal from the Q terminal (at B) of the RCA 1802 microprocessor commands the UART through terminal 18 (RDAV = Read Data Available) to accept information. The data is transferred in parallel to the 1802 microprocessor (Data lines DO - D3) when the command is given from terminal 19 (DAV = Data Available) of the UART. A signal from terminal D7 of the RCA 1802 instructs the Commodore 2001 microcomputer to configure for a 4-line input. Terminal D4 of the 1802 enables CMOS switch 4016, and data is transmitted to the Commodore 2001 microcomputer through data lines D0 through D3. The electronic balance and the 1802 microprocessor are synchronized by means of the circuit associated with transistor 2N2219A shown (at C) in Figure 9-10. The 2-millisecond pulse is obtained from the test system. The clock pulse of 38.4 kHz for the serial/parallel converter is generated by the 2.4576-MHz crystal controlled oscillator (at D) and the 4020 counter.

The RAM locations in the 1802 microprocessor for sorting and storing data obtained from the balance are shown in Figure 9-11. The timing signal transmitted from the 1802 to the Commodore is shown in Figure 9-12. Data line D7 instructs the microcomputer to configure for a four-bit input. Then, "A", the first four-bit nibble [D0 - D3 (HEX)], instructs the microcomputer

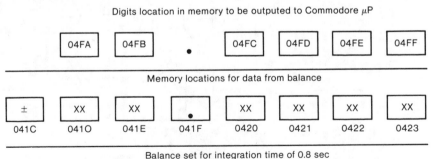

Digits location in memory to be outputed to Commodore μP

| 04FA | 04FB | • | 04FC | 04FD | 04FE | 04FF |

Memory locations for data from balance

| ± | XX | XX | • | XX | XX | XX | XX |
| 041C | 041O | 041E | 041F | 0420 | 0421 | 0422 | 0423 |

Balance set for integration time of 0.8 sec

Figure 9-11

RAM Locations in the RCA 1802 Microprocessor for Sorting and Storing Data from Balance

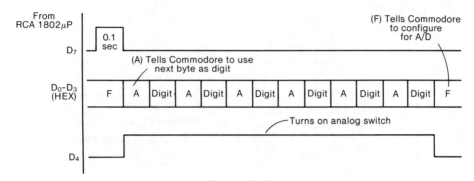

Figure 9-12
Timing Signals Transmitted from the RCA 1802
Microprocessor to the Commodore 2001 Microcomputer

to use the next byte as a digit rather than a value from the A/D conversion. The weight from the balance is in digital form, while the other data for the microcomputer—the pressures, the temperature, etc.—are analog signals and are entered through the A/D converter. The digital input is applied for 0.1 second and is followed by another "A", etc. until the entire six-byte output from the balance is entered. The next four-bit nibble, "F", instructs the microcomputer to configure again for the A/D input. The signal from the D4 terminal of the 1802 microprocessor turns on the analog switches. When D4 is "zero," the switches are open.

The program, entered into the 1802 microprocessor by means of a hexadecimal keyboard, controls the data transfer from the weighing balance to the Commodore microcomputer. The flowchart used to generate the program is given in Figure 9-13. The program, in machine language, is given in Figure 9-14.

The results from a test run are displayed on the video monitor and the printer (Figure 9-1) as controlled by the program entered into the Commodore 2001 microcomputer. The program given in Figure 9-15 prints in hard copy the total quantity of liquid delivered in milliliters and the flow rate in milliliters per hour, as ordered by the PRINT #5 instruction of the program. The time interval between the printouts is given by instruction 290. The time interval between printouts can be conveniently changed as desired simply by adjusting this one instruction. The video monitor displays additional information as instructed by PRINT instructions.

Improving a Laboratory Setup with a Microcomputer Test System

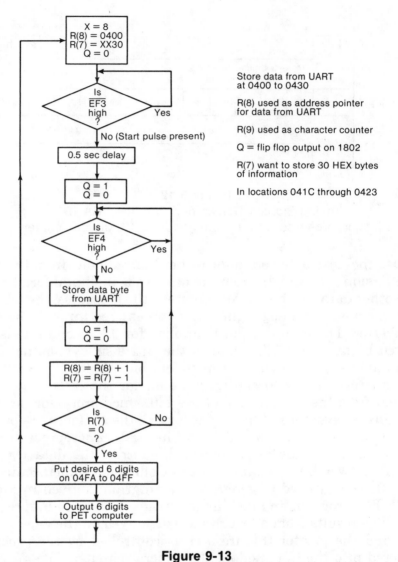

Store data from UART
at 0400 to 0430

R(8) used as address pointer
for data from UART

R(9) used as character counter

Q = flip flop output on 1802

R(7) want to store 30 HEX bytes
of information

In locations 041C through 0423

Figure 9-13
Flowchart for Programming the 1802 Microprocessor, which
Interfaces the Balance with the Instrumentation System

ADDRESS	MACHINE CODE (HEX)	COMMENTS
00	E8	X=8
01→06	F8 04 B8 F8 00 A8	R(8)=0400
07→09	F8 30 A7	R(7)=XX 30
0A	7A	Q=0
0B→0C	3E 0B	Loop to 000B if EF3 unchanged
		(no start pulse)
0D	C4	
0E→0F	F8 35	Delay variable
		35 gives ≈ .5 sec delay
10→11	A9 B9	
12→13	29 99	
14→15	3A 11	
16	7A	
17→19	7B C4 7A	Q=1 delay Q=0
1A→1B	3F 1A	Loop if EF4 is high
1C	6B	Data on input port goes to M(R(8))
ID→1F	7B C4 7A	Q=1 delay Q=0
20	60	R(X)=R(X) + 1 (increase R(8) for
		new location)
21	27	R(7) -1→R(7)
22	87	R 7.0→D
23→24	3A 1A	If D≠0 then 001A
25	EA	$\dot{X}$=A
26→2B	F8 04 BA F8 ID AA	R(A)=041D
2C→31	F8 04 B8 F8 FA A8	R(8)=04FA
32→35	0A 58 18 1A	041D→D, D→04FA, R(A)=041E
		R(8)=04FB
36→3A	0A 58 1A 1A 18	Second digit, R(A)=0420,
		R(8)=04FC
3B→3E	0A 58 18 1A	Third digit,
3F→42	0A 58 18 1A	Fourth digit,
43→46	0A 58 18 1A	Fifth digit,
47→4A	0A 58 18 1A	Sixth digit,
4B	E8	X=8
4C→52	F8 30 A8 F8 80 58 63	Output=80 (HEX)
53→5A	F8 08 A9 B9 29 99 3A 56	0.1 sec delay
5B→5D	F8 30 AA	R(A)=0430
5E→60	F8 FA A8	R(8)=04FA
61	EA	X=A D→0430
62→65	F8 1A 5A 63	Output=1A (HEX)
66→6D	F8 08 A9 B9 29 99 3A 69	0.1 sec delay

Figure 9-14
Program Based on the Flowchart of Figure 9-13 Entered into
the Microprocessor 1802 via a Hexadecimal Keyboard

Improving a Laboratory Setup with a Microcomputer Test System

ADDRESS	MACHINE CODE (HEX)	COMMENTS
6E→72	E8 F8 04 B8 63	Output=Digit
73→7A	F8 08 A9 B9 29 99 3A 76	0.1 sec delay
7B	88	R 8.0→D
7C→7D	3A 61	Branch to 0061 if D≠ 0
7E→81	F8 0F 58 63	Output=0F (HEX)
82→83	30 00	Loop to 0000

Figure 9-14
(continued)

READY.

```
5 S6=0:G=0:R=0:P=0:Q=0:U=0:W=0
15 PRINT"◻"
25 RESTORE:READS
30 READA:POKES,A:S=S+1:IFA=1THEN40
35 GOTO30
40 IFPEEK(135)<27THENPOKE135,27
45 DATA826,169,255,141,67,232,169,0,141,75,232,162,8,173
50 DATA76,232,141,151,3,202,16,7,173,151,3,141,76
55 DATA232,96,169,193,141,76,232,142,65,232,169,225,141
60 DATA76,232,169,128,141,150,3,141,65,232,234,234,234
65 DATA172,65,232,234,234,169,2,45,77,232,240,5,152
70 DATA77,150,3,168,78,150,3,240,7,152,77,150,3
75 DATA76,104,3,152,157,152,3,76,76,3,1
80 PRINT"PRESS" #5 IF PRINTER NOT USED. #9 IF PRINTER USED"
82 GETJ$
85 IFJ$="5"THENGOSUB100
90 IFJ$="5"THEN85
92 IFJ$="9"THEN95
94 GOTO82
95 GOTO500
100 F=0:PRINT"✱✱✱✱"
105 SYS(826):L=PEEK(920):IFL<20THEN105
110 SYS(826):L=PEEK(920):IFL>20THEN110
115 A=PEEK(921):B=PEEK(922):C=PEEK(923):D=PEEK(924):E=PEEK(925)
120 H=TI+15:IFG=0THENH=0
125 IFG=0THENTI$="000000"
130 SYS(826):IFPEEK(927)<20THEN130
135 POKE59459,240
140 I=0
150 Z=PEEK(59471):IFZ=15THEN150
155 IFZ<>10THEN150
```

Figure 9-15
Program for the Commodore Microcomputer

```
160 Z=PEEK(59471):IFZ=I0THEN160
165 A(I)=PEEK(59471):I=I+1
170 Z=PEEK(59471)
175 1FZ=10THEN160
180 IFZ=15THEN190
185 GOTO170
190 Z=PEEK(59471):IFZ<>15THEN170
195 POKE59459,255
200 K=I−1:M=100000:N=0
205 IFK>5THENF=8
210 IFK>5THENK=5
215 FORI=0TO5:IFA(I)>9THENF=8
220 N=N+(A(I)∗M):M=M/10:NEXT
225 PRINT"▢"IFA>60THENW=W+1
230 IFF=8THENPRINT"∗∗ERROR"
235 B(G)=N/10000:G=1
240 PRINT"BALANCE READS ";N/10000;" GRAMS"
245 PRINT" ▨▨▨▨▨▨▨▨▨ ":PRINT
250 B(G)=N−INT((B(0)∗10000+.1)):B(G)=8(G)/10000
253 PRINTB(G);" ML USED FROM START"
255 PRINT
260 PRINT"FLOW TIME ";INT(H/.036)/100000;" MINUTES":PRINT
265 P=0:IFH=0THEN275
270 P=INT((((B(G)−Q)∗(2.16E+10))/H)/100000
275 PRINT"PRESENT FLOW ";P;" ML/HR":PRINT
280 PRINT"PAST FLOW ";R;" ML/HR"
285 PRINT:PRINT" ▨▨▨▨▨▨▨▨ "
286 PRINT"PULSE COUNT";W:PRINT
290 IFH<216000THEN310
295 R=P:TI$="000000":U=10:Q=B(G)
310 PRINT"PULSE";A:PRINT"TEMP";B:PRINT"ROOM
    PRESS";C:PRINT"GAS";PEEK(926)
315 PRINT"CAPL VOLTS";O;O∗.0313725:PRINT"REF VOLTS";E;E∗.0313725
325 RETURN
500 OPEN5,4:PRINT#5,"ML USED     PULSE CT∗∗TEMP∗∗";FLOW (ML/HR)
501 PRINT#5,"GAS PRESS∗∗CAP PRESS"
505 PRINT#5," ":PRINT#5," "
506 PRINT#5,0,0,"∗∗∗∗∗∗∗∗∗∗∗∗∗∗∗∗∗∗∗∗∗∗∗"
507 PRINT#5," "
510 GOSUB100
515 IFU=10THEN525
520 GOTO510
525 IFF=8THENPRINT#5,"ERROR"
526 IFF=8THEN530
527 PRINT#5,B(G),R,W;"∗∗";B;"∗∗";PEEK(926);"∗∗";D
530 PRINT#5, " "
535 U=1:TI$:="000000":W=0:GOTO510
READY.
```

Figure 9-15
(continued)

Improving a Laboratory Setup with a Microcomputer Test System

```
READY.
5 86=0:G=0:R=0:P=0:Q=0:U=0:W=0
15 PRINT"❏"
25 RESTORE:READS
30 READA:POKES,A:S=S+1:IFA=1THEN40
35 GOTO30
40 IFPEEK(135)<27THENPOKE135,27
45 DATA826,169,255,141,67,232,169,0,141,75,232,162,8,173
50 DATA76,232,141,151,3,202,16,7,173,151,3,141,76
55 DATA232,96,169,193,141,76,232,142,65,232,169,225,141
60 DATA76,232,169,128,141,150,3,141,65,232,234,234,234
65 DATA172,65,232,234,234,169,2,45,77,232,240,5,152
70 DATA77,150,3,168,78,150,3,240,7,152,77,150,3
75 DATA76,104,3,152,157,152,3,76,76,3,1
80 PRINT"PRESS #5 IF PRINTER NOT USED. #9 IF PRINTER USED"
82 GETJ$
85 IFJ$="5"THENGOSUB100
90 IFJ$="5"THEN85
92 IFJ$="9"THEN95
94 GOTO82
95 GOTO500
100 F=0:PRINT"✱✱✱✱"
105 SYS(826):L=PEEK(920):IFL<20THEN105
110 SYS(826):L=PEEK(920):IFL>20THEN110
115 A=PEEK(921):B=PEEK(922):C=PEEK(923):D=PEEK(924):E=PEEK(925)
120 H=TI+15:IFG=0THENH=0
125 IFG=0THENTI$="000000"
130 SYS(826):IFPEEK(927)<20THEN130
135 POKE59459,240
140 I=0
150 Z=PEEK(59471):IFZ=15THEN150
155 IFZ<>10THEN150
160 Z=PEEK(59471):IFZ=10THEN160
165 A(I)=PEEK(59471):I=I+1
170 Z=PEEK(59471)
175 IFZ=10THEN160
180 IFZ=15THEN190
185 GOTO170
190 Z=PEEK(59471):IFZ<>15THEN170
195 POKE59459,255
200 K=I−1:M=100000:N=0
205 IFK>4THENF=18
210 IFK>5THENK=5
215 FORI=0TO5:IFA(I))9THENF=8
```

Figure 9-16
Modified Program for the Commodore Microcomputer

```
220 N=N+(A(I)*M):M=M/10:NEXT
225 PRINT"□";IFA>60THENW=W+1
230 IFF=8THENPRINT"**ERROR"
235 B(G)=N/10000:G=1
240 PRINT"BALANCE READS ";N/10000;" GRAMS"
245 PRINT"▓▓▓▓▓▓▓▓▓▓▓ ":PRINT
250 B(G)=N−INT((B(0)*10000+.1)):B(G)=B(G)/10000
253 PRINTB(G);" ML USED FROM START"
255 PRINT
260 PRINT"FLOW TIME ";INT(H/.036)/100000;" MINUTES":PRINT
265 P=0:IFH=0THEN275
270 P=INT(((B(G)−Q)*(2.16E+10))/H)/100000
275 PRINT"PRESENT FLOW ";P;" ML/HR":PRINT
280 PRINT"PAST FLOW ";R;" ML/HR"
285 PRINT:PRINT"▓▓▓▓▓▓▓▓▓▓▓▓"
286 PRINT"PULSE COUNT ";W:PRINT
290 IFH<216000THEN310
295 R=P :TI$="000000":U=10:Q=B(G)
310 PRINT"PULSE";A:PRINT"TEMP";B:PRINT"ROOM
          PRESS";C:PRINT"GAS";PEEK(926)
315 PRINT"CAPL VOLTS";O;O*.0313725:PRINT"REF
          VOLTS";E;E*.0313725
325 RETURN
500 OPEN5,4:PRINT#5,"ML USED      FLOW (ML/HR)      PULSE CT **
    TEMP ** ";
501 PRINT#5,"GAS PRESS ** CAP PRESS"
505 PRINT#5," ":PRINT#5," "
506 PRINT#5,0,0,"***********************"
507 PRINT#5," "
510 GOSUB100
515 IFU=10THEN525
520 GOTO510
525 IFF=8THENPRINT#5,"ERROR"
526 IFF=8THEN530
527 PRINT#5,B(G),R,W;" ** ";8;" ** ";PEEK(926)" ** ";D
530 PRINT#5, " "
535 U=1:TI$="000000":W=0:GOTO510
READY.
```

Figure 9-16
(continued)

A modification of the program is given in Figure 9-16. The major difference between the two programs is the PRINT #5 commands for the hard-copy printout. The current pulse count rate, temperature, gas pressure in the gas container, and liquid flow measured by the capillary pressure drop are given in addition to the total quantity of liquid weighed and the calculated

Improving a Laboratory Setup with a Microcomputer Test System

ML USED	FLOW (ML/HR)	PULSE CT ** TEMP ** GAS PRESS ** CAP PRESS
0	0	*************************
.0590	.11759	19 ** 44 ** 245 ** 176
.1176	.11713	18 ** 44 ** 245 ** 175
.1763	.11733	18 ** 44 ** 245 ** 176
.2352	.11774	18 ** 44 ** 243 ** 175
.2941	.11778	17 ** 45 ** 243 ** 177
.3539	.11959	17 ** 45 ** 243 ** 177
.4144	.12043	17 ** 45 ** 243 ** 175
.4746	.11984	18 ** 45 ** 241 ** 175
.5349	.12005	17 ** 46 ** 242 ** 176
.5955	.12066	17 ** 46 ** 240 ** 176
.6560	.12048	17 ** 46 ** 239 ** 176
.7166	.12067	18 ** 46 ** 239 ** 176
.7773	.12089	17 ** 47 ** 238 ** 176
.8378	.1205	18 ** 47 ** 238 ** 176
.8983	.12049	17 ** 47 ** 237 ** 176
.9587	.1203	18 ** 47 ** 237 ** 176
1.0193	.1207	18 ** 47 ** 237 ** 176
1.0797	.1203	17 ** 47 ** 237 ** 176
1.1402	.1205	18 ** 47 ** 236 ** 176
1.2007	.1205	19 ** 47 ** 238 ** 176
1.2613	.1207	18 ** 47 ** 238 ** 176
1.3219	.1207	18 ** 47 ** 237 ** 176
1.3825	.1207	18 ** 47 ** 237 ** 176
1.4432	.12088	19 ** 47 ** 240 ** 176
1.5035	.12008	19 ** 47 ** 243 ** 176
1.5638	.12009	19 ** 47 ** 243 ** 176

Figure 9-17
A Sample Printout Controlled by the Program of Figure 9-16

flow rate. The flow rates obtained from the balance and from the pressure drop across the capillary can be compared and used to calibrate the capillary equipment. The recorded data can be used to study parametrs of interest, such as the current pulse rate as a function of the temperature, and variations in pressure at the liquid discharge site. A sample printout is given in Figure 9-17.

CHAPTER 10

Capitalizing
on Additional Capabilities
of the Microcomputer

10.1 INTRODUCTION

The microcomputer can be used for many functions in addition to those which have been described in previous chapters. A spread sheet program used for financial purposes is helpful in organizing data. Laboratory workbook and report writing may be facilitated by using a word processor. A data-base manager is ideal for organizing work and controlling material coming into and going out from the laboratory. A financial package may help in keeping accurate accounts.

A hardware date card can provide the correct date for all the files. A hardware timer will synchronize the various parts of an experiment. A voice board can be a real-time reminder for tasks to be done. The availability of different mathematical, statistical, and other scientific routines allow faster analysis of the data collected. Also the computer can control the laboratory temperature and humidity, and serve as fire, smoke, and burglar alarms.

It is often advantageous to control the computer from a remote location by means of a terminal and a telephone connection. The equipment can monitor and store personal collections of scientific papers. It may be able to communicate with libraries and other data bases.

Some of these additional functions will be considered in more detail. In Chapter 5 you have extensions that are necessary for the laboratory microcomputer system to carry out additional functions without interfering with the experiment. When the laboratory computer cannot fulfill a requirement, linking it with another computer could become necessary.

10.2   SOFTWARE FOR LABORATORY MANAGEMENT

10.2.1   General

A wide range of functions can be carried out with the microcomputer if it is provided with the proper software. A discussion of programs which can enhance the usefulness of the microcomputer in the laboratory will follow.

To use these programs, certain additional skills may be required of you. The knowledge of computer languages may be helpful even though not absolutely necessary. This is especially true if the computer is to be used for a program that requires software that is not available or is incompatible. Then fluency in at least one of the computer languages is highly recommended for writing the needed software. Developing such software by an outside vendor is very expensive.

Chapter 3 presents a short introduction to the machine, assembler, and BASIC languages. This should give you a good foundation in writing of these languages, especially if a computer and some of the more advanced texts in these languages are available. PASCAL would probably be the next language to study for higher level programming. Once PASCAL is mastered, FORTH, FORTRAN 77, and C-language may be useful in writing programs for laboratory experiments.

10.2.2   Software Packages for the Microcomputer

Many recurring mathematical and statistical algorithms are useful in scientific data processing. A dozen of the many easily-accessible programs for algorithms written in BASIC and/or PASCAL are included in the following list.

Roots of quadratic equations
Linear programming
Matrix inversion
Mean, variance, and standard deviation
Linear regression
Bayesian decision analysis
Least square analysis

Fast fourier analysis
Normal distribution
Integration
Derivative of a function
Permutations

Programs in FORTRAN are more difficult to obtain. Algorithm programs are normally published in formats which are fairly easy to use as supplied. Altering them slightly or building them into another program is more difficult because only the source code—with a few remarks and maybe one or two applications—is given. Sometimes the source code is preceded by a short explanation of the nature of the program, perhaps with a mathematical formula.

Certain points should be considered in making programs easier to adapt for general use:

1. The program should be available in BASIC, PASCAL, and FORTRAN.
2. A short description of the purpose for the program and how it can be best applied.
3. A mathematical representation of the program is desirable with an explanation of all symbols.
4. The detailed method for translating this formula into the computer program.
5. An overall flowchart showing how the computer program executes the mathematical formula.
6. Detailed flowcharts for each section of the program are needed to supplement the overall chart.
7. The complete code should be given with remarks for each section.
8. Some examples of entering data and the computer's responses to the inputs for a few of the major applications.
9. Modifications of the program for different applications.
10. Programs available on floppy disks, cassettes, tapes, and perhaps those suitable for use over telephone lines.

Writing programs for general use in the assembler language is not recommended as this language varies for different computers. High-level languages, on the other hand, require relatively few changes to adapt them to different computers.

10.2.3 Other Programs to Utilize the Microcomputer

Several other programs may make use of the computer. One is a modem program which allows transferring files between computers. Such programs are available for most laboratory computers.

The date and time may be generated by a program. One hardware date card with an independent power supply can be used to give the correct date and time into all the files and records. This assures greater validity for the files.

An executive program is very useful because it can create a program for commands only. Such a program can execute any number of programs in a given sequence.

Programs are available which emulate different disk operating systems for a given system. This allows the use of programs created for other operating systems. For example, programs exist to use CPM and IBM programs on FLEX and vice versa.

Many hundreds of utility programs exist which greatly simplify the life of the computer programmer. Such programs may find a certain string in memory or in any file, organize files sequentially or alphabetically, or compare files byte by byte.

10.2.4 Software for Laboratory Management

Several excellent software packages exist to improve the efficiency of laboratory operations. Some of the more useful ones are:

1. Word Processor
2. Spelling Checker
3. Database Manager
4. Spread Sheet
5. Accounts Payable and Receivable
6. General Ledger
7. Inventory
8. Payroll
9. Mail Merge

These programs usually are written either in the assembly language or in Interpretive Basic. Interpretive Basic allows easier modification of the program but it runs much slower than the assembler language, for which changes are more complex.

Often the main program is written in BASIC and the frequently repeated modules in machine or assembler language. For less experienced programmers, this simplifies customizing the main program, which establishes the relationship between the modules.

Probably a well-written data-base manager is the most important of the additional programs. A database manager program creates any desired relationship between files, including any of those mentioned above, and will create new files in almost any desired form. A database manager may be considered the heart of the system.

10.3 HARDWARE DEVICES

Hardware devices can expand the versatility of a laboratory microcomputer in many ways. Components of the interface systems can allow the computer to extend its basic, single channel, binary-digital data capability to multiple channels with binary data, and also to analog and other forms of information. Interfaces which have handshaking control, and a software-controlled hardware timer, are especially helpful. Other hardware devices will be mentioned later.

10.3.1 Date Card

Many operating systems have a software timer and date system which are very accurate while the computer is switched on. If the computer power is interrupted, even momentarily, the data and time must be reentered. A date card overcomes this problem because it has rechargeable batteries for an independent power supply. It is set up once when it is inserted into the computer or when the computer is first switched on. Any time later, when the computer is turned on, the computer receives the correct date and time from the date card. Date cards have a quartz oscillator clock to insure the correct time and date. An independent date card can often be set up as a software-settable interval timer.

10.3.2 EPROM Programmer

Programs for certain laboratory operations may be needed at once, without waiting for them to be loaded and set up each time the computer is switched on. Such customized programs can be loaded permanently into an EPROM, from which it can be recalled as required. Commercial EPROM programmers have been developed to make loading of programs easier. EPROMs need certain voltages and a specific program sequence to be loaded properly. The requirements to load a program into the EPROM will now be considered.

All memory cells are in the "one" or discharged state when an EPROM is erased by exposure to ultraviolet light for five to fifteen minutes. The EPROM is programmed and a data byte loaded by raising the chip select pin to 12 volts—putting each data byte and its address on the data and the address pins—and applying an approximate 1-millisecond, 26-volt pulse to the program pin. To load the program into the EPROM permanently, this process has to be repeated sequentially more than a hundred times for each byte. Good EPROM programmers not only supply the necessary voltages at the proper timing, but also carry out the repeated loading for permanence.

10.3.3 Power Output Stage

For many applications the microprocessor may be required to drive devices with high power demands, such as motors, lamps, or relays. Most such devices are run on 120V AC. A special interface is needed to transform the 5V on the output pins of the microcomputer to that required for the driven units. Triacs are the simplest controls for the current through a motor.

A triac is turned on by a pulse and can be turned off only by the reversal of the AC voltage at the end of each cycle. The amount of current going through an AC device can be increased by shifting the trigger pulse to the end of the AC cycle or decreased by shifting it to the start of the AC cycle. An interface between the computer and triac translates the binary digital number into a variable time delay for the trigger pulse.

Most AC-controlled devices such as lamps, AC relays, and heaters can be operated by a triac. A power amplifier will be necessary to amplify the DC voltage coming from the DAC if DC power is needed. If only on or off control is necessary, electromagnetic or electronic relays can be used to actuate any devices from the computer.

10.3.4 Print Buffers

Printers used with microcomputers can print from 40 to 300 characters per second. Computers can send 100,000 and more characters per second to the printer. Printing short messages does not present a problem. However, computer time is too valuable to be used to feed long messages or tables to a printer.

A printer buffer solves this problem by quickly storing large amounts of data and controlling the functions of the printer as it slowly feeds out data at a rate suitable for the printer to receive it. Often the printer buffer is a small microcomputer complete with a processor, memory, and I/O buffers. Good print buffers can control the format of the printout or allow it to be set manually.

10.4 LABORATORY HEATING AND COOLING SYSTEM

10.4.1 General

One advantage of using a microcomputer is that any non-linear relationship between the sensor and output can be taken into account. Other advantages of a microcomputer are that it can automatically calculate in other influences on the temperature control, such as environmental (outside) temperature and load variations.

The effect of such a temperature program running at the same time as other programs in the same computer is normally minimal, because short temperature readings and control commands for the heater leave ample time for other programs.

10.4.2 Single Thermostat Control

Consider the single-thermostat microcomputer system, shown in Figure 10-1. The single microcomputer system shown

Capitalizing on Additional Capabilities of the Microcomputer

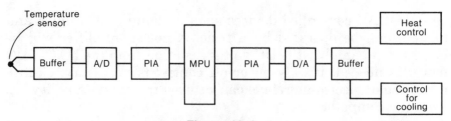

Figure 10-1
A Single Temperature Control System

in the middle of the diagram receives the temperature of the laboratory setup through a PIA, an ADC, and a buffer from the temperature sensor. This information is processed according to the program in the computer. Then appropriate signals are sent to the different heating and cooling control devices.

Figure 10-2 shows a basic flow diagram for operating a single thermostat computer system. There are two interlocked cycles, one for the temperature reading and the other for adjusting the control settings of the heating and cooling units. Although both the readings and control signals can be set for fixed time intervals, the program should be written so that only the reading cycle is periodic, while the heating/cooling cycle is activated only when necessary.

Coding of the program depends upon the microprocessor selected and the other equipment being used.

10.4.3 Multiple Thermostat Control

The time intervals between the temperature readings and the heater or cooler control commands may be in seconds or minutes. The computer can accept data in microseconds. Ample time is available for additional temperature sensors or heater control units which can be added by using multiplexers in the input and output sides of the microcomputer for better control.

A suitable arrangement is shown in Figure 10-3. A channel number is assigned to each sensor and to each heating and cooling unit to insure that each sensor controls the proper unit. When the microcomputer collects a data point from a sensor, it sends its channel number to the multiplexer which connects this input channel to the computer. The computer then puts the latest value from this sensor into the appropriate table in the memory.

This value and the information from the other sensors is used to calculate a control command for the particular heating/cooling unit. After the control command has been calculated, the computer sends the channel number to set the multiplexer on the output side for that heating/cooling unit, and then sends the control command. The PIA stores the input values until they are

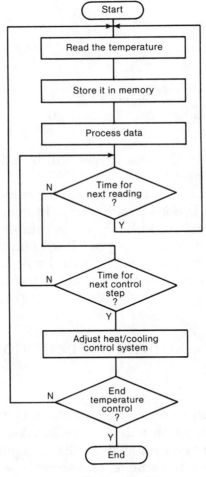

Figure 10-2
Flow Chart for Single Temperature Control System

Capitalizing on Additional Capabilities of the Microcomputer

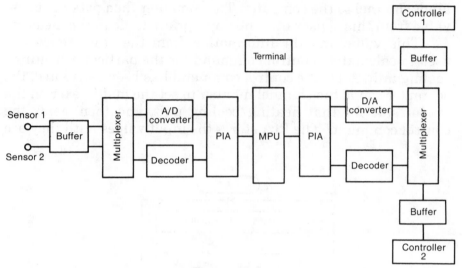

Figure 10-3
Block Diagram for a Dual Temperature Control System

read by the computer. Control values will be held until they are updated by the computer.

The system monitors itself after each cycle to guard against a malfunction. This is done first by detecting out-of-range values and then by searching for unlikely value combinations. A test is made for the proper functioning of all system parts. An alarm will sound if an error is detected. Control will be switched automatically to the manual backup system if the error could cause damage.

10.5 FIRE, SMOKE, AND INTRUDER DETECTION

10.5.1 General

A system similar to the temperature control system described above can be used to detect fire, smoke, or intruders. As with the temperature control system, the computer requires very little time to read the fire, smoke, and security sensors or to activate the various alarms. Thus, such duties will not interfere with the laboratory monitoring assignment.

10.5.2 System Layout

Several different sensors should be installed around the laboratory to detect fire, smoke, or intrusion. At least one or two smoke and heat sensors should be in each separate laboratory. Intrusion detectors such as ultrasonic, electromagnetic, infrared sensors, light-beam switches, or even TV cameras may be installed in strategic locations around the building. Alarms may include horns, flashing (red) lights, automatic locking of doors, and/or automatic notification of a security officer over telecommunications lines.

The hardware system, including all input and output connections, shown in Figure 10-4, is not too much different from the temperature system described in Figure 10-3; only the input and output devices differ. Similarly, the flow diagrams and the programs will not be essentially different from the temperature control system.

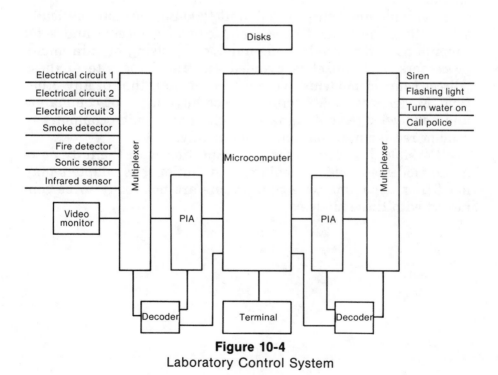

Figure 10-4
Laboratory Control System

10.6   TELECOMMUNICATIONS SYSTEMS

10.6.1   General

Remote setting and reading of temperatures and other sensor values by the microcomputer are usually done by telephone. A special code word must be used to gain access to the computer in order to prevent unwanted access.

Certain restraints should be kept in mind when accessing the computer by telephone. A modem certified by the telephone company must be purchased. The more common 300-Bd modems are considerably less expensive than 1200-Bd modems but also much slower. A 1200-Bd modem reduces the time on the line by a factor of four and may pay for itself if the connection time is long and the line rate high.

Baud speeds faster than 1200Bd are not recommended over telephone lines, especially over long distances, unless these lines are specially set up by the telephone company for the higher speeds.

Available modems for 300- and 1200-Bd, can automatically select the correct baud speed, and can also receive and send commands and dial telephone numbers by using built-in microprocessors. A handset is avoided and the error rate of these "direct connect modems" is much lower than that of any other type. Modems with a microprocessor have a set of commands and acknowledgement signals which allow a microcomputer to send or receive information automatically.

Possible difficulties exist in connection with the fully automatic modems in older telephone installations, as adapters may not fit, or telephone wire connections are not ready to be connected with these modems.

CHAPTER 11

Microprocessors for Control Applications in a Car

11.1 INTRODUCTION

Microprocessors are being widely used in automobile dash-boards, panel controls and displays, and for engine control. Dashboard applications are of a general nature, performing functions similar to those in examples given in other chapters of this book. Engine control is specialized. The use of microprocessors to control and optimize engine performance, to minimize exhaust emissions, and to improve fuel consumptions while maintaining acceptable drive performance will be demonstrated in this chapter.

11.2 ENGINE CONTROL PRINCIPLES

Each engine manufacturer has a different detailed approach to engine control, and as might be expected, much of the information is proprietary. However, in all approaches, certain variables are measured at given time intervals and are used to decide, through computations, actions to be taken to control the engine. A manufacturer may use different degrees of control sophistication for different cars. Usually, the more sophisticated the control system, the larger the number of monitored variables and the larger the number of controlled actuators. For example, exhaust gas oxygen may be measured in one system and not in another.

A system will be discussed in which eight variables are sensed and three actions controlled, as illustrated in Figure 11-1.

Microprocessors for Control Applications in a Car

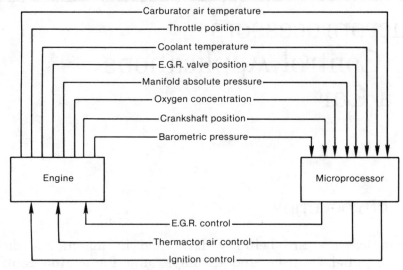

Figure 11-1
Essential Features of Engine Control

The values of the eight quantities are entered into a set of equations stored in the microprocessor. The results of mathematical calculations determine the optimum ignition timing, exhaust gas recirculation flow rate, and thermactor air mode. The eight variables that are being measured are: carburetor air temperature, throttle position, coolant temperature, exhaust-gas recirculation valve position, manifold absolute pressure, crankshaft position, barometric pressure, and exhaust-gas oxygen content.

11.3   REQUIRED HARDWARE

11.3.1   General

The center of the control system is the microprocessor and its affiliated components. Sensors collect the required data. Actuators respond to the control commands. The choice of interface hardware depends upon the particular microprocessor, sensors, and actuators used. Section 11.3.2 describes sensors and Section 11.3.3 describes actuators for a microprocessor-controlled spark-ignited automobile internal combustion engine. A microprocessor implementation is discussed in Section 11.4.

11.3.2 Sensors

11.3.2.1 Crankshaft Position Sensor

The instants at which pistons reach specific positions must be known in order for the electronic control assembly to control the ignition timing. The piston position is determined from the relative crankshaft position. Such a sensor could consist of an electromagnet mounted at one end of the engine block and a ring with lobes pressed onto the end of the crankshaft. When the crankshaft rotates the ring lobes cut the magnetic flux lines of the electromagnetic sensor (Figure 11-2).

The passing of a lobe is detected by the sensor through a change in voltage, or a current waveform. If the crankshaft rotates twice during a single distributor rotor revolution as in a four-stroke cycle engine, the four equally-spaced lobes, ninety degrees apart, will indicate the positions of the eight pistons in an eight-cylinder engine. The voltage pulses generated by the lobes moving past the electromagnetic sensor are sent to the microprocessor for analysis. The microprocessor converts the pulses into precise crankshaft position information for optimum ignition timing. It also derives engine speed (RPM) information to control the spark advance, which is equivalent to the centrifugal advance in mechanically controlled engines.

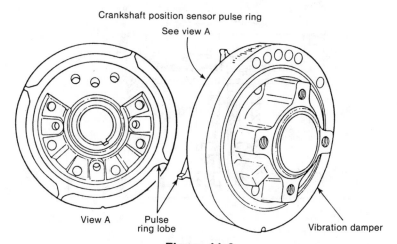

Crankshaft position sensor pulse ring

See view A

View A   Pulse
          ring lobe   Vibration damper

Figure 11-2
Crankshaft Position Sensor (Reprinted with permission of
Ford Motor Company, Dearborn, MI)

11.3.2.2 Throttle Position Sensor

Engine operation can be classified into three major conditions: (a) closed throttle (idle or deceleration); (b) partial throttle (normal operation); and (c) wide open throttle (maximum acceleration). The throttle position sensor can be a variable resistor (potentiometer) with voltage applied across its end terminals. It is mounted on a bracket and coupled to the carburetor throttle shaft. The variable voltage output corresponds to the three modes described above. This information indicates driver demand and is used by the microprocessor to determine the proper spark advance, exhaust-gas recirculation flow (EGR), air/fuel ratio, and thermactor air mode.

11.3.2.3 Exhaust-Gas Recirculation Flow Sensor

The exhaust-gas recirculation (EGR) flow is measured and controlled by the position of a tapered plunger attached to the diaphragm of a pintle valve (Figure 11-3). The valve is actuated against the pressure of a spring by vacuum from the intake

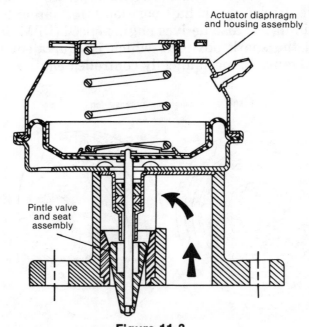

Figure 11-3
Valve for Exhaust-Gas Recirculation Control (Reprinted with permission of Ford Motor Company, Dearborn, MI)

manifold vacuum. The shape of the pintle valve and the seat of the EGR valve are designed so that the displacement of the pintle valve is directly proportional to the EGR flow. The sensor is a variable resistor attached to the valve with a reference voltage obtained from the microprocessor. The output voltage from the sensor is directly proportional to the pintle valve position. The microprocessor checks the valve position several times each second, compares it to the computed desired position, and commands the valve actuators to correct any improper valve position.

11.3.2.4   Intake Manifold Absolute Pressure Sensor

The manifold absolute sensor monitors changes in the intake manifold pressure which result from engine load, speed, or atmospheric variations. Manifold pressure is defined as the difference between atmospheric pressure and manifold vacuum. The sensor contains an aneroid capsule which is sensitive to pressure variations. An electronic circuit converts the capsule position into an output voltage proportional to the manifold pressure.

11.3.2.5   Barometric Pressure Sensor

Atmospheric pressure varies with weather conditions and altitude. A vehicle requires less EGR flow when driven at a higher altitude than it does at sea level. The sensor can be mounted on the engine side of the firewall. It receives a reference voltage from the microprocessor and provides an output voltage proportional to the atmospheric pressure.

11.3.2.6   Coolant Temperature Sensor

The coolant temperature may be sensed by a thermistor in a watertight, heat-conducting, corrosion-resistant housing mounted in a water passage. The resistance of a thermistor is temperature dependent. A constant current applied to the sensor will result in a voltage across the thermistor which varies with the temperature. This output voltage is fed to the microprocessor.

11.3.2.7   Inlet Air Temperature Sensor

A thermistor, similar to the one used for the coolant temperature sensor, is mounted in the air cleaner body near the duct and valve assembly to read the air inlet temperature. Since this sensor need not be airtight or watertight, the housing usually has a series of holes around the thermistor to reduce the response time to sudden changes in inlet air temperature.

11.3.2.8 Oxygen Sensor

An exhaust-gas probe is mounted in the exhaust-gas stream. This sensor measures the oxygen concentration in the exhaust gas. It generates a high output voltage (such as 0.6V to 1.0V) when sensing a rich exhaust-gas mixture (low oxygen concentration) and a low output voltage (such as 0.2V or less) when sensing a lean exhaust-gas mixture (high oxygen concentration). This constantly changing voltage signal is used by the microprocessor for performance analysis and to control the air/fuel ratio.

11.3.3 Actuators

Actuator mechanisms used to set ignition timing, adjust EGR flow rate, and control thermactor air flow to maintain high catalytic converter efficiency will now be described.

11.3.3.1 Ignition Adjustment

The microprocessor signals the ignition module at the proper time to break the coil primary circuit. The collapsing field generates a high voltage in the coil secondary winding. The distributor rotor transmits this high voltage to the appropriate spark plug. Since the microprocessor determines the timing of the spark, the distributor construction is simpler than that of a conventional distributor. It does not need a centrifugal or vacuum advance mechanism. Therefore, no calibration springs or weights are needed.

11.3.3.2 Exhaust-Gas Recirculation Control

The EGR flow is determined by the position of a pintle valve which is controlled by the EGR flow sensor and the microcomputer (Figure 11-3). The valve is actuated against a spring-loaded elastic diaphragm by air pressure from the thermactor bypass valve. This air flow is manipulated by two solenoid-operated valves. One valve is normally open, the other is normally closed. The control scheme can be explained with the aid of

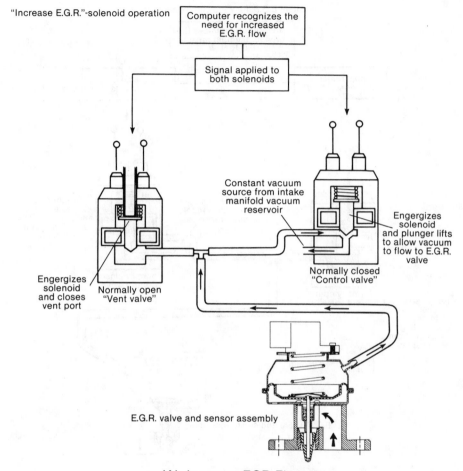

"Increase E.G.R."-solenoid operation

Computer recognizes the
need for increased
E.G.R. flow

Signal applied to
both solenoids

Constant vacuum
source from intake
manifold vacuum
reservoir

Engergizes
solenoid
and plunger lifts
to allow vacuum
to flow to E.G.R.
valve

Normally closed
"Control valve"

Engergizes
solenoid
and closes
vent port

Normally open
"Vent valve"

E.G.R. valve and sensor assembly

(A) Increase EGR Flow

Figure 11-4

Exhaust-Gas Recirculation Control (EGR) Method (Reprinted with
permission of Ford Motor Company, Dearborn, MI)

Figures 11-4A to 11-4C. When increased EGR flow is needed, the
microprocessor sends signals to energize both solenoid valves.
The vent valve closes and the vacuum valve opens, as shown in
Figure 11-4A.

Vacuum is applied to the top of the EGR valve diaphragm
when the EGR flow is increased. The flow is sensed and
expressed in terms of a voltage proportional to the position of the
stem of the valve. This voltage is compared to the reference volt-

Microprocessors for Control Applications in a Car

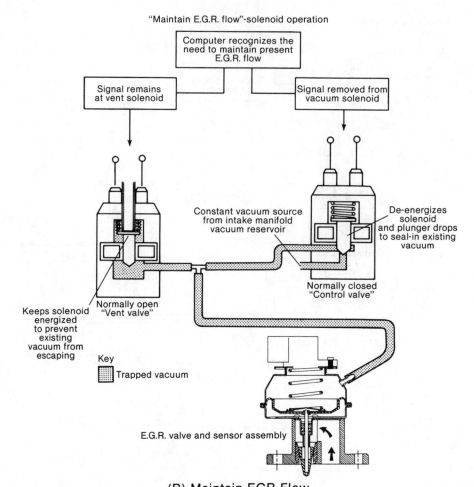

"Maintain E.G.R. flow"-solenoid operation

(B) Maintain EGR Flow

Figure 11-4 *continued*

age supplied by the microprocessor, representing the computed desired flow. The normally open vent valve continues to be energized and the normally closed vacuum valve is deenergized when the flow is correct. Both valves will be closed and the vacuum trapped in the system to hold the EGR valve, diaphragm, and pintle valve in their present positions and maintain the desired EGR flow (Figure 11-4B).

To reduce EGR flow, the power is removed from the solenoids of the normally open vent valve and the normally closed vacuum valve. The vacuum on the diaphragm drops, allowing the valve

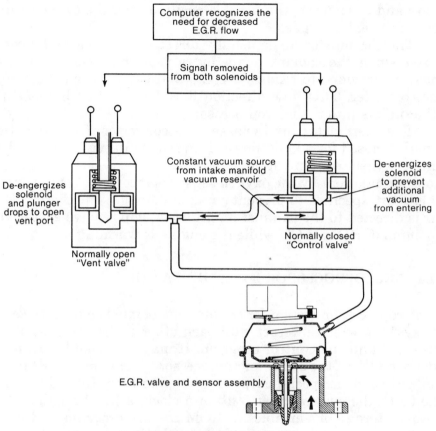

(C) Decrease EGR Flow

Figure 11-4 *continued*

to start closing, thus reducing the EGR flow (Figure 11-4C). The microprocessor returns the solenoids to the condition shown in Figure 11-4B when the valve is set for the specified EGR flow.

11.3.3.3 *Thermactor Air System*

The efficiency of the catalytic converter is dependent on the temperature and chemical composition of the exhaust gases. Extra "thermactor" air is provided by a belt-driven pump to increase this efficiency. The air stream can be routed in any one of three directions by means of a bypass/diverter valve, depending upon the information received from the sensors by the microprocessor. These values include the engine coolant temperature and time curve, the throttle position, and the oxygen content of the exhaust gas.

The thermactor air is usually directed to the catalytic converter when the coolant temperature is normal. Sufficient air must be provided to oxidize the HC and CO molecules leaving the converter. This flow direction may be modified because of other inputs into the microprocessor.

The thermactor air bypasses the converter if the throttle remains closed for a long time or if the time interval between the "high-oxygen concentration" and the "low-oxygen concentration" signals sent by the oxygen sensor is incorrect. Correct time values are specified to prevent catalyst damage. The thermactor air is directed to the exhaust manifold to help remove excessive amounts of HC and CO while the engine is warming up.

11.4 MICROPROCESSOR IMPLEMENTATION

A microprocessor system for engine control must contain several subsystems which interact with each other under the control of the CPU and the control program. It may be possible to use a commercial off-the-shelf microprocessor. Some manufacturers build their own special-purpose microprocessor. In addition to the CPU, the system must contain a clock, a RAM for the temporary storage of variables, a ROM for the program and constants, registers, and an interface for the input/output devices. Each engine model may require a specific engine control protocol and a particular set of equations and constants, stored in the ROM. The same controller may be set up for many vehicle/engine combinations by selecting the proper ROM for that particular vehicle/engine combination.

One multiplexed, 8-channel A/D converter with a 4-bit, latchable output capability may be used to transfer the information from the output voltages of the eight sensors to the designated locations in the RAM. Power amplifiers are needed at the output ports to interface the processor output levels with the solenoids to control the several valve positions.

CHAPTER 12

Practical Aspects
of Microcomputer Standards

12.1 INTRODUCTION

As the number of microcomputers and their support devices increase rapidly, it is becoming much more difficult to apply a device or software developed for one processor to another. The user who cannot find a special device for an existing microcomputer must spend many hours building one or must have one made at a relatively high cost. Manufacturers may also suffer because they must make or provide devices or software compatible with those of competitors, or they will lose business.

Fortunately there is now a strong tendency to create standards, especially by the original equipment manufacturers. Other manufacturers must match their equipment to that of the successful basic computer producers. New developments do not always come from one manufacturer, and a confused set of standards develops.

Many complex considerations must be considered before microcomputer standards can be made generally acceptable. The extremely rapid development of microcomputers is a major problem. A standard may be outdated before it is even issued. In the microcomputer field, most standards which have been accepted and are in use today pertain to the areas in which there has been relatively little development. These include bus standards, telecommunication protocols, and high-level languages.

12.2 BUS STANDARDS

12.2.1 Bus Standards Based on Motorola's Microprocessors

12.2.1.1 Hobby Computer Bus Standards

The S-50 bus is the only major bus standard for 68XX-based microcomputers because the 68XX microprocessor made it possible to reduce the number of bus pins from 100 of the S-100 bus to 50 without decreasing the flexibility of the system. Design changes reduced the number of control signals and provided only one set of power pins on the bus. This pin assignment for the S-50 bus left four pins unassigned.

A recent minor special reassignment of the S-50 bus pins allows the 6809 to address one million bytes instead of 64K bytes. This reassignment to twenty address lines necessary for one million bytes was made in such a way that boards for 8K, for 64K, and for one million bytes can be plugged into the same motherboard without any alterations. An 8K system on the expanded 68XX bus, using an old 8K memoryboard designed for a 64K bus system may be expanded by putting in new memoryboards for a one-million-byte system. This can be done without changing programs, computerboard, or interfaces.

Microprocessor manufacturers are starting to produce a new S-64 bus system to accommodate the full capability of the 68000 processor with more address lines (24) and data lines (16). The motherboard is arranged to accommodate the 6809 processorboards.

12.2.1.2   *Other Motorola Microprocessor-Related Buses*

Motorola designed the Exorcisor system for its microcomputer development system. This 86-pin bus has an expansion capability for a 16-bit data bus to accommodate the 68000 microprocessor. This bus system, originally designed for the 8-bit data bus, is quite popular because the Exorcisor system is not only a well-designed and low-cost development aid for 68XX-based microcomputer systems, but it is also a versatile and compact stand-alone system which can be used for many other purposes.

The Exorcisor system is limited to two interrupt lines and only can be switched between bus masters with 68XX microprocessors. Use of the 68000 removes these limitations.

Motorola also makes several kits to expand the capability of their microprocessors into different areas. A 60-pin bus system is offered which can be used with 16-bit microprocessors.

12.2.1.3   *Motorola Buses for the 16/32 Microprocessors*

Motorola and other companies using the 680XX in their products have developed expanded buses for these microprocessors.

Motorola developed the VERSA bus system to make full use of the mini and large computer capabilities of the 680XX. Several companies in the hobby and small industrial applications field have developed buses which use the full capabilities of either the 6809 or the 68000. Such systems can directly address up to 16-million bytes.

12.2.2   Bus Systems Designed for Intel's Microprocessors

12.2.2.1   *The S-100 Bus*

MITS Inc. developed the S-100 bus system for their first successful small business computer system, the ALTAIR 8800. It was a tremendous breakthrough in its time. Even though the ALTAIR 8800 is no longer produced, the S-100 survives as the most popular bus for microcomputer systems.

The 8008 system has some weaknesses, as did most early units. The address bits and pin numbers on the address bus appear to be at random. Connecting devices are confusing and can lead to crosstalk between the address lines. Inconsistent assignment of signal polarity on the bus causes difficulties in designing and debugging. Two devices can be granted control of the bus simultaneously due to the bus control design.

Other problems result from the inconsistent use of the spare pins by manufacturers of special devices for the S-100 bus. These problems are being resolved by an S-100 standard developed by IEEE. Continued rapid development of microcomputer technology is resulting in changes to the S-100 bus. Even minor bus changes can mean that certain special devices for the S-100 bus are difficult to use.

Not all signals in the processor appear on the S-100 bus because some of them are generated by the system controller. This creates difficulty in using the bus with other microprocessors.

There are major differences between the S-50 and the S-100 buses. The data lines on the S-50 bus are bidirectional, whereas those on the S-100 are unidirectional. Therefore, twice as many data lines are needed on the S-100 as on the S-50 bus. The S-100 has eight interrupt lines compared to two on the S-50 bus. The S-50 has less than half as many control lines as the S-100 bus because the system controller is incorporated into the 68XX processor. Errors in the design, construction, and operation of the microcomputer are reduced by the need for fewer pins.

Practical Aspects of Microcomputer Standards

12.2.2.2 The Heath H8 Bus

The Heath H8 bus is specially designed for the H8 Heath Kit microcomputer systems. The number of pins on the bus was reduced to 50 by techniques similar to those used for the S-50 bus. The random relationship between the address bits and the pin numbers has been eliminated, the data lines are bidirectional, and all basic control signals are available on the bus. But, because it is difficult to use this bus with other microprocessors, it is rarly used except with the Heath Kit microprocessor line.

12.2.2.3 Other Buses for Small Microcomputer Systems

Low-cost, single-purpose microcomputer systems usually use direct connections between their components instead of a bus system. Reducing the number of connections increases the reliability, lowers the price, and reduces size because fewer parts are needed. These systems have an advantage over those with a full bus system in applications for which they are suitable. A system with a bus is cheaper when you need flexibility, because all signals which occur in a single-purpose system must be translated before they can be used in a bus system. This translation can be inexpensive for a simple additional device. It may become very expensive when all the signals for the bus must be translated.

Low-cost microcomputers have non-standard connections (proprietary buses) between their components. The larger, more expensive computers offer greater flexibility with standardized bus systems. The bus is a minor part of the cost in a large microcomputer. It can be a major item of the total cost in a small low-cost computer.

The least-expensive, adequate computer for the job is the best for a specific unchanging application. If there is a need to enlarge the system in the future, buying a computer with a full bus and provisions for expansions is indicated.

12.2.2.4 Bus Systems for Sixteen-Bit Microprocessors

The well-designed Multibus from Intel is especially suited for Intel's 16-bit microprocessors. It has 86 pins, which are assigned for 16 bidirectional datalines, 16 address lines, 8 multilevel interrupt lines, 5 bus arbitration lines, and spares. Control signals are specifically chosen for the Intel family of microprocessors, whose I/Os and memories require separate handling.

12.2.3 Other Bus Systems

12.2.3.1 LSI Bus

DEC designed a special bus for their LSI-11 microprocessors. The 16-bit data bus is bidirectional and multiplexed with 16 address bus lines. The DEC and Motorola designs use the I/O as part of the memory.

12.2.3.2 Texas Instrument Bus

The TI TM990 system has a 100-pin bus. All the pins are assigned to include 16 bidirectional data lines, 16 address lines, and 16 interrupt lines. Of the remaining lines, 4 are used for additional address lines to access one million bytes. Other pins allow bus control of the DMA, different bus masters, a memory-mapped I/O, and a special CRU operation (Communication Register Unit) to speed up communication.

12.2.3.3 The CAMAC Bus

The CAMAC (Computer Automated Measurement and Control) system was initiated by the United Kingdom Atomic Energy Research Establishment to create a unified and easily-adaptable system for the automatic measurement and control of systems. It is an outstanding system for a specific industry. The CAMAC bus collects data from and gives commands to 24 stations. The 24 station call-up lines with 4 additional lines, are able to control 16 different devices at each station. Five function lines define the 32 different functions which can be performed by each station. Twenty-four read and 24 write lines on the bus allow the system to transfer high-precision numbers.

The CAMAC system and its bus are accepted by the atomic and similar industries where many remote locations are monitored and controlled.

12.2.3.4 IEEE 488 Communications Bus Standard

The goals for the IEEE and CAMAC buses are similar—in that they collect data and control from several remote stations.

The CAMAC system was designed for use in heavy industry. The IEEE 488 interface bus is aimed at the small laboratory operation, using 8-bit microcomputers. The 488 has 16 lines plus 7 ground lines. The 16 lines are divided into 8 data lines, 3 for the data transfer bus and 15 for the control lines. Forty-six different 3-character commands can be sent to and received from up to 14 devices.

The 488 bus has become very popular in laboratory instrumentation and industry because of its simplicity. The bus can transfer data at a rate up to 1 Megabyte/sec at distances up to 65 feet. This distance can be increased by the use of modems connected to the telephone network. However, the rate of transmission is reduced sharply. Some microcomputers, such as in some Commodore PCs, use the IEEE-488 link. In others, a bus extender such as that made by Vistar Corporation must be used to convert the microcomputer into an IEEE-488 bus controller.

12.3 TELECOMMUNICATIONS STANDARDS

12.3.1 Short Range Standard—RS 232

The RS 232 standard is probably the one used most in the computer industry. It governs the flow of serially transmitted information between computers, terminals, and other equipment. Some details of this standard have already been described. It is suitable for distances up to 50 feet at low speeds up to 20K bits per second, conditions which are common in a computer center.

This standard has 20 assigned signal lines: 4 are for the transmission and reception of serial signals, 12 are control signals, 3 are timing signals, and 2 are ground/shield lines. These amount to twenty-one assignments. Two control signals, CH and CI, as they perform the same function, one for sending and the other for receiving.

RS 232 C is the most frequently-used version of this standard. It has a maximum voltage range from $-3V$ to $-25V$ for a MARK sign, and from $+3V$ to $+25V$ for a SPACE sign. The range from $-3V$ to $+3V$ is undefined to prevent overlap and is not used. A control signal is ON if it is between $+3V$ (up to $+25V$), and "OFF" if it is in the range of $-3V$ (to $-25V$). The internal resistance of the driver should be greater than 300 Ohms when the driver power is off and the receiver load should be between 3K and 7K Ohms.

The standard specifies 25 pins. The cable connector is usually a 25-pin miniature connector from Cannon, Cinch, or Amphenol.

All control and monitor signals to determine the condition of the transmitter, receiver, line, and the modem are included in the standard by thirteen control signals. No control signals are needed if the connection between the computer and the terminal is short and the three-wire connection suggested in Chapter 3 is used.

12.3.2 Long-Range Telecommunication Standard RS 449, RS 422-A, RS 423-A

The RS 449 standard extends the range and speed of the RS 232 to world-wide communications at speeds up to two megabits per second. To achieve secure communications at these extended ranges, ten additional functions are added, requiring the use of two connectors (a 37-pin and an optional 9-pin connector). The use of balanced circuits, not required by RS 232, is another difference. There are 4 transmission lines, 20 control lines, 3 timing signals, and 3 ground connections.

Standard RS 449 covers the functional and mechanical characteristics of a long-range telecommunication standard. Standard RS 422-A gives the electrical characteristics of this standard for balanced circuit operation. Standard RS 423-A describes the electrical characteristics for unbalanced circuit operation. A requirement for long-range telecommunication standard 449 was downward compatibility to the RS 232. Contact the Electronic Industries Association in Washington, D.C., for a more detailed description.

12.4 SOFTWARE STANDARDS

12.4.1 Disk Operating Systems

Only two major general disk operation systems are available at this time for the small computer market having a standard bus: the Flex system and the CPM system. The Flex system was designed by TSC and is now used for all disk systems operating 68XXX microprocessors including the popular Radio Shack Color Computer. The CP/M system was invented by Digital Systems and can be used on all systems with the S-100 bus. Low-cost home computers with special buses must have an additional interface to the S-100 bus system to use the CPM disk system. Both disk operating systems are used frequently and are about equally powerful. Thousands of commercial programs exist for each of these systems and programs exist to translate from one system to the other. Most major microcomputer manufacturers have designed disk operating systems for their own line of microcomputers.

12.4.2   Other Software Standards

Many other software standards are under consideration, such as micro assembly language mnemonics, extending high level languages to microprocessors, and microprocessor software benchmarks. Over a dozen such projects are underway in different IEEE and other society committees. High-level language developments such as BASIC, PASCAL, FORTRAN, FORTH, C-Language, or operating systems such as Unix are in addition to these developments. These have been adapted recently to the more powerful microprocessors having at least 56K and a disk operating system. Unix type systems normally need a minimum of 128K. This imposes few restrictions as even smaller microcomputer systems can be equipped with 128 or 256K. Some of the adaptations for the language operating system differ little from the original versions. They may even contain some improvements.

APPENDIX I*
Quick Reference to Electrical Symbols

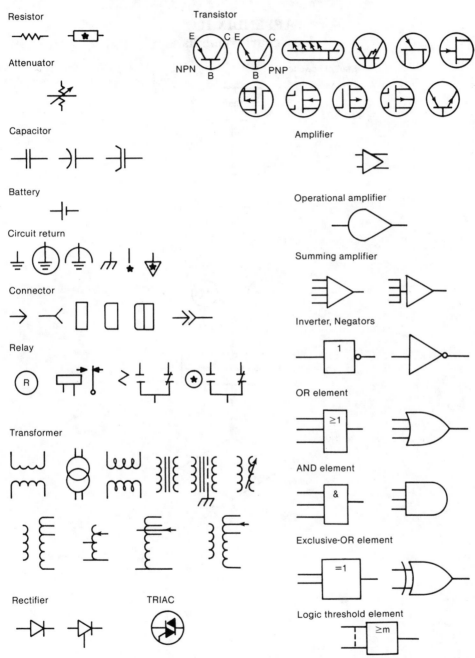

Resistor

Attenuator

Capacitor

Battery

Circuit return

Connector

Relay

Transformer

Rectifier

TRIAC

Transistor

NPN   PNP

Amplifier

Operational amplifier

Summing amplifier

Inverter, Negators

OR element

AND element

Exclusive-OR element

Logic threshold element

*These symbols were taken from the IEEE Standards books *IEEE Std 315, 1975,* and *ANSI/IEEE Std 91, 1984.*

APPENDIX II
Flowchart Symbols

Start of flowchart

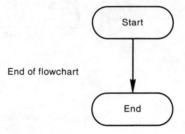

End of flowchart

Continuation of flowchart

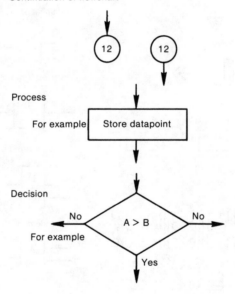

Process

For example

Decision

For example

Index